KY4/06

VANITY
WILL GET YOU
SOMEWHERE

JOSEPH COTTEN

VANITY
WILL GET YOU
SOMEWHERE

Mercury House, Incorporated
San Francisco

Published in the United States by
Mercury House
San Francisco, California

Distributed to the trade by
Kampmann & Company, Inc.
New York, New York

Interior design by Thom Dower

Manufactured in the United States of America

Library of Congress Cataloging-in-Publication Data

Cotten, Joseph, 1905–
  Vanity will get you somewhere.

  Filmography: p. 219
  Includes index.
  1. Cotten, Joseph, 1905– . 2. Moving-picture actors and actresses—United
States—Biography. I. Title.
PN2287.C638A4 1987   791.43′028′0924 [B]   86–23703
ISBN 0–916515–17–6

For Patricia,
who is my world

Foreword

Once upon a time I read a book called *Old Men Forget*. It was the story of a man's life, written by the man, Alfred Duff Cooper, and I thought then, and I still do, that *Old Men Forget* is the best ever title for a book of autobiographical wanderings.

Fact, per se, is valuable to the statistician, the research scholar, the detective; but let us be eternally thankful for the clouded memory that diffuses cold fact into colorful form, and the clouded memory that, abetted by time, transforms tears into laughter; and, yes, even that clouded memory that often solidifies itself into a crystal ball of invention.

Joseph Cotten

Acknowledgments

There are so many people to whom I am grateful for encouraging me to write this book, that I feel like an actor at an awards ceremony who thanks everyone who has had anything to do with an entire career. So why don't I begin by thanking my agent, Dorris Halsey, who had enough confidence in me after reading forty pages to say, "Jo, don't let anyone assist you with your writing. You have your own style; I like it, and I can sell it." Let me thank Sidney Sheldon for recommending Dorris Halsey to me. Among my many friends I would acknowledge Aliza Caillow and Alex Paen. Their encouragement was a great help to me.

I am grateful to Carol Costello, editor, for her marvelously flattering critique. It massages my already overstimulated vanity. Thank you, Alev Lytle, executive editor, tireless worker and a friend indeed. Of course, I bow deeply to Bill Brinton for becoming a publisher and for having the good taste to publish this book.

Joseph Cotten

BOOK
ONE

1

I was born in 1905 and grew up in the section of Virginia known as Tidewater. In the summer the heat in my home town of Petersburg, which sits on the banks of the Appomattox, can be seen rising in wavy layers from the tin rooftops of the city. From a distance, the paved streets appear to shine through those waves of heat, offering the optical illusion of recent rainfall. The summer is hot. It is humid, it is long, and it is beautifully unhurried. And the winters are just as extreme.

It is those bitter cold days in Grandma's house that I remember with such vivid joy. When the icicles hung long from the eaves, when the snow piled in drifts around the house, it always meant that I would be confined indoors, and that after breakfast, after the table had been cleared and the rest of the family had left the dining room, Grandma would rustle (she rustled whenever she moved) herself into her rocking chair by the crackling fire, and when I had perched myself on the carpet at her slippers (which always matched her dress) she would tell me a story.

They were fascinating stories, romantic and colorful stories about her life as a young girl in Washington, where she danced in the White House at the president's inaugural ball. Stories of the Civil War, stories of danger, and courage, and loyalty.

In the summertime the storyteller in the family was Uncle Benny. When the really unbearable weather came, during late July and August, the whole family went down to his cottage at Virginia

Beach. All the houses at Virginia Beach were called cottages. Uncle Benny's was named The Randolph Cottage. It was a large two-story frame house with a huge living room facing the ocean, and it was surrounded by a wide veranda. Running straight back from the living room was a long hallway with four or five rooms off each side. Upstairs and downstairs, there were about twenty rooms.

We all stayed there through Labor Day.

Weekends were lively. My father would arrive with Uncle Benny in his motorcar, driven by his chauffeur, Ernest. Other relatives and friends arrived, filling the back garden with carelessly parked motorcars.

The swimming was absolutely marvelous, and it was hard to keep us children out of the water. Uncle Benny was more disciplined about his swimming. He called it a dip . . . and a dip it was, because no sooner had he gotten wet than he saw Ernest standing at the top of the wooden steps leading from the beach, holding a silver tray bearing a julep with snowy powdered sugar sprinkled over the mint sprigs.

Uncle Benny bade his fellow swimmers a hasty goodbye, walked up the steps past Ernest, who followed him, and went directly to a hammock on the veranda where he reclined, took a sip, and started to rock. As he rocked, he sipped, and as he sipped, he rocked. The children all gathered round to hear Uncle Benny's stories, and listen to him sing songs that no one else knew. He sang romantic songs about beautiful girls. He always started out with a comic one, and when we all laughed after the first verse, he took a deep swig from his mint julep and came up with powdered sugar on his nose. Uncle Benny never took a chance on missing a laugh. "More, more, Uncle Benny!" we cried. "Did you hear that, Ernest?" said Uncle Benny as he handed him his glass. "More, they said."

One weekend he asked me to tell a story that he had told the week before and act it out. It was my most exciting weekend. My brother and cousins laughed, and Uncle Benny finished his drink and applauded, rocking gently in his hammock.

I knew the family wanted me to work for Uncle Benny when I grew up, and the idea of having a car and a chauffeur and spending weekends rocking and sipping those wondrous-looking mint juleps had appealed to me considerably in the past. But after I had acted out his stories weekend after weekend, a new idea began to form in my mind. Yes, Uncle Benny might have a hand in my future, but not in the way the family imagined.

The more my parents sifted the evidence, the clearer it became to them that Jo Jr.'s concentration at school was limited to his classes in manual training and drama. Mathematics plagued me to such an extent that my younger brother Whit (with his superior knowledge in that department) was constantly on his feet answering questions, while I, his older brother, sat in perplexed density in the same classroom impatiently awaiting the bell that would release me to the locker room and football practice.

But always I dreamed of the theatre. I knew I could never make my parents understand. I was wrong. They understood me far better than I understood them. I feared my father. I would go to my mother to ask a favor. "Have you asked Daddy?" she'd say.

"He doesn't understand."

"He understands, child, your father is a good man. Do as he says."

Father *was* a good man, but why was this sweet old-fashioned lady so twinkling in his presence, so demure, and yet flirtatious with her eyes, her gestures? It never occurred to me that my birth and that of my two brothers was the direct result of these two people making love. In those days, I'm sure I was not alone in thinking that my parents never had sexual intercourse. That glorious never-never land was something they had not experienced: a secret that we children had invented and must not tell them about. Obviously our arrival on this planet was entirely due to the stork.

Of all the grown-ups Uncle Benny seemed sadder but wiser to me. The look in his eyes, the occasional sigh, his savor and gentle swallow of a mint julep spelled S E X. Yes, Uncle Benny had tasted the joys of the flesh.

But it was actually my father who helped me begin my career in the theatre—my father who so much disapproved of my desire to become an actor, who so much believed that his sons should learn a good and respectable trade like Uncle Benny's banking. My strict, aloof, but beloved father telephoned his sister in Washington and asked her to help me.

He telephoned her in "Big" Washington, for my father, because of his birth, still maintained affectionate family ties in "Little" Washington, North Carolina.

Aunt Florida, so named by my grandfather because she was the only one of his seven children to be born outside his native state, was an entrepreneur in "Big" Washington. She brought concerts and recitals to the Capital. Aunt Florida had on more than one occasion allowed herself to be victimized by my dramatic readings from, well, anything . . . Shakespeare, the Bible, Mother Goose, the Funny Papers . . . anything. She arranged for me to have private lessons at the Hickman School of Expression, commencing almost at once. The year was 1923, and I was eighteen years old.

Mr. Hickman was English, and exposure to his accent would certainly help in changing mine, said Aunt Florida, although, she went on in her classic cracker tongue, just being "up North here" should iron out the problem, as though a Southern accent automatically disappeared as one crossed the Potomac.

My parents underwrote my living expenses in Washington. But I insisted on paying my tuition fee.

I confided in Uncle Benny. I told him I had decided to make acting my career (after all, it was his applause that had encouraged me to do so), and he very kindly offered to give me much-needed financial assistance.

"Come to the Union Trust Company, and we shall sign your first contract," he assured me good-naturedly.

And so I made an appointment with Uncle Benny at his office one day. When I arrived at the Union Trust Company, I told his secretary that I had a very important business matter to discuss with him. I was ushered through a door which bore the word: PRESIDENT. I walked in and nervously sat down in front of his most impressive desk, and waited for the president to speak.

I did not mention money for a while. I was sure he needed no reminding of why I was there.

Uncle Benny asked me questions about the theatre. An aspiring actor should have known the answers, and when this one didn't he tactfully supplied them. He knew the amount of money I wanted to borrow, and after I had signed a note that said "payable on demand," he handed me a bank check made out to the Hickman School of Expression for $150.

The $150 paid Mr. Hickman, but I needed to make some money for my own expenses as well. I had not yet learned to act, but I knew that I could play football.

Every Sunday I left the School of Expression and expressed myself in a rougher and more lucrative fashion on a semipro football team. I thought I was very good and began to wonder why indeed my team was called semipro.

I finally got up enough courage to discuss this with the coach. "Why, if we are professionals, are we called *semi?*" I timorously asked him.

"You get twenty-five dollars a quarter?" he replied.

"Yes sir, but I only play one quarter."

"Well, Cotten, when you are signed up by a team that requires your special talent for all four quarters, then you will be a professional," was his illogical comment.

I walked gloomily to join my pals at the crap table in the locker room, where every week I lost most of my twenty-five dollars.

My teammates all had jobs on the side. (That was really why it was called semiprofessional, I suppose.) I had only Mr. Hickman and his School of Expression. In my mind I wasn't even a semipro football player. But that *semi* bothered me so much I vowed that one day the word *professional* would be applied to me—even if it had nothing to do with football.

Mr. Hickman's voice lessons were valuable. Beyond that, I learned that private acting instruction should be prohibited by law. How can an actor express himself in a room? A painter needs only a brush and an easel in a room; a composer needs only a pencil and a piano in a room; a musician, through his instrument, can communicate in a room; but what and to whom does an actor communicate in a room? Nothing! An actor must communicate to an audience; it is the audience who teaches him to act, and this can take place only in a theatre.

"But how do you get on the stage?" ask the hopefuls.

"Well," said Burgess Meredith, "you . . . you go on the stage."

It was summer when I collected my diploma from Mr. Hickman and journeyed south to Petersburg, where I would stay until I paid off the note held by Uncle Benny. I had worked as a lifeguard at Wilcox Lake during previous summer school holidays. Tilton Wilcox owned the lake, and I sent him one of those "How-about-it-again-this-summer?" letters.

Tilton welcomed me back to the lake. "Which do you want, the day shift or the night shift?" he asked.

"Both shifts," I said. "I'm trying to pay off a big note at the bank."

"Both shifts are yours," he said. "When do you want to start?"

"Right now," I said.

I had my swimsuit with me.

"You sure are determined to pay off that loan," said Tilton. "The lake is all yours." He bowed to me and went off about his business.

I looked over "my lake" with great pride. From that moment on, I worked day and night until I was in the happy position of being able to pay off my debt.

Uncle Benny's jacket was hanging over the back of his black chair as he waved me to a seat. His chair swiveled and squeaked. The electric fan swiveled and hummed as it blew clouds of Uncle Benny's cigar smoke through the iron grillwork of a partially opened window. "How's everything going at the lake?" he asked.

"Fine," I said. "We call it the Sixth Great Lake."

"Can you name the other five?" asked Uncle Benny.

I rattled off four. "And, er . . . and, er . . ."

Uncle Benny interrupted my faltering. "Funny how so many people can't remember Superior. On the map, you'll find it at the very top of all the lakes, which is probably why it is called Superior. It has a sharp nose that pierces Duluth, a very cold city with many warm citizens."

"Have you ever been to Duluth?" I asked.

Uncle Benny took a big puff on his cigar. His eyes followed, with a nostalgic look, the cloud of smoke passing through the grillwork and reorganizing its shape for its unhurried flight skyward. "Yes," said one of the handful of romantic bankers in the history of finance. "Yes," he said. "Many years ago . . . I had a dear friend in Duluth, and I visited her on several occasions."

He reached for a pitcher, which was cooled with real ice. He poured me a glass of ice water. "I want to pay up that note I have here," I said, placing an envelope on his desk. Uncle Benny's thoughts slowly left Lake Superior and returned to Lake Wilcox.

"To the penny," he said, "including interest." The note was on his desk. "Tear up this piece of paper," he said. I tore it up. "Where now?" he asked.

"Times Square," I said.

"Here's another piece of paper, the kind of note you do not tear up." Uncle Benny placed a crisp fifty-dollar gold certificate in my hand. "Give my regards to Broadway," he said.

My arrival in New York in 1924 evoked a welcome somewhat less elaborate than a ticker tape parade. I existed through a miserable, lonely year for, although ours was not a demonstrative family, I loved my mother and father deeply and I missed them. If only I had been older and they younger, what good friends we could have been!

I worked mostly for Mr. Elfenbein and his shipping clerk, Mr. Kantor, in their paint warehouse downtown on West Broadway . . . not exactly the Broadway I had had in mind. My vanity was fading into despair. Where was the applause, the public gratitude for my sacrifices? For whom had I become a high school dropout so that I might unselfishly share my talents, my charm? I began to question the true motivation of my generosity, my duty, my dedication to the theatre. The brilliance of the image in the mirror was beginning to mottle. Self-confidence was turning into self-consciousness. There come times in life when the anguish seems unbearable, but most of us do survive. Perhaps these pangs are felt more acutely in early years because their lodging place in the system has not yet become numb from overexposure.

I had no idea of how to find friends among strangers. But Becky Pollard saved me. Becky, with her lovely red hair, her marvelous outgoing personality, and her overprotective family, had recently moved to New York from Tidewater. She shared my love of the theatre, and she was very good about riding the subway with me and sitting in the balcony. However, since most of her beaux called on her in black ties and fancy motorcars, I dared not impose on her friendship too often. Looking back over the years, I think I was a little in love with her for a long time.

The treadmill was accelerating, and my pace was weakening. Instead of approaching the Great White Way ahead, I was slipping gradually but steadily into the dark abyss behind.

But . . . there was Ruby.

Ruby was sitting across the table from me in a neighborhood cafeteria. We both rose to leave at the same moment. Outside, I walked beside her and the words we said to one another Noel Coward would have claimed with pride.

"My name's Jo, and I'm harmless," I said.

She said, "Your name's Jo and you're fresh." I really thought she meant it. I stopped. "My name's Ruby," she said. Our walk continued. Her face was very pretty, her hair was very blonde, and her clothes were very tight. Her general appearance might have been described in *Vogue* as "overstated chic." An earthy appraisal such as, "on you it looks good, Ruby," I would have considered more accurate.

She stopped in front of a large apartment building. "I live here," she said.

"May I see you to your door?" I asked, and whether Noel Coward wrote that one or not, it got me to her door. When she had trouble with the key, I said, "Here, let me help you," and that got me *through* the door. When next it opened, Ruby held it for my exit at seven thirty in the morning and I was on my way to join Mr. Kantor in Mr. Elfenbein's paint warehouse on the wrong Broadway.

Earlier Ruby had made coffee. "May I see you again?" I asked.

"Next Thursday," she said.

"But that's a week from now! Not sooner?"

"Next Thursday," she said and added, "Come early, we'll see a movie."

"How about six thirty for a bite before the movie?"

"OK," she said, "six thirty next Thursday."

For almost a year Ruby and I had dinner every Thursday, went to a movie and then back to her apartment. She always seemed happy to see me. She was warm and friendly and responsive whenever we were together, but as the weeks passed, I wanted to feel closer to her. Maybe I wanted her to feel closer to me. She didn't even know my full name, and never asked for my phone number. She changed the subject when I asked any questions relating to her personal life. I felt as if I were prying when I scanned the mail boxes downstairs and discovered her surname. "What kind of love affair is this?" I asked myself. "It's no kind of love affair," I answered myself. "How can two first names have a love affair?" Our bizarre arrangement had become eerily unromantic. My monologue continued. "I'll just display a little indifference," I said.

The following Thursday night I dined alone in a cafeteria far away from "our place" and spent the night alone in my own bed, staring wide-eyed at the ceiling. During the next week my twenty-odd years of accumulated wisdom, somehow influenced by last Thursday's "coitus interrupted," led me into cooler, saner, less rigid distinctions between a love affair and just an affair.

On Thursday at six thirty, I pushed her apartment button. The buzzer that opened the door had always been prompt before. I waited. I pushed the button again. No reply. I walked away with the independent dignity of a beggar.

I needed to get away from New York for a while. First I went home to think things over. I got a ride to Virginia with my landlady's brother, who was driving from New York to Miami to help his uncle spend a newly acquired fortune. The real estate boom in Florida had produced a golden echo that was luring multitudes toward both its shores and the Everglades that divide them.

Highway 1 passed through Petersburg, and he was kind enough to leave the highway and drop me at my family's house. As we drove through the streets of Petersburg, he said, "Can't see why you'd want to stay in a sleepy town like this, with all that easy action going on in Miami. I'm getting mine while it's there; it can't go on forever." I wished him good luck, lifted my bag out, and watched his car fade away toward the land of milk and honey.

Life more or less took up where it had left off. My parents didn't say much. They were aware that nothing positive had happened to me, and their evasion of specifics was, I am sure, meant as kind consideration. I fell easily into old habits. I mowed the lawn, danced with the same girls at the country club every Saturday night, swam at the lake every morning and tried to keep a cheerful face.

But some of the bits and pieces had developed rough edges, and I was feeling some friction before they all dropped into place. "Howya doin' up there?" "Don't you find our drawl fascinating?" "Flo Ziegfeld signed you up yet?" These questions were beginning to test the sincerity of my smile; indeed, the veracity of my answers.

"Home on a visit?" This seemed an impersonal, polite inquiry, and it came from a local detective I had known when he had been an officer in uniform. We were strolling up Sycamore Street. I said, "I think so, but I'm not sure."

"Where is it you live now, didn't your father tell me Washington?"

"New York last," I said.

"Say, I don't mean to put you on the stand," he said.

"I know you don't," I replied.

"Remember old Judge Clements?" he asked.

"I remember his name," I replied.

"Well, when the judge was wrestling with a tough decision he used to say, 'Sometimes we must bow to older judgments.' "

"I guess that's the way it is," I said. "I was thinking of trying Florida."

"I've got a daughter in Florida," he said. "Where were you thinking of going?"

"Oh, I don't know. They tell me most anywhere is booming right now. Sarasota, maybe. I read that the sand there is snow-white."

"What about Miami?" he asked.

"What about it?"

"Did you know that for twenty-five bucks you can buy an excursion round trip from here to Miami next weekend?"

"How long can you stay there?" I asked.

"Tell you what," he said, "if you want to go to Miami, I'll make a deal with you; my daughter is in Miami, she's not well, and she'd like to come home to her mother for a while."

We crossed Washington Street to the Atlantic Coast Line Railroad depot. He gave me fifteen dollars, I added ten to it, and I bought a round trip ticket to Miami, leaving next weekend. The detective knew the ticket agent. The ticket agent gave him a blank envelope and a stamp. The detective wrote his daughter's name and address in Miami on the envelope, gave it to me, and said, "When you get there, just put the unused part of the ticket in this envelope and mail it to my daughter. Have a nice trip."

At supper that evening I told the family about my plans to invade Miami. I also told them of my deal with the detective. My mother said, "Seems to me, son, you've bought yourself a one-way ticket to Florida," and she abruptly left the table.

I left my bag in the checkroom of the Miami terminal, a neatly painted and vastly overcrowded wooden structure with gingerbread accents. I had never been this far from home before, and I felt a slight sense of cutting the umbilical cord from Petersburg when I placed my return ticket inside the envelope, sealed it, and posted it to the detective's daughter before I left the station.

It was not yet noon when I started up Flagler Street toward the beckoning royal palms that lined Biscayne Bay. By the time I reached Halcyon Hotel, with its graceful stairway leading up to a broad wooden terrace crowded with rattan rocking chairs, I was strolling with three old pals from Virginia who were filling me in on the easy fortunes to be made in Miami. On the Halcyon terrace I ran into more friends. The talk was ENORMOUS—a million here, a million there. The group traded inside information and then dispersed.

An old chum from Richmond took me in his rickety Ford to collect my bag from the station, and drove me to the Rancocas, where I took a room. "Everybody lives here," he said.

The Rancocas was within walking distance of downtown, and before the sun had set that day, I had shaken myself awake from that euphoric dream in which I saw myself trading the Everglades for Tampa Bay and then buying all of Miami Beach. I responded with a realistic "thank you" to Charlie Sergeant, the classified manager at the *Miami Herald,* when he offered me thirty-five dollars a week as an ad salesman.

The boom was dwarfing Florida. At that time Miami was too small to accommodate the hordes that were arriving every day. The crowds were so dense that an ordinance was passed making it illegal to unfold an acreage map in the streets.

But the abundance of bodies gave birth to a marvelous idea by my friend Woody Fath. We had been walking one day on Flagler Street when he noticed the crowds of people fighting to get into restaurants, and how some of these people even attacked soda fountains selling thin, dried-up sandwiches.

"But Woody, we'd go crazy trying to make sandwiches; we'd never be able to compete," I said.

"Who said anything about our making sandwiches? You always say you make the greatest mayonnaise of anyone."

"So I do," I answered proudly, "but we're not going to get rich selling mayonnaise, even though mine is the tops."

"I agree with you for once; your mayonnaise is the tops. That's why, when we pour it over all those lovely potatoes we'll cook, we'll call it 'Tip Top Potato Salad,' and since most of the people in the

city are obliged to eat lunch in a soda fountain standing and grab-
bing at any available crumb, our Tip Top product, which will be
easily attainable and reachable in cups on our two-decker royal blue
display trays, should sell as fast as we can deliver it."

With $126 (our combined savings) and a station wagon thrown
in by Mr. Beach, the manager of the Rancocas, we rented a newly
built showroom on Grapeland Boulevard, out in the wilds near
Coral Gables, and entered into a serious contract with the Dixie
Cup people to supply containers. They offered us a free top-
capping machine, and free printing of our product's name on every
cup if we ordered a million cups. We did, and I'm sure that today
the Grapeland community is still using waxed Dixie Cups that bear
the inscription "Tip Top Potato Salad."

The business went well, but I had to work full time on the *Miami Herald*, so I had little social life.

Rebecca Pollard had moved to Miami with her family. Becky
loved to dance, the town was full of big bands, and some of our rou-
tines on the ballroom floor would cause Adele and Fred Astaire to
quake in competition.

Becky was a good sport in assisting me with my new responsibility as a potato salad tycoon. I would pick up my titian-haired beauty
in my slightly gimpy Maxwell and drive directly to the plant. Becky
would find an apron to cover her emerald green satin frock, and
while I mixed several gallons of mayonnaise, she peeled bushels of
potatoes faster than an entire KP squad.

But peeling potatoes was not as easy for her as she pretended.
She cut her hand once, and it bled all over one of her many glamorous gowns. Next time she brought an extra flimsy creation and
hung it up while she peeled potatoes in a royal blue beaded number. In my haste to get our chores finished, I splashed mayonnaise all over Becky's gorgeous beaded dress. I was devastated.
The dress must have cost a fortune, and I wondered how much it
would set me back if I offered to have it cleaned. I offered,
and was most grateful to have it flatly refused. "Mummy will
know exactly who to send it to, if it's worth it," she said airily,
then seeing my guilty face, she added, "Don't worry, just turn
around while I take it off and jump into this chiffon thing." I turned
my back. She changed and started vigorously peeling away
again.

This interruption behind us, we spun off in the direction of the country club and Paul Whiteman's orchestra.

Becky and I had perfected a rather professional and bold-looking few steps that we managed to incorporate into any dance. Foxtrot, tango, waltz; you name it, we did it. The orchestra used to play happy tunes, so I would lead Becky off rather quickly into our "routine," which consisted of our doing three fast turns, in time with the music, then she twirled once on her own, I caught her hand and pulled her into my arms for another three fast turns, and then she'd do her single again. It was very successful and we loved people stopping and watching us.

This night Becky had already changed dresses once. We arrived on the dance floor a little late, and when we went into our routine, I saw, to my horror, my beautiful redhead skidding across the entire length of the ballroom floor until her momentum came to a thunderous stop as she slid into the bass drum. Everyone stopped and rushed to the damsel in distress. I got there as fast as I could, just in time to see Becky remove a long potato peel from the heel of her dainty shoe. She looked up at me wide-eyed. "Why, I do wonder wherever that came from? Seems to me they should keep this club cleaner." I helped her to her feet and wrapped the remains of the chiffon dress around her. We made a formal complaint at the desk, then swept out in dignified splendor.

In the car Becky laughed till she cried. "Some of that potato peel must have gotten in my underwear when I changed dresses," she said. "Oh my, wasn't it fun?"

One night I looked at her lovely face. "Becky," I said. She put her fingers to my lips.

"I must tell you, Jo Jr., I'm engaged to marry Bill."

I couldn't say a word. I knew Bill van Lennip, and I had suspected they might be sweet on each other. But now I felt lost.

"You just haven't found the right girl yet," she said, "so you think you are in love with me. But girls are wiser than boys, and I say that you and I are 'best friends.' That's really much better than being in love, because best friends never change. Tell me you will always be my best friend, Jo; I know I will need you."

"I'll always be your best friend, Becky. I'm sorry about your dresses and the potato peel."

She laughed and kissed me gently on the cheek.

Alas, dear Becky danced out of my life during one of those raging hurricanes that remind us that September is here. Her fiancée, Bill van Lennip, charged into town in his white Stutz, and whisked her away to Cambridge, Massachusetts.

Woody peeled potatoes nonstop after she vanished. Good as he was at potato peeling, he was not half as decorative as Becky, and I found my interest in mayonnaise waning.

Our venture was doomed to end in failure; in our innocent anxiety to become millionaires, we had omitted to get a license for making and selling food. The health authorities put us out of business because of this omission.

I guess I was not meant to be a tycoon, but I still make one hell of a good mayonnaise.

2

Eddie Hay was entertainment editor on the *Miami Herald*. When he had time he would review a performance at the Miami Civic Theatre, to which I gave more time than I did the *Herald*. When he was too busy in Miami Beach reviewing trashy spectacles put on by the hotels and night clubs that bought those big plush ads, he would also sometimes accept copy from me.

Once I reviewed with shameless admiration a play in which I acted the lead, and guess whose picture appeared above the piece. We at the Civic Theatre were cunning enough to persuade the society editor of the other paper, the *Miami News,* and an executive of the Florida Light and Power Company to serve on our board. This resulted in columns in the *News* about people who attended our performances and who wore what. From Florida Light and Power we got large placards on the front and back of every trolley car in town announcing our opening nights, which grew into premieres to be envied by the Metropolitan Opera.

Dr. Seeley was a patron of the Miami Civic Theatre, and in 1930 he generously wrote a letter that allowed me to get more than one foot in the New York theatre. Dr. Seeley's letter was to his friend, Burns Mantle, the drama critic of the *New York Daily News.* Mr. Mantle received me politely but was not at all encouraging. "I can't get you on the stage," he said. "Just what do you want me to do?" He held out both hands as if the next note would be high C.

"Give me a letter of introduction to David Belasco," I said.

"Dear boy, what good will a letter do?" he asked.

"One got me in here to see you," I said. I expected Mr. Mantle to say, "Touché, young man." Instead, I got the back of his head as he twirled in his chair and dashed off a letter to "Dear Governor" (as Mr. Belasco was called by some) and then twirled back and handed me the letter.

The letter from Mr. Belasco's secretary, Mr. Curry, acknowledged receipt of Mr. Mantle's introduction. He added, "Mr. Belasco will be having a dress parade of his new play, *Dancing Partner,* on Wednesday morning at eleven. Why don't you pop into the auditorium around noon and ask for me?"

On Wednesday noon, the population of Greenwich, England, could have set their clocks when I "dropped in" on the dress parade. The auditorium was dark, except for a small strip of illumination on a desk constructed over some of the seats. On this desk lay Mr. Belasco's script and his notes on lighting, scenery, costumes, etc. His clinically white hair glowed in the soft reading beam.

The entire cast, elegantly costumed for an evening party in Biarritz, were aimlessly wandering about, appraising each other and being minutely examined by Mr. Belasco. Mr. Curry presented me. Mr. Belasco said, "Excuse me just a second. Now try the pink one, Miss Purcell." Miss Purcell removed the red scarf and tried the pink one. "Now the red one again, please." Miss Purcell discarded the pink for the red. Mr. Belasco turned to me, and said: "Tell me, Mr. Cotten, which scarf do you prefer on Miss Purcell, the red or the pink?" I hesitated. He said casually, "Personally, I prefer the pink."

My hesitation was over. "No question about it, sir."

"No question about what?" he said, looking at me as if I'd just given him a backward slap in the face with my gloves.

"No question about the pink being the more becoming color, sir," I managed to say without pulling down a forelock of hair, which was probably standing straight up in fright anyway. Mr. Belasco turned to the stage. At his first syllable, everything froze.

"Miss Purcell, Mr. Cotten prefers the pink scarf. Will you please discard the red."

While the wardrobe mistress darted onto the stage to remove the red scarf, the entire acting company peered over the footlights, looking for "Mr. Cotten," who was doing his utmost to render himself invisible.

"Burns Mantle writes me that you want to get into the theatre and don't expect to start at the top," said Mr. Belasco.

"Yes, sir."

"Go up to the office, ask for Burke Simon, and he'll give you a contract. Mr. Reynolds, our stage manager, will call you about when to start . . . and I promise you it won't be at the top."

General soft laughter from Mr. Curry and a host of assistants, a "thank you, sir," from New York's latest discovery who with long, proud strides made his exit up the aisle.

Mr. Reynolds had been Mr. Belasco's stage manager for many years, and my first call from him was to report at the theatre at 11:00 A.M. for the evening performance.

Mr. Grimes, the backstage doorman, interrupted his sewing to greet me, then left his little office and ushered me to Mr. Reynolds. We crossed the unlit stage and I introduced myself to Mr. Reynolds, who was working on a dimmer control for offstage orchestra volume with the house electrician, Louis Hartman. Louis Hartman had one eye and was one of Broadway's most inventive lighting talents. Mr. Reynolds said to me, "Come, I want to show you about the doors." We got halfway across the stage when he stopped and turned back to Mr. Hartman. "Oh, Louis, I am going to show Cotten here about the doors. Will you please have the carpenter lower the house curtain?"

"Certainly," said Mr. Hartman, then added, "Oh, do you have the key, sir?"

Mr. Reynolds felt in his pockets, then said, "Oh, yes, excuse me." While Mr. Reynolds crossed back to Mr. Hartman to hand over the key, I stood stage center, wondering, "What doors? What key?"

I followed Mr. Reynolds to dressing room number one. "This is Mr. Overman's room," said Mr. Reynolds. "His position in the cast entitles him to the star room, which is larger." He pointed to the only other room on the ground floor. On its door was a large bejeweled star, and outside was a small anteroom for the comfort of visitors. "But being a gentleman, he has surrendered it to Miss Granville, because it is larger." He added, "You must have noticed at the dress parade the other day that Miss Granville is also larger."

"Yes, sir," I said. It was about the only thing I ever did say to Mr. Reynolds.

"Now about the doors." He beckoned and I followed him to

number one. "At precisely two minutes before eight, you will knock on Mr. Overman's door and announce half hour, like this." He gave three gentle taps with his knuckles, after which he said, "Half hour please, Mr. Overman."

"Yes sir."

"I'm not finished."

"Yes sir."

"Mr. Overman will respond with a 'thank you,' after which you will move on to Miss Granville's room, and then upstairs to the rest of the cast."

"Yes sir."

"Now try it," said Mr. Reynolds.

I gave three discreet raps on door number one and said, "Half hour please, Mr. Overman."

"Very good," said Mr. Reynolds. "What do you do next?"

"I now go to Miss Granville's room, and do the same thing."

"Wrong," said Mr. Reynolds, "Mr. Overman hasn't acknowledged your call yet."

"But Mr. Overman isn't in there," said the stupidest assistant stage manager in the history of stupid assistant stage managers.

Mr. Reynolds tweaked the waxed point of his moustache and gave me a look I hoped never to see again—but did.

As he stared at me, he spoke loudly and slowly, with pauses in between each word. *"I know that Mr. Overman is not in that room at this moment, Cotten, but what will you do tonight after you knock and get no response?"* Mr. Grimes interrupted his sewing again, and I saw his head peering at us from his office doorway.

"Yes sir," said Mr. Reynolds's assistant.

"That is no answer, Cotten, this is what you will do."

Mr. Reynolds gave three more knocks, this time quite strong raps, then in a voice just under a shout announced, "Please Mr. Overman, half hour, please Mr. Overman."

"Now try that." I did. "Not bad," said Mr. Reynolds, "and when he does not respond to this second call, what do you do?"

My hand was reaching for the knob of dressing room number one when Mr. Reynolds' voice paralyzed my move.

"That is exactly what you do *not* do, Cotten."

"Yes sir."

"When you get no response after the second announcement, come to me. I will do the door opening. Come to me whenever you're uncertain about anything, Cotten."

"Yes sir."

That evening, after act one had been called, I assumed my position beside Mr. Reynolds in the stage left wing. I had my own lighted manuscript stand. Mr. Reynolds was watching the seconds tick off, his hand on the button that would signal the carpenter across the stage to take up the curtain.

The carpenter suddenly appeared. "Where's the key to the curtain, sir?" he panted to Mr. Reynolds.

Mr. Reynolds looked at me, then to the carpenter. "Didn't Cotten here give you the key?" he asked.

"No sir," said the carpenter.

Mr. Reynolds was panting now. He looked at me with very wide eyes and very white teeth. "What did you do with the key to the curtain?" he asked.

"You didn't give it to me, sir."

The stage manager patted his suit . . . empty pockets. The empty-headed assistant stage manager spoke up. "I remember you giving a key to Mr. Hartman earlier today, sir, could that have been . . . ?"

"Where's Louis?" snapped Mr. Reynolds.

"He's up high on the board," replied the carpenter.

"Climb up there as fast as you can, Cotten. Fetch that key and give it to the carpenter. We've got to get the curtain up."

I went up that ladder faster than a graduate of Annapolis. At the top was a man. "Where's Mr. Hartman?" I gasped.

"In his shop, I suppose," said the man.

"Where is his shop?"

"Under the stage."

"Do you happen to have the key to the curtain?" I appealed.

"The carpenter has the key to the curtain," he replied.

On the way down the ladder, I heard a loud swishing sound. It was the curtain, going up on time. It verified my suspicion that there was no such thing as a key to the curtain. I returned to my post, stage left beside Mr. Reynolds. His eyes remained glued to the script as he said, "You won't lose that key again, will you, Cotten?"

One night, after my three soft taps on the door of dressing room number one, followed by, "Half hour, please, Mr. Overman," Mr. Overman's voice said, "Come in please, Cotten," instead of the usual "Thank you." I entered.

He was making up. "Close the door," he said. Click.

"Yes sir?"

"You know the scene I have in the garden with Miss Granville?"

"Yes sir."

"You remember the laugh I used to get when I ordered the stinger?"

"Yes sir."

"You remember the laugh I used to get when I referred to my white tie as an off-white tie?"

"Yes sir."

"Why do you think I don't get those laughs any longer, Cotten?"

I was flattered that Lynne Overman was seeking my advice, but just in case his question was rhetorical, I offered no remedy. Instead I answered: "I can't imagine why, sir."

"Well, finish calling your half hour," he said, "then stop by here on your way back to the stage and I'll tell you why I've lost those laughs."

I was more than a minute behind now, and I raced to the top floor, finished the call, then back to Mr. Overman's dressing room.

"I'm not getting those laughs because of that damned white handkerchief," he said.

I gave the only answer I could think of, "Oh."

Mr. Overman continued, "It's not only the biggest white hand-kerchief in the history of the theatre—Barnum could use it to cover three rings—but lately she has taken to waving it at exactly the wrong times, and that's why I am not getting those laughs."

"I see, sir."

Mr. Overman said, "I'm sure it's just a thoughtless gesture that has crept into her performance. It's embarrassing for me to mention it to her, but somebody should. That kind of thing could become a naughty habit. Besides, the scene needs those laughs."

"I'll tell Mr. Reynolds," I said.

I told Mr. Reynolds.

"Don't tell me," he said. "Tell her."

"Me, tell Miss Granville?" wheezed I.

"She'll be dressed when you call act one. Do it then."

A shaky hand tapped beneath the radiant star, a trembling voice announced, "Act one please." "Thank you," came the reply.

"Miss Granville, I have a message for you, please."

"Come in." She rose from the dressing table as I entered. Mr. Reynolds was right. She was large. At this moment she looked gigantic, standing there smoothing out her satin gown, arranging the 10,000 beads that cascaded to her knees, and patting oh such a lot of hair, with oh such a lot of things in it.

"It's this," I said. The handkerchief was considered a prop, and Matty, the master of properties, a meticulous gentleman, had permitted me to remove it from its position on the offstage table.

"What about it?" glared the queen.

"Well," I stuttered, "in the garden scene, Mr. Overman was, well, was rather hoping that you could, well, sort of control the animation of the handkerchief, during a couple of his speeches."

Charlotte Granville grew six inches, then asked, "Mr. Overman sent me that message? Well young man, you tell Mr. Overman to go fuck himself."

"Thank you, ma'am," I said as I held the door for her regal sweep to the stage.

I went to my post.

"Did you tell her?" asked Mr. Reynolds.

"Yes sir."

"What did she say?"

"She, er, she, well, she seemed to be very sorry about the whole thing. I'm sure it will never happen again," said the assistant stage manager as he looked to heaven.

The four eyes offstage left were focused on the garden scene, and when Mr. Overman ordered his stinger, it looked as if forty wind machines were focused on the handkerchief. No laugh.

I received from Mr. Reynolds that look I hoped never to see again, and never did, until a few seconds later, when Mr. Overman's "off-white" reference was softly zephyred away—alas, not by the god of the west wind, but by that lethal weapon, the white handkerchief, whose slightest quiver renders impotent the broadest statement of comedy.

After the curtain calls, I was alone at my offstage post, gathering up manuscripts, and I noticed that Mr. Overman had remained on stage. He was unknotting the off-white tie with one hand, with the other he summoned me.

"Yes sir?"

"Did you mention that handkerchief bit to the stage manager?" he asked.

"Yes sir."

"Did he mention it to her?" he asked in the direction of the dressing room he had gallantly ceded.

"He asked me to mention it to her."

"Did you?"

"Yes sir."

"I don't know what you told that woman, but you obviously didn't make it clear."

"I'm sorry. I tried to."

"Well, tell her this. If she waves that white handkerchief again, I'm going to kick her in her big fat ass."

"Yes sir."

"What did I say?"

"You said if she waved the handkerchief again, you'd kick her in, well, in the ass."

"What kind of ass?" he said.

"Big fat ass, sir," I managed somehow to say. I never saw Mr. Overman laugh so loudly. He was doubled over as he made his way to his dressing room.

I knew now the time had come to stop trying to be diplomatic and bare the black truth to the stage manager. I was sure that Mr. Reynolds would consider it important enough to be handled by the theatre's general manager, Burke Simon, or even by Mr. Belasco himself.

"So he said to tell her he'd kick her in the ass, eh?" said Mr. Reynolds. I wanted the record to be accurate this time.

"Her big fat ass," I said.

"Well, tell her," he said, and walked away.

And there I was, the next night, face to face with Miss Granville behind her star-studded door. I tried my best, I stuttered, I swayed from foot to foot, I simply could not repeat that threat to her.

She spoke, "Is it still something about the handkerchief?"

"Yes ma'am."

"Did you tell Mr. Overman what I said?"

"Yes ma'am."

"Well, tell him again."

Again, I didn't tell him.

Mr. Hartman had developed what he called a warm blue light. It was in this romantic illumination in the garden scene, when the handkerchief once again waved in front of Miss Granville, that behind her, the neat, patent-leather-covered foot of Lynne Overman scored the precise bullseye.

The play ran on for weeks. The handkerchief was washed and ironed every day and delivered by the wardrobe mistress to the master of properties, who placed it in its usual position on the prop table, where it was to languish, for it never made its appearance again on the stage.

The Governor's last production was *Tonight or Never*. I understudied Melvyn Douglas. During the run of the play Helen Gahagan, the star, and Melvyn fell in love and announced their intention to marry before the close of the play. Mr. Belasco gave them his blessing. He was an old man now and pneumonia brought down his final curtain before the nuptials. But Melvyn and Helen had found true love that lasted them a lifetime.

My tedious apprenticeship at Mr. Belasco's theatre was made more than bearable by a pretty young girl who lived in my building. She was very French, and, young as she was, she took over my free time completely. She also decided to "tutor" me in the art of lovemaking.

"You are very lucky to 'ave met me, Joseph, some day you are going to make many women very 'appy!" said Lizette at about four o'clock one morning to a blissfully exhausted assistant stage manager.

Her hair was always shining. When I wouldn't allow her to come to the theatre, for fear of overstepping my rather tentative position, she would wash her hair and greet me with a soft, uncurled mane. I found her irresistible and wise; I had never really known a girl intimately. Oh, I had "loved" Becky when I was a boy, although she had realized it was only puppy love. Reflecting back, Becky was the only other pretty girl I knew.

"Lizette, do you love me?" Her answer was a breathy whisper in my ear. I do not think she said anything.

When I was not at the theatre, we would go window shopping. It was not my favorite pastime, but she so enjoyed looking at the beautiful, expensive dresses.

"When you are famous, you buy me beautiful dresses, eh cheri?"

"Of course I will," was my answer.

The thought of marrying her had crossed my mind—but some awful chill would run up my spine at the idea of taking her home to mother. Why? She was pretty, she was young, her accent was adorable. How stupid I was. Of course I'd marry her. But not for some time. I was young too, a budding actor. Too young to get married. How does it go? "This year, next year, sometime . . ." She may have guessed my thoughts, for she had never mentioned marriage. It may not even have entered her pretty head.

"Take me 'ome, Joseph. If we walk too much, you will get tired."

She certainly was solicitous about my well-being. I wasn't the least bit tired, but I knew what she meant and pretended to let her lure me back to my apartment, which she had called home.

And so it continued. I worked hard at the theatre, for I was learning. Then back to my one room apartment, where I was also learning.

During one of the rehearsals of *Tonight or Never* Lizette snuggled up to me backstage and said, "You know, matinees are the most exciting."

Since by now I felt I was an authority on the theatre, I replied somewhat pompously, "If matinees are so great, why is it we always open a play in the evening?" She started to laugh, a little too loudly. I didn't like that laugh, and I wondered why I hadn't noticed before that it jarred me.

"Silly Joseph, I 'aven't taught you very much. Do you 'ave a re'earsal tomorrow afternoon?"

"No," I said.

"Then, tomorrow afternoon we will 'ave a matinee, wisout an audience. Come to my room at three o'clock." She turned and walked away, her derriere very subtly swaying as she left the theatre.

Ruby had taught me one well-remembered lesson: If you do not show up for an appointment, or rather an assignation, *end of the affair.*

The next afternoon at three o'clock I went for a long walk in the park and thought very seriously about my acting career.

Adieu, Lizette, and thank you so much.

"Edward Goodnow is at the Lincoln Hotel, interviewing men for next season at the Copley Theatre, Boston. All women's roles have been set," read an item in agent Cliff Self's folder. The Copley Theatre was a cultural fixture of Boston.

I made a beeline for the Lincoln Hotel. The fact that I had understudied Melvyn Douglas weighed in my favor, for the Copley was to open its season with *Tonight or Never.* They had engaged Helen Gahagan's younger sister, Lillian, as guest star for a two-week run, although it was the normal policy of the house to put on a play every week.

I was engaged.

So were Shepperd Strudwick, Raymond Jones, Richard Whorf, and Francis Cleveland (son of *two* presidents of the United States).* We were all about the same age and shape: really a touch too old for juveniles, a bit immature for leading men, and certainly unfit in age or experience for character parts.

God bless the Copley Theatre and Ed Goodnow. The thirty plays produced there that season gave the actors, all playing a variety of parts, years and years of experience in just a few months.

Lynne Overman once suggested that a certain line in his part was "corny," and I remember Mr. Belasco's cold answer coming slowly through the upturned corners of his slightly rouged lips: "Nothing, Mr. Overman, is 'corny' if you believe it."

Oversimplification or not, I filed it away as gospel, and throughout those thirty plays, my hypnotic belief in what I was doing kept my confidence always, or nearly always, above that mercifully adjustable line of self respect.

Shep Strudwick, Dick Whorf, Raymond Jones and I—the "adjustable quartet"—found it difficult, but we had ignorance and arrogance on our side. We also had the aid of a touch of rouge for youth; clown white in the temples for maturity; and grey beards for grandfathers, or even fathers. (Any character described as over

---

Grover Cleveland was the twenty-second and twenty-fourth occupant of the White House, and is officially listed as two presidents.

forty automatically got a few veins on the hands with Stein's blue eyeliner, and all men over the half century mark were played with a noticeable stoop.)

But as our makeup became less obvious, our performances became more subtle. We began to learn technique and, more importantly, we managed to keep the audience from noticing our new-found knowledge. We listened to each other, and we listened to the audience. Laughter in the wrong place was bad; applause was music to our ears.

In our first play, *Tonight or Never*, Lillian Gahagan had a few musical spots. (She played the part of an opera singer.) Our utility man, who acted as her accompanist and coach, couldn't play a note, so I called someone who could. Lenore La Mont was in New York and she agreed to come and play the "real" (offstage) piano in synchronization with the muted stage instrument.

I had first met Lenore two months earlier at the Miami Civic Theatre during rehearsals of *Paris Bound*. Franklin Harris, professor of harmony at the University of Coral Gables, was an old friend of hers and had persuaded her to help us by playing backstage for the on-stage actor.

During rehearsals of *Paris Bound* I spent most of my time in the vicinity of the backstage piano. She played extraordinarily well, and I invited her to a Sunday afternoon concert. The next Sunday, she offered to play for me at her house.

She had come to Florida with her two-year-old daughter, Judy, to make the best of life in a warm climate, leaving her husband in Columbus, Ohio, to dictate the terms of their divorce. Under these circumstances, I considered dates for lunch, dinner, picnics on the beach, dancing, and making love not out of order, and she agreed. They say the way to a man's heart is through his stomach. I soon discovered that the way to a woman's heart is through her two-year-old daughter's stomach. Judy loved chocolate malts. I would take her for a drive and indulge her in as many chocolate malts as her little heart—or rather her little stomach—desired. Through her I became addicted to them myself and have remained so.

When summer came, Lenore went to New York. When summer came, I went to New York. Actually, I went to New York every summer, but not because the weather was more comfortable than in southern Florida, where at least a cooling trade wind sometimes brushed the shores. I went there to be with Lenore, to see old plays, and to try to wiggle my way into a new one.

On weekends I would usually take an overnight ride on the Atlantic Coast Line Railroad to Petersburg to visit my family. Their lives seemed to roll onward. My brother Whitworth had entered Duke University, and although he made the football team, he astonished the athletic community by becoming an honor student. Our youngest brother, Sam, had arrived in Petersburg on Ground Hog Day. His appearance, twelve years after Whit's, was called a "surprise arrival"! As far as I could determine, every newborn child was a surprise arrival.

And now I was standing beside Lenore, at her backstage piano, at the Copley. She was practicing "Vissi d'Arte" with the onstage actor. Two of the crew were shifting his piano, trying to find the most advantageous angle for masking the keyboard and his fumbling hands from view of the audience. Lenore sized up the onstage, offstage piano arrangement and said to me, "This seems to be where we came in."

"We've got to stop meeting this way," I replied.

Getting married in Boston was impossible. We were both tied up all day and all night in nervous preparations for opening the new season, and the city fathers had long since given up anything as simple as Paul Revere's "one by," "two by" code as a bureaucratic formula. Now we faced all sorts of exasperating legal barriers, such as medical tests, filing advance intentions, and enough other complications to cause one to speculate on whether any couple in the state of Massachusetts ever managed a legal union. With Dick Whorf's help we succeeded in October of 1931.

Neither of us knew what the future held in store. Wherever we lived and however poor we were, we had to have a piano for Lenore. It would be difficult, if not impossible, for her to live without one.

This was the early thirties, and my next intent was to crash radio. I started by finding out all the names of producers and directors and going to their offices to wait for an audition. At one of those auditions I met another actor—a young man named Orson Welles.

3

I know little about Orson's childhood and seriously doubt that he ever was a child. His mother and father died very early in his life. Though strongly opinionated, he talked very little about himself. He asked a lot of questions and listened intently to the answers. While he was in prep school (Todd), he wrote and illustrated a book on the works of Shakespeare. I found a copy years ago and asked him about it. "Oh, that old thing," was his reply. I referred to it again much later. "Didn't we cover that subject before?" he replied.

It seems a well-known fact that he went to Ireland to study art when he was about sixteen. "Why did you pick Ireland as a place to study art?" I once asked him.

"Because the Abbey Theatre is in Dublin," was his answer.

It was becoming evident to me that cross-examination would never become my chosen field, but I did learn that it was as a member of the Abbey acting company that he was seen by Alexander Woollcott, the eminent American critic, recommended to Katherine Cornell, and engaged by her for a couple of her plays.

When I first met Orson, he was a free soul, having just lost the binding title of Child Prodigy during adolescence, and having not yet had the more mature title of Genius thrust upon him.

We were in Knowles Entrekin's office at CBS on Madison Avenue. Knowles was *the* dramatic director, and actors got cast in CBS radio shows by "looking in" on Knowles, or on Courtney Savage, *the* dramatic producer.

Knowles introduced us, since Orson and I had "looked in" simultaneously, and during our chat Orson put the contents of his pipe in the wastepaper basket and set the office afire. I remember Knowles saying at a later time, "That young man certainly left an impression!"

We were rehearsing for one of CBS's "School of the Air" series (this one was about rubber trees in the jungle), when a couple of the lines suddenly took on a double meaning and very rude connotations. Instead of biting our tongues and ignoring the moment, Orson and I lost control and broke into choirboy giggles. Knowles stopped the rehearsal and warned us. He used words like *schoolchildren, nonprofessional,* and *bad manners.*

"I see nothing funny about the line 'barrels and barrels of pith,' " he said. Thick silence in Studio Two. Eyes of all actors remained glued to their scripts. Knowles continued, "Will Mr. Cotten or Mr. Welles please tell us what is funny about the line 'barrels and barrels of pith' so that we may all join in with their laughter?"

The atmosphere of the studio made Grant's Tomb seem like a boiler factory; and then Knowles made the mistake of the day. "And now, ladies and gentlemen, if indeed that is what we all are"—glares at you know who—"we will now go back to the beginning of the scene."

Back to the beginning we did go, and when Ray Collins read the line, "Barrels and barrels of pith," there was an explosion of laughter in Studio Two at CBS that would have rocked the very timbers of Madison Square Garden. Ray Collins himself never finished the word *pith.* His manuscript simply slid from his helpless fingers. Most of the other actors doubled over, the sound man hid behind his bulky equipment, the orchestra sought refuge in the shadow of the bass fiddle, and the two culprits fled the building in hysterical tears.

After a few days, when Knowles's face had lost its angry crimson color, he allowed it to smile as he shook hands and accepted apologies.

It was a damaging experience for Orson and me, however, as we were now considered an unreliable influence and were never cast in parts on the same show. It was not until some years later when CBS gave Orson his own show that we worked together on the air again.

We did, however, work together on the stage—in the justly famous Mercury Theatre.

When Orson started the Mercury Theatre with John Houseman in 1937, he had $5000 in the bank. With this $5000 he intended to produce *Julius Caesar* as his first "commercial" play.

To produce a commercial vehicle with that little money, no sets, no costumes, and no stage seemed impossible. But *impossible* was not in Orson's vocabulary.

Orson had three things going for him. One was Abe Feder, the greatest lighting expert ever. The second was the head of Brooks Costumes, who had seen and admired Orson's acting and directing at the Federal Theatre. The third was himself.

Brooks Costumes offered Orson some very old uniforms left over from the highly successful World War I play, *What Price Glory?* Orson graciously accepted the famed antiques and had them dyed black and fitted with shiny gold buttons from Woolworth's. Wardrobe complete.

They painted the walls of the theatre red. The black uniforms against the red were strangely dramatic. There were no sets, just different sizes of platforms that created a multilevel stage.

Julius Caesar opened, a modern version with wondrous lighting. When Joseph Holland, playing Caesar, raised his arm to speak, he looked for all the world like Mussolini. The play took on an eerie likeness to what was happening in the world.

Orson decided to have a second company and send it on tour with one small addition. In this new production the gentleman who played Caesar wore a small moustache. When *he* raised his arm to speak . . . well, the only person who might not have been able to see the resemblance to Adolf Hitler would have been the author, William Shakespeare.

After *Julius Caesar,* Orson produced at Mercury Theatre *The Shoemaker's Holiday, Heartbreak House,* and *Danton's Death* and, from a radio station, the sensational "War of the Worlds."

We were a young, enthusiastic group who reveled in Orson's boldness of production. In most of these plays were Martin Gable, George Coulouris, and a terribly talented, handsome young actor named Joseph Cotten.

Jimmy the Greek would certainly be safe in offering staggering odds on the fact that no one, not one single person, ever engaged in a dull conversation with Orson Welles. Exasperating, yes. Sometimes eruptive, unreasonable, ferocious, and convulsive, yes. Eloquent, penetrating, exciting, and always—never failingly even at the sacrifice of accuracy and at times his own vanity—witty. Never, never, *never* dull.

Orson and I lived a few blocks apart in the Village and saw each other often. Lenore and I had an apartment in Waverly Place. By now I had acted in several plays on Broadway, but with the exception of *Accent on Youth* with Constance Cummings (later with Claudia Morgan and Sylvia Sidney), they were flops, even though the titles included *The Postman Always Rings Twice* with Richard Barthelmess and Mary Philips, and Owen Davis's *Jezebel*, Miriam Hopkins's first starring role on Broadway.

These two became famous as films. Bette Davis won an Oscar for the latter, for which the Ethel Barrymore Theatre paid me a salary of sixty dollars a week for ten weeks, with four weeks of rehearsals thrown in free.

Forty-eighth Street had become the Bermuda Triangle to me. The Vanderbilt Theatre was there, and the Vanderbilt Theatre was a glutton for harmless, light comedies. It gobbled them up faster than the authors could turn them out.

One of my agonizing tilts at the Vanderbilt was called *Absent Father.* The review in the *New York Times* appeared under the large black italic headline: *"Lucky Father."* How could this theatre, I wondered, defy the simplest law of physics and operate a front curtain that went down more often than it went up. The gloomy sound of that final dropping was matched only by that of the stage door when it slammed on our exit into the chill of the grey concrete alley.

My lack of ability, hereinafter softly referred to as "limitations," was becoming evident. Actually, my limitations were enormous, but it is unfair of me to make that judgment today about that day which was nearly half a century ago. Without the natural physical endurance of youth, with its blessed ignorance, its lofty arrogance, and vanity strong enough to be mistaken for graciousness, all actors would end their careers early, uttering Hamlet's last words, "The rest is silence."

My security in my chosen craft began to waver early one evening during a conversation with Orson and Lenore. Since the fascinating subject was my career, I was modest enough to keep my mouth shut. At last someone included me in the conversation. Orson said,

"You're very lucky to be tall and thin and have curly hair. You can also move about the stage without running into the furniture. But these are fringe assets, and I'm afraid you'll never make it as an actor."

Lenore poured a drink. I drank it. Orson went on, gently pointing out a deficiency here, a handicap there. I heard him saying, "A lazy tongue, still with a regional accent, no training in the classics, and a stubborn resistance [he was too charitable to say "inability"] to submerge and twist personal characteristics to fit specific roles. Nope, I'm afraid you'll never make it as an actor."

Now I needed oxygen.

Then he added, "But as a star," here I heard the referee stop counting to ten. "But as a star, I think you well might hit the jackpot." Orson gave me that starring role in a farce called *Horse Eats Hat*. I still keep a copy of the script, and I'm sure that it brought me to the notice of a great actress.

It is unbelievable, but undeniable, that there was a time in the late thirties when Katharine Hepburn was known as "box office poison." That was when she returned to New York and, with a slight assist from her galvanic personality and her natural chic, single-handedly restored color to the fading reputation of author Philip Barry, as well as confidence to many timid stockholders in the Theatre Guild, which produced *The Philadelphia Story* in 1939.

On our evening off before the Monday opening night in each of our tryout cities, Katharine had invited her quartet of leading men—Van Heflin, Frank Fenton, Dan Tobin, and me—to her hotel suite. She poured champagne, and we clicked our glasses while muttering all sorts of toasts, such as "Cheers," "Up the gum tree," and other equally bright twisters to avoid any reference to that theatrical superstition, those two words we were all eager to scream, *Good Luck!*

The small miseries of tryout were behind us now. We were in New York. The stage door we entered tomorrow evening would be in Shubert Alley. The curtain that went up tomorrow would be in the Shubert Theatre. Not the Shubert Theatre in New Haven. Not the Shubert Theatre in Boston. This Shubert Theatre would be just across the street from Sardi's, on West Forty-fourth Street, in New York City. And tomorrow, when the curtain went up in that theatre, we knew that from the audience across the footlights would storm in our direction an icy blast to chill our hearts, paralyze our tongues, and shake our knees. No one had ever devised a calendar that would permit a play to open on its second night, but Katharine tried. She invited her quartet for our usual pre-opening night drink. "But not to my house," she said (she lived in Turtle Bay), "I'm in the Waldorf Towers."

Her four gallants were poor support. Unsteady hands clinked the glasses. Frozen, overdone smiles slashed our faces. Katharine herself indulged in a moment of unconvincing acting. She had chosen the Waldorf instead of her house for this night of fear because she could pretend she was still on the road. We looked toward Grand Central Station, which was masked by drawn curtains. "We're simply in another tryout town," she said in a loud and unconvincing voice to four grinning stooges.

"Like Akron," one of them managed to sputter.

"That's right, like Akron," said Katharine.

I went back to Waverly Place, but the more I bit my nails, the less Washington Square seemed like a rubber factory.

To celebrate the 500th performance of *The Philadelphia Story* Phil Barry gave a party at Passy, which he took over in its entirety for the occasion. Sardi's must have been as deserted as the Vanderbilt Theatre that night. Everybody from Broadway, that is everybody who owned a white tie or a tiara, was at Phil's party.

The few "private people" were conspicuous. They were mostly those "men of the theatre," known to Al Woods as "butter and egg men" (later, more respectfully as "angels") and currently dignified as "investors." One needed no secret service training to spot a member of this philanthropic fraternity. His arm was certain to be enlaced in that of the ingenue's understudy, and her arm was certain to be enlaced in Cartier memorabilia. Most of the backstage crew were there and they all danced with Katharine Hepburn, whose shining, triumphant night it was.

I was standing facing the bar, when a soft hand grasped mine and turned me around. I looked down into the eyes of Tallulah Bankhead—the blinking eyes of Tallulah Bankhead I should say—although what I assumed to be a come-hither flutter, I was later to learn was a nervous tic. She had seen *The Philadelphia Story* three times. My performance, she wanted me to know, as if I didn't, was one of the most skillful light comedy achievements of the decade. My timing was "impeccable," my charm "overwhelming," and my personality "hypnotic." I listened, enraptured, and with great strength restrained my little finger from touching my raised eyebrow.

Her flattery was intoxicating, when suddenly it stopped. Her eyes no longer blinked; they now clicked as she realized with utter disgust to what extremes her exaggeration had carried her. Her eyes now stared at me wildly, as if I had insulted her. "And now, go and fuck yourself," she said, and walked away.

Besides conquering Broadway, Katharine had tamed the lion's roar at MGM. They bought the movie rights to the play. Our last performance in New York after a long, long run was far from one of those weepy closings. It represented only a temporary shutdown while Katharine went to California for the making of the film version. We were all to gather again in a few months to commence an extensive national tour, which had already been arranged. And so I decided to try California.

My movie agent in New York, Leah Salisbury, had some sort of reciprocal arrangement with Leland Hayward in Hollywood, and Leland was to represent me while I was on the West Coast. I looked forward to meeting him. Katharine Hepburn had told me fascinating stories of what a paladin he had become in the realm of studio operations and influence. When Leland moved, he darted; when he relaxed, he kicked the shoes off his tiny feet and snuggled them under a battery of telephones on his desk. He never stopped asking questions, and he stored the answers with computer accuracy under his crew-cut pate. When I arrived in California, he guided me around town, introducing me to producers and directors.

From sea to shining sea was a distance of 3000 miles. In 1940 that meant three nights by civilized railway or seven days by motorcar. The direct flight from Los Angeles to New York got all the way to Albuquerque before a necessary stop. The result was that Broadway and Hollywood names, customs, and money were much less integrated than they are today. I found it an exercise in tact trying to explain just how I had participated in *The Philadelphia Story*, a "property" that just now was starting at MGM.

"I was in the stage version," I said.

"Oh, been trouping, eh?"

"Not exactly," I said. "This stage version was in the Shubert Theatre in New York." A stare. "But you're right. We're going 'trouping,' as you say, just as soon as the movie is completed."

On our way to my next interview, Leland suggested that perhaps he could explain in "simpler terms" just what version of *The Philadelphia Story* I had been in. At our next stop, he did just that with childlike clarity and diplomacy. "Good for you," said the producer. "Which part did you play?"

"C. K. Dexter Haven," I tossed away as if I were saying "Franklin Delano Roosevelt."

"No, no," said the producer, "I mean did you play the Jimmy Stewart part or the Cary Grant part?"

Before I could field this one, Leland came to my rescue. At least he meant to come to the rescue, but he missed the bus. His answer only gave the impression that I was slow. "He just spent a solid year creating the Cary Grant part," he said.

We were back in Leland's office now. His feet were enmeshed in his beloved communications system, and he was sipping what he considered the South's one and only contribution to international culture, a Coca-Cola.

"Your history in *The Philadelphia Story* is a hard nut to crack," he said.

"Speaking of cracks," I said, "That one about 'spending a solid year creating the Cary Grant role' is certain never to win you a crocodile attaché case from the Department of Protocol."

"Confusion gets us nowhere," said Leland, "let's change the subject. You and Orson Welles still good pals?"

"Still good pals," I said.

"Let's call him," said Leland, picking up one of his foot warmers faster than John Wayne could draw a gun. I stopped him.

"He's out of town. I expect to see him in a few days."

"He's been making big waves out here," said Leland. "No pictures yet, but loud trumpets whenever he moves. Maybe nobody in Hollywood ever heard of the Shubert Theatre in New York, but everybody certainly knows about the Mercury Theatre in New York. Yes, I think we'll change the subject . . ."

The slightest hint of attainment too often bears the magnified definition of instant success; and success is often greeted with envy and sarcasm. David Selznick once said to his public relations director, "I don't care what they say about me; just make sure they spell my name correctly."

Maybe Orson Welles felt that way. Maybe we all do. The first time his name appeared in a national column, he came into the theatre waving the paper above his head. "O. O. McIntyre mentioned me today," he sang out.

"What did he say?" we shouted back.

Orson said, through a roar of laughter, "He said I was a flash in the pan."

His Mercury Theatre productions had given Broadway a blood transfusion, and his Martian invasion radio broadcast had brought him international renown, including a comment from Hitler on the instability and hysterical nature of the American public. He was the first director to be given final editing and cutting decisions on his film. (Historically, the producer reserved this right.) Green eyes were watching him; claws were becoming exposed. I am not sure he realized it, and I am speaking in retrospect, but I don't believe the industry would have been disappointed if he had fallen on his face.

All of the above is my observation, my memory, my opinion of Orson's image and the position to which his career had brought him in Hollywood. Even then I'd known him too long to vouch for its analytical precision. True knowledge strikes after short exposure. Three days in Istanbul confirms us as authorities on Turkey. Two days in Rome, and we begin to debate Gibbon. A vintage opinion acknowledges exigencies.

No art director would have been nominated for an Oscar had he used Orson's offices at RKO as a model for a movie producer's headquarters. There were two or three cluttered rooms, several assistants, and a secretary named Shiffra, who seemed to run everything. The largest bare wall of Orson's office was covered with rows and rows of sharply defined drawings . . . visuals, they were called, and the man who did them was called a visual artist. Orson explained that he was preparing a movie, and these visuals on the wall allowed him to "see" the film just as the words in the manuscript allowed him to "hear" it. The visuals ran along his wall in sequence, and he used them as an experimental jigsaw puzzle, substituting a two-shot here for a close-up there, etc. "We haven't finished the script yet," said Orson, "Herman Mankiewicz is writing it with me, and we're reading what we've got at his house tomorrow afternoon. Why don't you join us?"

The Mankiewiczes lived in a large, comfortable house in Beverly Hills. Around the pool were sprinkled about a dozen chairs. Blue-bound manuscripts, sharpened pencils, pitchers of iced tea were in evidence. I met a lot of people.

"Well, shall we?" said Orson, leading the way to the garden. He then told us where to sit. Shiffra handed out scripts.

"We've never actually heard it," said Herman.

"I think I'll just listen," Orson said. "The title of this movie is *Citizen Kane*, and I play guess who." He turned to me, "Why don't you think of yourself as Jedediah Leland? His name, by the way, is a combination of Jed Harris and your agent, Leland Hayward."

"There all resemblance ceases," Herman reassured me.

These afternoon garden readings continued, and as the Mercury actors began arriving, the story started to breathe. Many evenings we would assemble in Orson's office and see the story tell itself through his visuals. The artist had seen most of the cast by now, and the characters began to look like Ray Collins, Everett Sloane (who played Bernstein, pronounced Bernsteen, a name that was snitched from Orson's godfather, Dr. Maurice Bernstein), Paul Stewart, and George Coulouris. Even William Alland, over whose strong shoulders most of the scenes were shot, was heard to say, "Yep, that's my back all right."

I began to believe that those numerous jokes about armpit on the Pacific, W. C. Fields's "Don't buy anything there you can't bring home in The Chief," and George S. Kaufman's *Once in a Lifetime* were just a lot of sour grapes. So this is how they make movies, thought I. Why didn't somebody tell me about this before?

Lenore found us a house. It was high in the hills and overlooked what seemed like a large part of the world. The house was owned by a beautiful chubby blonde lady who told us that it had been a gift to her from a "friend of Mr. Ziegfeld" for whom she had once worked in the New Amsterdam Theatre. One of the conditions of our lease was that she was to have reasonable visiting rights on the back porch with a bluebird who was in love with her, or "vice versa."

She showed us what she meant. Standing on the porch, she held out a palm filled with seed. Then, in bluebird baby talk, she called her lover. From a nearby tree it swept down, landed on a railing and pecked its dinner from her hand. It was a joyous omen.

How could I miss? I was abiding on Wonderland Avenue in Hollywood in a house owned by an ex-Ziegfeld girl who dined every night with a bluebird.

One afternoon Paul Stewart, Everett Sloane, and I were living it up in Orson's office. Shiffra had given us some chilly glasses, and we were applauding the fine performances we were giving in the visuals on the wall. Orson came in and suggested we take a look at a movie set, and we followed him through a garden of blooming roses, down a hedge-lined street to a soundstage. He pulled a heavy door open, and we followed him inside. It was very still. The light was much dimmer than outside, the temperature much lower. We could hear a voice or two, almost whispering, somewhere far off.

Orson put his finger to his lips to motion silence and beckoned us to follow him, which we did on tiptoe. We arrived at a lighted set. A small crew was quietly adjusting lamps and furniture. One of them was seated behind the biggest black box ever built. It was ornamented with shining wheels and handles; it rolled in a track. It was a movie camera. Paul, Everett, and I paled. This monster drew from our eyes the same look the Sabine ladies must have given the invading hordes of Romulus.

Orson introduced us to the crew and to the cameraman, Gregg Toland. "Shaking hands" was a literal description of our meeting. We mentioned the black cyclops. "Oh," said Gregg, patting his camera, "you'll come to love this little gadget."

Gregg was right. Like all truly talented artists, he was generous with his knowledge and assistance. He was amused by the awe of the uninitiated. He had a keen sense of others' problems, and he accepted them as part of his own. He would destroy an entire lighting plot rather than have it impose one uncomfortable moment on an actor. In this way he was like Orson, who in his whole career as a director never led an actor or even allowed an actor to make a move alien to his own nature or utter a self-conscious line of dialogue. This is one of the reasons, I'm sure, that all actors felt safe in his hands. He was uncanny at instant personality perception. I have seen him change the whole concept of certain characters to take advantage of an inspirational, on-the-spot discovery of a natural human quirk. Harlequin always wears the same mask, the same costume; but under this conventional exterior it is the actor's interpretation of Harlequin that stirs attention or boredom.

Citizen Kane finally began in August of 1940. Most of the actors' starting dates were weeks apart, which meant that some of the Mercury players had become screen veterans before fellow actors had been baptized. Orson promised each of us an unruffling, comfortable first day consisting of long walking silent shots, short reactions, inserts of fingers pushing doorbells . . . nothing that might give the tongue cause to divorce the voice.

One afternoon, about two weeks before I was to start, Orson telephoned. "We've run into a bit of bad luck," he said, "I've sprained my ankle."

"Are you in pain?"

"Maurice [Orson's godfather, a doctor] has fixed that," he said.

"Where are you?"I asked.

"In a wheelchair," he said.

"Anything I can do?"I asked.

"There certainly is," he said.

"Name it," said I.

"You can start tomorrow," heard I.

"Tomorrow . . . tomorrow, Orson, I haven't even got a final script."

"One is on its way to you, and don't worry, it's a very cozy scene, just you and Bill Alland, and you'll have a wheelchair too."

I almost dropped the phone. This was the most difficult scene I had in the entire picture. As a matter of fact, it wasn't a scene; it was a monologue with scanty interruptions. It was Jed Leland as an old, old man sitting on the sun deck of a sanitarium reminiscing about his friend Kane. I had never played a character role of any consequence before. (We certainly won't count those bent-over old gentlemen in white gloves bearing silver trays, or those clown-white-in-the-hair ancients described as "Banker Number 3.") Orson and I had never discussed Jed Leland seriously. Knowing the

in-joke origin of his name would bring me low marks in any character analysis poll.

I opened the door that evening and there stood a young man
bearing a large blue-bound manuscript. He was one of Orson's assistants. "I'd like to explain about tomorrow," he said. "May I
come in?" He sat down and continued. "This is the final draft. I
have marked tomorrow's pages here with a paper clip."

"So I see," I said, feeling the thickness of the clipped pages with
the nonchalance and delicacy of Daniel stroking the lion's jaw.

"I won't keep you," said the young man. "Mr. Welles thought
you might like to study the lines. You still have a few hours."

"What do you mean a few hours, it's only seven o'clock," I said.

"I'm getting to that," he said. "I take it you don't know about
the rubber makeup process."

"You may take it that I haven't the slightest notion of what
you're talking about," I said.

"As you know, you are an old man in this sequence. Mr. Seidman, who invented this process, will be applying the liquid rubber
himself. It's a tedious process for all concerned, and he'd like you
in his chair in the makeup department quite early."

"How early?"

"Four A.M. If you can make it three thirty, he'll be happy to
give you breakfast and discuss your skin allergies, if any." He
laughed, "Thank goodness you had those early wig fittings. That's
one item that will cause us no trouble. Good night. I shan't see you
on the set. Mr. Welles is keeping it strictly closed."

At four A.M. a weary, confused actor presented himself to Mr. Seidman's makeup chair. Mr. Seidman seemed to be alone in this vast
makeup department.

"Coffee?" he asked.

"Please," I said, "black with one sugar."

He snapped his fingers and shouted, "Black with one sugar."
Then he said, "Sit here and relax. Now puff out your cheeks like
this." He mimed blowing up a balloon. I puffed out my cheeks and
with a brush, he covered them with a coat of sticky liquid rubber.
"Don't pant like that," he said, "just breathe naturally and hold
that position as long as you can. . . . Perfect," he said when my
cheeks finally collapsed.

I leaned toward the mirror and said, "Mr. Seidman, I am acting the part of a nice old gentleman, not a relief map of the Rocky Mountains."

"You'd be surprised at what the camera doesn't see unless we place it within its view," said Mr. Seidman. "How about some more coffee?"

"I haven't had any coffee yet," I said.

He looked at the makeup shelf in disbelief, then in full tones he shouted, "Where's Mr. Cotten's coffee?" It was now about five thirty, and the only answer to his shout was an echo. We continued our cheek puffing and rubber application routine. About seven o'clock the coffee arrived. More puffing, more coffee. Then the wig. Wigs are stuck on with spirit gum, called spirit gum, I presume, because it contains enough ether to anesthetize the spirit. I tried to peep occasionally at my lines in the script, but my peeping position was never compatible with Mr. Seidman's puffing and sticking positions. About eight o'clock, assistant directors came popping in. The dialogue was always the same.

Assistant: "Wardrobe's ready. When may I take Mr. Cotten to wardrobe?"

Seidman: "You may take Mr. Cotten to wardrobe as soon as he is finished in makeup."

Finally Mr. Cotten was finished in makeup, or to be accurate, Mr. Cotten had been finished by makeup. I was led down the street to the wardrobe department. Mr. Seidman never left my side and never ceased dabbing here and brushing there as we moved along. He kept muttering, "I don't like that wig line at all."

Wardrobe was simple . . . a pair of old bedroom slippers, a pair of old pajamas, and a bathrobe that was more wrinkled than my face. We headed toward the set. Mr. Seidman kept dabbing, and the wardrobe man carried several other choices of pajamas and bathrobes. We were picked up along the route by two or three assorted escorts who were looking at their watches and accelerating the pace. My stomach was heaving. I saw a sign that read MEN, and popped in.

The set was buzzing with activity. Orson wheeled himself over to greet me. "You've had quite an ordeal," he said. "How about some coffee?"

"I've given up coffee for a while," I said, but I didn't tell him how I had given it up.

Gregg Toland, the cameraman, gave me a cheery "good morning," made a gesture, and we were at once bathed in a sunny glow of illumination. "Would you please sit in your wheelchair?" he asked. A property man rolled the wheelchair to its white-taped marks on the floor, and I got into it.

"Let me hold this for you," he said as he pried the manuscript from my talons.

Orson and Gregg now examined my face with a thoroughness that could not have been bestowed on King Tutankhamen by the earl of Carnarvon when they first met in Luxor. Orson was looking through the camera and Gregg was a step or two away squinting at me through what appeared to be a lavender monocle, which he wore dangling around his neck. They would pause for whispered conferences while Mr. Seidman would dab away. I turned my head left, I turned it right, I stared straight ahead. Gregg finally said, "You're right, Orson, it is the eyes."

Orson wheeled up. "You simply don't look old," he said. Mr. Seidman suddenly looked a hundred. "Oh nothing to do with you, Maurie," said Orson, "it's the eyes, they are simply too young for the face."

"I don't know what Mr. Seidman can do about making up my eyeballs," I said.

"Please call me Maurie," he said.

"I'm not sure I'll ever know you well enough. As of this minute I am resigning from the movies."

"The car is here," shouted an assistant. Another one explained that before I went to work I had to see the doctor.

"Insurance, you know. Come with me. You come too, Maurie, and keep an eye on that makeup." I shuffled myself, swaddled in wrinkles from head to foot, into a shiny limousine. When we stopped, we were in front of an office building on Wilshire Boulevard in Beverly Hills. I followed close behind the assistant and Maurie, wishing I were the invisible man.

The elevator was crowded, and I recognized Burgess Meredith as one of the passengers. When he saw me he cried, "Good God!" Our exit on the doctor's floor saved me from a reply. The doctor reacted in no unusual manner whatsoever at what he saw standing before him. He did his routine check, signed something, and said, "Goodbye."

In the lobby, the assistant said, "Let's just stop in here." We went into a Wilshire shop whose sign read something like "Dr. Greenspoon. Optometrist." Dr. Greenspoon greeted me as if I were fully dressed and in my right mind.

"The studio called. I think I can help you." He brought out a black case. "These are called contact lenses," he said. "Usually we make them to order, let's hope a couple of these fit reasonably well."

He used a rubber suction device similar to a baby bottle nipple picking up the lens and pressing it on my eye. He removed it from the eye by pressing the nipple on the eye and then pulling. Flurp. "There you go," he would say. "Out." During our fitting sessions there were several flurps followed by "Oops" instead of "There you go . . . out."

He looked at Maurie's brushes and powder puff. "You the makeup man?" Maurie nodded. "The idea is to take some of this harmless red dye here and paint some blood vessels on the lens, then we fill the lens with some of this harmless white milky liquid, place it on the nipple, and with Mr. Cotten's head bent over we simply press upward and into the eye, giving, I hope, the effect of old eyes." This is the kind of speech we used to end in radio scripts with the direction "N.D.S.N.," which means "Nobody don't say nothing."

The doctor continued, to Maurie, "Think you can handle this little operation?"

"No," came quickly from Maurie.

"Well, I guess I'd better come along to the set," said the doctor.

The chauffeur held the door. The man in the white smock led the way. The old man in the bathrobe followed. Behind him was the man with the brushes and the man with the brief case. For a moment, the traffic on Wilshire Boulevard came to a stop.

Shooting that day was torture for all concerned. The harmless milky liquid behind the lens rendered me completely sightless, the wig line was forever being repaired by Maurie, and as the camera would creep closer and closer to my face, the humming of its motor became audible and hypnotized me into a frozen and silent trance. Orson was patient, encouraging, and helpful in every way. Uncomfortable though I was, I could not let him down.

The one thing we had prepared early—the wig—turned out to be the problem. "The problem is," said Maurie, "when you raise your eyebrows, the forehead wrinkles, and the wig pops loose in front."

"Well, at least we know the problem," I said.

"Do you suppose," said Maurie, "that you could possibly talk without moving your eyebrows?" I looked in his mirror.

"I notice the rubber is beginning to crack around the corners of the mouth. Besides not moving my eyebrows, perhaps I could also talk without moving my lips."

Six o'clock finally came. Flurp. Dr. Greenspoon released me from his lenses and Maurie released me from his uncooperative wig. Orson congratulated me, and the crew assured me that I had lived through the unhappiest day I would ever spend in a studio. It is forty years since then, and I can say they were right.

Two or three days later, Orson telephoned. He told me how pleased he was with the scene. "There's just one thing," he paused.

"The wig," I said.

"The wig," he repeated.

"I don't think I can face it again, Orson," I said.

"Think of it this way," said Orson, "that first try was just a bad dress rehearsal. And you know that successful openings always follow bad dress rehearsals."

He was right. How many actors get a second first day? I knew they were making a new wig, but just for insurance I went at once to Tex's Tennis Shop and picked up a Helen Wills tennis sun visor which masked the entire top of the brow, including, of course, that troublesome hairline.

After a few days, when I returned for the retake, the visor was the most popular thing—animate or inanimate—on the set. We started shooting at nine, and before ten Orson shouted, "Cut and print. Many thanks and go home everybody."

One thing I discovered very early in my career is that to play a drunk scene you do *not* get drunk. Such realism is disastrous.

Orson and I decided we would wait until the end of the day to shoot the scene in which I got drunk and told my old friend Kane just what I thought of him. He worked me the entire day on other scenes and then, very late at night when fatigue had obviously set in, he said, "Now get ready for your drunk scene." Throughout the night, we shot that scene. It is my favorite scene in the picture, at least my favorite scene of which I was a part. It turned out that extreme fatigue and drunkenness are very similar in effect. Thank goodness the former is somewhat easier to control. The unintentional verbal slip of "dramatic *crimitism*" for "dramatic *criticism*" was left in the final version.

Mine was a heady beginning in the movies. With Orson in a wheelchair and a "stop date" on my time to enable me to return to my contractual obligations in the road tour of *The Philadelphia Story*, the *Citizen Kane* production department had no choice other than to concentrate the schedule on scenes in which I appeared. I spent long days, every day, at the studio. My role in the picture was immense, almost large enough to justify a change in the title to *Citizen Leland*.

There was always the script, of course, to remind me that the story did concern other characters, and there was always the fact that no matter how much my part seemed to shine because of the absence of production continuity, the title of the film was *Citizen Kane*, and the man sitting there recuperating in a wheelchair was not only the director but was also starring in the title role.

But even such realistic reminders only scratch the surface of an actor's vanity. Once the days of rehearsal are past, most honest actors will tell you that concentration on the overall play steadily narrows. Paper clips begin to tab certain pages of the manuscript, heavy marks begin to underline certain scenes and certain bits of dialogue . . . always yours. There are more than a few actors who can't tell you the plot of their own films until after they see them.

As Orson's leg mended and he began acting in my drunk scene, I was strongly reminded that all of Gregg Toland's spotlights were not meant for me. I remembered the story of the actor who boasted that he alone was solely responsible for the greatest spectacle ever filmed. He played the soldier who ignited the fuse that destroyed the entire city of Atlanta. When he attended a showing of *Gone with the Wind*, he had to admit that Rhett Butler was a better part.

I don't know who first said, "The show must go on." Probably some box office person. What is this stupid compulsion that drives us on and on through impending disaster, never allowing the curtain to drop, never surrendering as long as the lights are glowing? Maybe that is it! The lights! Maybe those shining, artificial sparkles cast their hypnotic powers on us and tempt us to soar beyond all natural abilities.

It was during one of Orson's solo scenes in *Kane* that I saw him seized by this show biz impulse to save the scene at any cost. In the story, the scene takes place just after Susan Alexander (Kane's mistress) leaves Kane and Xanadu. Kane, in a jealous and passionate fury, goes to Susan's room and literally destroys it. The scene was frightening to watch and to hear. The set dressing department must have found thousands of destroyable props: bottles, bowls, boxes, mirrors, furniture, and draperies. Kane destroys it all with his own two hands. Rehearsals had been thorough. There could be only one take. Another setup would require days. Every move, every light was set—exactly. The camera rolled, the operator peered through his finder and whispered, "Whenever you're ready, Orson."

And Orson with his two hands started the destruction of the set. Crash. Bang. Split. Crunch. Chairs splintered, bottles broke. Chanel Number Five, Joy, Ashes of Magnolia, and other exotic scents filled the air and told us the property man believed in realism. Silk draperies slit and hung, limply defeated. Crash! More glass, more mirrors, more pictures from the walls. Suddenly, Orson was destroying the room with only one hand, wildly swinging away to kill any object still intact. The other hand was concealed behind him, hidden from the eye of the camera, but those of us who were watching from the side could see the blood and the long gash across the hidden hand. He looked around to be sure the job was finished according to plan, and then he made his exit from the scene and sat down near the camera. He was panting as he calmly said, "Cut." The assistant had called a car, and in the hospital Orson's hand was stitched by a doctor who admonished him for not stopping sooner, thereby diminishing his loss of blood.

"Blood," said Orson, "I've got plenty of blood. It was the perfume I was worried about."

Everything we did during that movie was, to the motion picture people, extraordinary. Many times after working all night long we would sit on the curb at RKO and have cocktails at 6:30 A.M. instead of 6:30 P.M. Normal Hollywood actors and technicians were just arriving to start work and have their morning coffee. To them we were that crazy bunch from New York, either insane or alcoholics.

We were neither. We did things our way, which was, of course, Orson's way.

Two days before I was to rejoin Katharine Hepburn in New York for our *Philadelphia Story* cross-country tour, I went to the studio to say goodbye to the cast and crew. Orson sent me to the makeup department. When I reappeared on the set, there was the wardrobe man with everything I had worn in the picture, including that damn visor.

"Just let's get a few shots of you, in case Robert Wise [now a most successful director, then Orson's editor] and I need them to fill in during certain scenes here and there," said Orson.

I was photographed in every outfit, either walking through his office, in the street, or sitting applauding at the opera. The old man makeup was put on. It took forever, and we did numerous shots on my hospital balcony, including my opening a box of toothpaste and finding a precious cigar.

We shot all day. We shot all night. At eleven o'clock the following morning, Orson said, "I think we've covered everything, Jo, you've just got time to run over and do those three radio shows before you catch your plane. Have a good trip, and . . . thank you." He patted me on the back, and I almost fell at his feet.

"Thank you, Orson," I said. And I meant it.

Citizen Kane cost under a million dollars, and therefore came in on budget. We made a classic without knowing it, and in forty-odd years I have yet to have an interview without being asked about it. It has never been out of any list of the top ten best films ever made. And today, one of the most memorable utterances on film is still Orson whispering, "Rosebud."

Before I left Hollywood, George Schaefer (the president of RKO) told me that *Citizen Kane* was set to open in February at the Radio City Music Hall. I had often been to the Radio City Music Hall and seen only the most important pictures there. It had been a dream of mine that one day I might appear in a movie in that illustrious theatre. Imagine my pride, my undiluted ecstasy on hearing that the *first* movie I had ever appeared in was to open there. It was too good to be true.

Off I went to New York, and thence all over the United States with *The Philadelphia Story*. We played in so many different cities, we did so much traveling, that it was like being in another country. Hollywood seemed, and was, so far away. I didn't know what was going on there. I was sailing on my pink cloud, enjoying acting with Katharine again and dreaming of February, the opening of *Kane*. How noticeable would my billing be at the great Radio City? It mattered not one iota. What mattered was that we had made it.

Not until quite some time later did I hear of the goings-on in Hollywood: the intrigue, the blackmail, the threats, the bribes.

Of course I knew we'd been treading on thin ice with the obvious similarities between Kane and William Randolph Hearst. I also knew that Mr. Hearst was a most powerful man. I was to discover just how powerful.

The Radio City Music Hall turned down *Citizen Kane* because Louella Parsons—Hearst's right hand—had threatened the theatre. Schaefer was offered a sum of money to destroy the picture and the negative. The whole motion picture industry was threatened if they showed the movie. Hearst's newspapers would bring skeletons out of closets . . . and there were many of them.

Poor George Schaefer, as far as I could gather, was a hero. He refused to be bribed; he refused to be bullied. He could only get bookings in one or two art houses.

Although people who had sneaked in to see the picture raved about it, none of our names were mentioned in the Hearst newspapers and, of course, none of us was mentioned in Louella Parson's column (which was probably a blessing). But what I found personally rather baffling was that, after *Kane*, I made several movies in which my name was above the title, which thrilled me, but Mr. Hearst's newspapers always managed to review these pictures without mentioning my name! It was quite a feat, to tell the entire story of a film and leave out the leading man.

However, David Selznick finally intervened successfully, and we were delighted to find ourselves back in print, if not in favor.

The Radio City Music Hall still haunted me. Somehow, I felt I had been cheated out of a childhood ambition. Imagine my delight when, some forty-odd years later, my dream came true. I appeared in a movie called *Heaven's Gate*. It cost over 40 million dollars and was the most expensive picture ever to open in the Radio City Music Hall. I figured it had to be great and that perhaps it had been worth waiting this long after all.

Well, this picture certainly had one marked distinction: it was such a disaster that it *closed* the Music Hall. Heaven help *Heaven's Gate*. All that heaven could do was to open the gate and let it in . . . but not out.

4

The year was 1942 and we had started rehearsals for *The Magnificent Ambersons,* which Orson had adapted in two weeks of uninterrupted work at sea on a chartered yacht.

I was now playing love scenes with beautiful Dolores Costello, and in addition I had the pleasure of working with talented Ann Baxter as my daughter.

Ann Baxter came over from Fox studio and made a test, which Orson directed. He invited me to see it with him and Stanley Cortez, the cameraman. It was an exterior scene. Ann had a line that referred to "that little clump of trees over there," and she indicated with her eyes where the trees might be, over to the right. So real was her acting that Orson, Stanley, and I turned our gaze over to the right of the projection room expecting to see a clump of trees.

Ann's grandfather, Frank Lloyd Wright, lunched with us at the studio a couple of times. Mr. Wright was a handsome, meticulously tailored gentleman who had strong, fascinating opinions on architecture and its relation to living. Actually he had strong, fascinating opinions on everything, and he invited controversy.

"Seems to me the novel is an awkward medium to translate onto film," he threw out during lunch. There sat Orson, in the middle of "translating to film" a novel that he had adapted.

He took the bull by the horns and said, "The novel is an intellectual assimilation. Have you read *The Magnificent Ambersons* lately?"

"Last night," replied Mr. Wright.

"The same story on film, sir, is purely a visual assimilation," said Orson, "and until you see it I think you should withhold final judgment."

The next time Mr. Wright came to the studio, Orson showed him about an hour of rough cut *Amberson* film. Later, at lunch, Mr. Wright delivered an erudite lecture on the fusing of novel and film as an ideal marriage. And of course, *The Magnificent Ambersons* was a beautiful story.

Every one of Orson's pictures involved ensemble acting. He rehearsed all of us for two months before we started shooting, and he even made a recording of the whole thing in case he got so fascinated with the mechanics that he started to lose touch with the story. I miss those rehearsals. I miss good stories, too, but from time to time we find them again, and the adrenalin starts to flow.

The minute *Ambersons* was finished, Orson invited me to join him in adapting *Journey into Fear* from Eric Ambler's novel into a screenplay. When Eric saw the movie, he was delighted with it and said it bore so little resemblance to his book that he'd be able to sell it again. *Journey into Fear* starred Dolores del Rio and several Mercury actors, including Orson and me.

Dolores del Rio was the second most beautiful woman in the world. (The holder of the blue ribbon is to enter later in these ramblings.) Dolores lived in an aura of dreamland exoticism. Her house and its decor were poetically conceived by Omar Kiam, who, for the uninformed, was a fashionable Los Angeles decorator. The aroma of her garden was heady, and the protective wall of thick green leaves was cooled by a trickling fountain. Looking in the back seat of her limousine, a keen observer might glimpse a quick impression of her cuddled under layers of fur, her black eyes sparkling with humor and the joy of living.

Fred Othman, a Hollywood correspondent and national voice, also had a cynical sense of humor. His clear blue eyes sparkled rather than penetrated, and he was fond of applying realism to Hollywood myths and exploding them in his column.

Fred wrote items like, "Dolores del Rio is so ethereal she sleeps on air. Not air foam, not air cushion, just air." "Ever hear of an orchid omelet? Ask Dolores del Rio's cook." "Would you believe Dolores del Rio is so exotic she uses butterfly wings as a back scratcher?"

Fred's sarcasm went on until he had exhausted Dolores's patience as well as Webster's and Roget's synonyms for ecstasy and falseness.

Fred was assigned to interview Dolores and she invited him to lunch at her house.

Ah, Shangri-La at last, thought Fred as he sharpened his wit and the pencil that soon was to write, "The Reminiscent Miss del Rio."

They went into Dolores's dining room. On the table, in front of Fred, sat a chaste terra cotta Pompeian jug. Dolores said, as she extended her glass, "Will you be good enough to pour the nectar, Mr. Othman." Fred poured the nectar. They clicked glasses. The butler appeared and presented to Dolores a large silver tray, on which was artistically arranged a mound of perfect dew-dripping gardenias. Dolores took three; Fred took three. Nothing else was passed. Dolores started eating her gardenias. Fred started eating his. He took out his notebook as he asked a question. Dolores talked about her movie career, and when their gardenias were finished, she rang a bell and the butler passed them again. After that, another bell, more gardenias. When they were all consumed, Dolores arose and, pointing to the door, said, "We'll have coffee by the pool." Fred stood back for her to pass. As she did, she stopped at his chair and picked up a woody gardenia stem from his plate. "Naughty Mr. Othman," said Dolores, as she munched on the stem, "you left the best part."

Journey into Fear was the last movie done by the Mercury company. Orson immediately headed into the wilderness—Times Square— where his next stage performance was awaiting his attention.

After Orson left, I headed for my agent's office. Leland Hayward hung up three or four telephones and settled back. "We have a couple of offers for you from major studios," he said. "For me, it'll be a cinch; I simply pick up your check every week for the next seven years. Also for you it'll be a cinch; you simply go to work whenever they call you and do everything they tell you for the next seven years." He showed me the figures. "On the other hand," said Leland, "you can go to work for David O. Selznick. He is an independent, and I think you're more comfortable with independents. Life in his stable, however, will be no cinch for you or for me. I don't need to tell you that he produced *Gone with the Wind.*"

David Selznick and I met for a drink one sunny afternoon at a table overlooking the swimming pool at the Beverly Wilshire Hotel. That was before the value of land caused such institutions to persuade us that dark crowded corners were more comfortable for social communication. One of the things David said was, "I don't make my pictures, I remake them." He explained, "We know construction, we know formula, we recognize the value of stars, but the public taste in its particular relation to this moment in history changes before our pollsters can record it. Our previews in Palm Beach bring the same audience reaction as our previews in Liverpool. I make pictures, but the public tells me how to remake them."

Maybe the public told him how to remake films (he certainly never underestimated the public's intelligence), but he had his own natural gift about stories. His own innate taste manifested itself over and over again in both his masterpieces and in his lesser-known pictures.

He loved his chosen profession so fiercely that it was impossible to work for him without sharing that love. In many ways he reminded me of Orson. They both had more than the normal amount of energy, and they both expected that level of energy from their coworkers.

In 1943 I made two pictures simultaneously: *Gaslight* with Ingrid Bergman for MGM, and *Since You Went Away* for David. *Since You Went Away* was a long and successful war film. David wrote the screenplay from Margaret Buell Wilder's novel. It was directed by John Cromwell. Claudette Colbert, Jennifer Jones, Shirley Temple, Lionel Barrymore, Monty Woolley, Hattie McDaniel, and Agnes Moorehead, among many other fine performers, were in the cast.

I played a naval officer who was hopelessly in love with Claudette. I say hopelessly because her husband was my best friend and he was away at war. In those days movies were far more moral than they are today, and Claudette and I behaved in a most proper fashion. Thinking about it now, it is very refreshing.

Her daughters in the picture were Jennifer and Shirley.

Claudette, with her huge, expressive eyes and million dollar legs (that she seems to have shown only in *It Happened One Night*), was one of the most complete, humorous, hard-working, and delightfully, almost shockingly, honest creatures I have ever worked with.

One day, while sitting quietly between rehearsals, she said, "Is it true, Jo, this talk I hear around the lot?"

"What talk?" I said innocently. "I haven't heard a word."

"If you haven't heard about it, then it's not true," she said with an air of finality.

We played our scene, and the "gossip" she had heard was never mentioned between us again.

Several days later, Alfred Hitchcock came on the set and said to me, "I suppose David and Jennifer are going to get married as soon as his divorce is final. I had a letter from England today." Well, well, well.

England knew about it, and apparently everyone in our studio knew about it. Heavens knows, the *world* probably knew that the shy, quiet, beautiful young girl named Jennifer Jones, and the volatile, gregarious, and brilliant David Oliver Selznick were passionately in love and indeed were going to get married.

Claudette and I, each thinking that we were sitting on a powder keg, remained silent. The picture was not in any way affected by their romance.

The only person on our set who behaved in rather a furtive and giggly fashion was young Shirley Temple. Years later she told me that she had been going through a schoolgirl crush on *me*, and she kept pleading with John Cromwell, the director, "Don't you think Mr. Cotten should kiss me in this scene?" We made *Since You Went Away* such a long time ago that I cannot recall if the director did let me kiss her in the picture. I hope so. In any case, I am most flattered that she wanted me to.

Actually it was Jennifer who (in the picture) was supposed to have a schoolgirl crush on me. The poor girl had to gaze at me adoringly nonstop. One day, we were shooting a large party scene. Jennifer was overdressed and trying to look grown-up. They were photographing from the ceiling down, a complicated and enormous shot. The director, the cameraman, and David were way up high, shooting the scene. I looked at Jennifer. She had shifted her adoring look from me to David, and he was just gazing down at her. "Have you ever seen such an ugly man in your life?" I said very seriously to Jennifer.

She wheeled round at me, white with fury, and said, "Mr. Cotten, I don't agree with you at all." Then she turned around and dashed off the set.

I was glad Claudette was not there to witness my ungallant behavior, and Jennifer's complete giveaway!

To her undying credit, Jennifer laughs about it often, and says, "I only wish I'd known how evil you were. I would certainly have ignored you."

That would have spoiled the fun. *Since You Went Away* was one of the best pictures that ugly man made.

It was during *Gaslight* that we started thinking of ourselves as slaves, slaves bound in golden chains, or "solvent serfdom" as it is finally becoming known.

David Selznick liked to work and he worked hard, but he accepted leisure as an earned reward and treated it with responsibility. He loved parties. Big parties, particularly big Hollywood parties. "Where else in the world could you gather so many beautiful people in one room?" he said frequently, and frequently he did gather rooms, tents, seacoasts jammed with beautiful people. They all came, not to be surprised by the menu (the ham and turkey at one end of the table, a huge rib roast at the other, and in between always corn pudding or baked beans, without which David considered any dinner incomplete), but to be struck by the infectious joy which his enthusiasm for social communication generated. If anyone merely thought of leaving his party, he sensed it and a quartet of violins blocked the door. Driving home from David's parties required no headlights. The sun had always risen.

A large group of film investment bankers and their wives were in town, and of course they were entertained all day and all night by the local royalty. David's party for about forty of them was a dinner at his "luxurious Beverly Hills mansion," a phrase for which the press has never found a substitute. His "stable of stars," which his two-legged properties were called, was ordered out on parade for the occasion. The party was in the middle of the week, and the working members of his stable, particularly those of us with early calls the next day, began to feel the weight of the yoke.

It was arranged that I would bring Ingrid Bergman directly from MGM as soon as we had finished filming *Gaslight* for the day and changed into our party clothes. Instead of party clothes, however, we went to the wardrobe department, where Ingrid changed into a waitress's outfit, complete with white apron, cuffs, and that pretty white thing on the head. I slipped into a rather handsome white jacket, and we sneaked through the Selznick back door into the kitchen. We knew the butler, Stevens, and through the swinging door we marched with hors d'oeuvres, awaiting applause on our entrance. Next to a disastrous soufflé, our act was the flattest thing ever to pass through a kitchen door.

I never realized before, but we simply do not notice the faces that belong to the hands that pass all those little things before dinner. Edie Goetz (Louis B. Mayer's daughter) was heard to say, "That maid bears a strong resemblance to Ingrid Bergman, doesn't she?" Then she returned immediately to her chatting with Mr. Money. Our trays were now empty, and we sheepishly crawled back to the kitchen. Stevens had put Ingrid's evening dress in a guest room, and she started up the backstairs to change.

"We can't give up now," I said. "Come on, let's try once more."

"All right," she said, "but you must promise to stay between me and the man with the red moustache. My tray seems above his reach."

Stevens gave us more hors d'oeuvres, and I followed Ingrid. Just before we entered the living room, a waiter bearing a tray full of drinks came our way. Each of us took a drink, knocked it back, and returned the glass to the tray before the waiter knew what had happened.

The man with the red moustache approached Ingrid. "Don't leave me," she whispered.

"Never," I said, as I took another glass from a passing tray. I downed it, but the waiter kept walking so I put the empty glass on my tray of hors d'oeuvres. It was a little unbalanced.

As the moustache got closer to my Swedish friend, I leaped in between them, stamping my feet like a Spanish dancer and twirling my tray above my head. The red moustache moved to his left and reached his arm out, not quite in the vicinity of Ingrid's tray. I grabbed my empty glass and put it in his hand, took Ingrid by the arm, and said, "Come along, Martha, we only agreed to work for an hour. Remember, all our children are waiting up for us."

I had taken Ingrid by the arm with which she was holding her tray. It crashed to the floor. The barman appeared again and tripped over Ingrid's tray. She grabbed two drinks and knocked them back, just before his tray clattered to the floor.

"These people are a disgrace," said red moustache, slurring his speech.

"You, sir, are no gentleman," I said, and gave his moustache an impertinent tweak. It came off in my hand, and I was staring into the face of Errol Flynn. "What the devil are you doing here?" I said.

"I don't know," replied a very glassy-eyed Errol. "Where am I, and who's the sexy Swedish chick?"

All eyes were on us.

David said, "Ingrid, Jo, how wonderful to see you both. But why did you think this was a costume party?"

"Isn't it?" said Ingrid.

"And what's he doing here?" David continued, glaring at Errol.

"He's just a leprechaun we brought along for a gag," I said, then, quietly to Errol, I said, "Goodnight, the back door's just behind you."

"Gotta be more action out there. Goodnight, old boy." He turned and walked as if on eggs until he disappeared out into the darkness.

After he'd left, I held Ingrid's hand and did a deep bow. My head swam. As she curtsied, Ingrid said, "Get me out of here, I feel ill."

I was about to help Ingrid when a very large lady flung herself into my arms and said, "Let me curtsy too." She had obviously enjoyed herself at the bar.

I caught sight of Ingrid running out of the back door, when my lady "friend" closed her eyes and collapsed. I used all my strength and lifted her up. Stevens came to my rescue. I placed all four hundred pounds of her into his arms and said weakly, "She's all yours, Stevens. Help her get herself together."

Dinner was buffet style, and fortunately there were no placecards. A lady dripping with emeralds and diamonds approached me, gushing like one of her own oil wells, and said, "That was a very amusing little joke, Mr. Cotten, but where's that beautiful Ingrid Bergman?" Happily, before I could reply, she said, "She's so graceful, when she did that curtsy. Where is she?"

"She has to get up very early to work in a picture, so she sneaked home to bed. Ladies have to get up earlier than we do to look and feel beautiful," I said in a rather prudish way. I hoped my eyes weren't crossed, and I also hoped most fervently that Ingrid would not make an anticlimactic reentrance. Somehow I knew that whatever she felt like, she was too professional to face the gladiators again.

Mercifully, people started to leave. I didn't feel well. I had a pain in my left side. I found a comfortable chair and sat gingerly in it. David came across the room, and I stood up holding my side.

"That was a funny idea, Jo, but if you were going to put on an act, you shouldn't have gotten drunk; or were you kidding?" He looked at me hard and said, "No, you weren't kidding."

"I'm sorry, David, but our act was such a flop we needed booze for courage."

"You may call it courage," he said, "but I call it *chutzpah*." Then, "What the devil's the matter with your side?"

"I think I have a hernia."

I thought I heard David say "*Oi vay*," but it could have been my imagination. I did hear him ring the bell loudly, then he said, "Oh, my chauffeur took Ingrid home. Where is Stevens, didn't he hear the bell?"

Stevens came limping in, holding his right side! "Sir," he said painfully.

"Hernia?" asked David flatly.

"Yes, sir," said Stevens.

"Sit down, Stevens, I'll get my own drink while you two tell me what happened."

"Well . . . ," we started in unison. Then Stevens said to me, "You first, sir."

"David, this lady fell into my arms. She didn't feel very well, she just fainted. So I picked her up and gave her to Stevens as fast as I could."

"You threw her to Stevens?" Sheer horror on David's face.

"No, no sir, please let me explain. The lovely lady was not accustomed to alcohol, and so she, eh, eh . . . she collapsed. The lovely lady was very large, very regal," he added rather unnecessarily. "Well, as you know, a completely collapsed body is a dead weight. Mr. Cotten and I have just suffered a little hernia each."

I moved away from Stevens. We were beginning to look too much like Frick and Frack.

"Where is this lovely lady now?" asked David.

"I called her chauffeur in. She told me his name . . . eh, Adam, I think it was. Anyway, he helped her to her car and took her home. Very regal, very generous she was," said Stevens with a delicate cough.

David said, "I'm sure. Jo, you'd better sleep in my dressing room. I hope poor Ingrid feels better tomorrow, but after what you put her through, I doubt it. Maybe she should take the day off. I'm sorry about your hernia, but I should have thought you would have known that it takes two people to lift up a person who has passed out."

Stevens closed his eyes at the words *passed out.*

David continued, "Stevens, call Dr. Smythe at 8 A.M., and ask him to come and check you both. In the morning I may delay two pictures and hire a temporary butler."

"I'll be better tomorrow," we both said in unison.

"Goodnight," said David.

This time I waited.

"Goodnight, sir."

"Goodnight, Boss," I said feebly.

David Selznick and I were destined to become close friends. We traded too many ugly insults to permit the cultivation of any other relationship. Honesty can be hurtful and things are sometimes best left unsaid, but David said everything he felt without bothering to think twice. I have never learned to be tactful. I have embarrassed many people with this problem, but David was never embarrassed. He understood, and he admired straight talk.

I think it was the Mocambo caper that extracted our fangs. It was a time of the big bands. The big bands played soft music for dancers who were not embarrassed by physical contact in public. Actually, they were never known as big bands until they became almost extinct.

On this night, shortly after we had finished *Duel in the Sun* in 1945, the big band was playing "duel in the parking lot" music for David and me. There existed a wide difference of opinion between us concerning just how World War II could have been ended, just how peace should be brought to the world. We were sincere, we were positive, we were loud, and we were belligerent. Heads were turning, and waiters were busying themselves about the table with large waving napkins. Emil Coleman, the conductor, sent a message, "Will a waltz help?"

I snarled. David said, "I think we'd better step outside." We stepped outside, into the Mocambo parking lot. We squared off.

"Take off your glasses," I said to David.

"Take off my glasses?" he shouted. "Without my glasses, I can't see to hit you!"

So instead of twenty paces at dawn, it was a hilarious handshake at midnight and the end of our ridiculous feud.

One of the many things we had in common was "extravagance." David would often come to my house and sit back comfortably while I showed off my talents as a host. David lived at all times like an emperor.

When I was first under contract to him, we were both in New York. I invited him to lunch with me at Pavillon. Upon arrival, David said, "You can't afford to buy lunch here. I know what I'm paying you."

"I am the host," I replied. "What would you like to drink? A martini?"

David nodded in assent, and I summoned the waiter who bowed to David in recognition.

"How much are your martinis?" I asked. The waiter almost fainted, and David looked stunned for a split second.

"Do you want two martinis?" asked the waiter in a whisper.

"No," I said, "I want to know how much the martinis are."

The waiter's knees buckled just as a recovered David said firmly, "You heard Mr. Cotten. He said how much are the martinis?" The waiter fled into the back of the restaurant.

After a brief pause, the captain appeared, clicked his heels, and asked, "Did you want two martinis?"

I repeated my question about the price. Finally, Mr. Soulé, the owner, appeared. Leaning over the table, he said quietly, "Mr. Cotten, the barman has just told me that the martinis are eighty cents." (Remember, this was 1943.)

"Eighty cents!" said David. "We just had one across the road for much less. I don't think we want another, do we, Jo?"

"Oh, let's stay here, even though their prices are ludicrous." Then, very grandly, I ordered two eighty-cent martinis.

The waiter, having been revived from his total collapse, arrived with the two wondrous drinks. Just as he was about to set them on the table, the captain rushed over saying, "Stop, don't put those drinks down!"

I was beginning to think there was poison in them. "I have just discovered the martinis are ninety-five cents," he informed us.

David set his shoulders back and said, "That's the quickest inflation I've ever heard of. Let's drink them before the price goes to $1.50!"

We had a fine lunch. David relished all the indignity I had put him through. When I asked for the bill it was the smallest check Pavillon had ever written.

On the plane going back to Los Angeles, we relaxed in our comfortable seats, and David said, "That's what I really like about you, Jo, you have class. I always say 'first class or no class.' Have some champagne; it's paid for in the tickets."

My first job for David, in 1942, was a loan-out to Universal for *Shadow of a Doubt.* Alfred Hitchcock, another of David's "properties," was loaned out to direct it. Hitch, in his later years, thought this the best of his films, and it is certainly mentioned to me as often as *Citizen Kane* and *The Third Man.* What few people seem to have noticed in the credits, however, is that the screenplay, with the exception of the children's dialogue, was written by Thornton Wilder. As far as I can determine, this is Thornton's only contribution to the screen, and I cannot remember any shooting script that suffered so few alterations during production. All the actors agreed that the author's words were not only easy to learn, but a pleasure to speak.

Before we left for Santa Rosa, California, I had a meeting with Hitch to discuss the role of Uncle Charlie, a man high on the most wanted list of the FBI and one with a most complex philosophy, which advocated the annihilation of rich widows whose greedy ambitions had rewarded their husbands with expensive funerals.

"What's worrying you?" asked Hitch.

"I've never played a murderer before, and here I am looking in the mirror at one who's nationally known as The Merry Widow Murderer."

"And you want me to tell you how a murderer behaves," stated Hitch.

"You're the expert," I said.

"Come with me," he said. He should have said "I'll come with you," for we got into my car. On the way into town, he told me that he never drove.

"Know how," he said. "Matter of fact, taught my wife and my daughter to drive . . . but inside my own private driveway. Whenever I see a policeman, I simply go all to pieces."

"I suppose the sight of a policeman brings out a tinge of guilt in all of us," I said.

"I'm not talking about a tinge," Hitch replied. "I'm talking about real panic."

"What do you suppose Uncle Charlie feels whenever he sees a policeman?" I asked.

"Oh, entirely different thing," said Hitch. "Uncle Charlie feels no guilt at all. To him, the elimination of his widows is a dedication, an important sociological contribution to civilization. Remember, when John Wilkes Booth jumped to the stage in Ford's Theatre after firing that fatal shot, he was enormously disappointed not to receive a standing ovation."

We were driving now on Rodeo Drive in Beverly Hills. "Pull over and park wherever you can," he said. "Let's get out and take a walk." We strolled.

"Take a close look at the men you pass and let me know when you spot a murderer." I was beginning to catch on. I paused to look in a shop window. "No, no," said Hitch, dragging me away, "it's murderers we're looking for, not thieves."

"How about that man there with the shifty eyes?" I pointed. "He could be a murderer."

"My dear Watson," Hitch replied, "those eyes are not shifty, they've simply been shifted. Shifted to focus upon the pretty leg emerging from that car." The rest of Claudette Colbert followed the pretty leg to the pavement.

"What you're trying to say is, or rather what I'm saying you're saying is, that a murderer looks and moves just like anyone else," I said.

"Or vice versa," said Hitch. "That completes today's lesson. This walk has exhausted me, let's stop in here."

We were in front of Mike Romanoff's, and I knew now why he had piloted me to Rodeo Drive on our search for a murderer. Hitch had his usual steak. I ordered an omelette. "Never ate an egg in my life," said Hitch.

"Really, never?" I asked.

"Never one egg. I suppose eggs are in some of the things I eat," he said, "but I never could face a naked egg."

"I'll change my omelette to something else," I said.

"Oh, no, please, other people's taste don't bother me at all," he assured me.

"What about other kinds of eggs?" I asked. "How about caviar?"

"As far as I'm concerned," he said, "it's not another kind of egg. As you put it, it is an egg; or if you will, it are eggs."

I asked him, "Wouldn't you say that an epicure who never tasted an egg was an incomplete epicure?"

"I never claimed to be an epicure," said Hitch. "I think you'll find that most of those exotic descriptions we attain are usually inaccurate and always come from remote sources."

I drove him home. On the way he told me that he meant to use Franz Lehar's "Merry Widow" waltz over all the grim references and sights of murder. He was getting out of the car. "I think our secret is to achieve an effect of contrapuntal emotion. Forget trying to intellectualize about Uncle Charlie. Just be yourself. Let's say the key to our story is emotive counterpoint; that sounds terribly intellectual. See you on the set, old bean." He went into his house.

And so we went to Santa Rosa to commence *Shadow of a Doubt.*

Hitch had hoped to find a local youngster who could play the part of the little girl in the picture, and he picked out one on the street who was with her mother and father. She turned out to be a very good actress, with Hitch's patient guidance. After the picture her family sold their market in Santa Rosa and moved down to Los Angeles with great expectations. Like so many talented youngsters and moviestruck parents, expectations never came to fruition.

While location scouting, Hitch found the exact house he wanted in Santa Rosa. It belonged to a doctor and his wife. Again, his personality prevailed. He talked the doctor and his wife into renting their home to the studio. Hitch thought the house looked like a middle-class dwelling on a middle-class tree-lined street. But, like the little girl's parents, the doctor and his wife were stung by the magic of movies entering their lives, and as proud home owners, they wanted their house to appear at its very best.

When Hitch arrived to film, he found to his horror that the beautifully and artistically run-down house was now spick-and-span, a thoroughly painted and renovated structure.

The studio's painters immediately came in and spackled it down with a lot of muddy-looking gook. Sometimes we achieve our goals cruelly, at the expense of innocent people. When the picture was finished, Hitchcock had the house repainted to the owners' requirements.

I have read often that I received the Academy Award for best performance by an actor that year. This is due to obvious carelessness on the part of the vote counters and a double-cross by that wretchedly wonderful actor Paul Lukas, who actually did win. P.S. I wasn't even nominated. Teresa Wright, however, was nominated, but when the envelope was opened, the Oscar was handed to a young newcomer for her first role in *The Song of Bernadette*. Her name, Jennifer Jones.

Hitch had very strong feelings about women in his films. To him the most feminine and most vulnerable women were usually blondes, with the exception of Teresa. I suspect that Ingrid was his favorite, although Grace Kelly became a big star under his direction. He also guided Vera Miles, Tippi Hedren and many others. He loved blondes and couldn't understand women not bleaching their hair for the privilege of working with him.

Like all of us, this genius of an extrovert had superstitions. His best known was that he had to appear in all his own pictures, and somehow he always managed to appear in them. However difficult and however seemingly impossible, he made it. In *Life Boat* with Tallulah Bankhead, there was no way he could be in the little boat with the survivors, but he managed to have a piece of newspaper float by in the water. On the front page was a photograph of you know who.

I visited Hitch at Fox Studios during the making of that picture, and on that day the camera photographed the survivors as the boat rocked to and fro. The cameraman went over to Hitch and whispered, "This is most embarrassing, but as the boat goes backward Tallulah goes backward, and with her legs wide apart. We get a very good view of her with no pants on, do please speak to her." Hitch was for once insecure.

"Try it again," he said. The cameraman tried it again.

"It's very obvious, sir, that she has no pants on. Please speak to her."

Hitch lifted his stomach, stuck out his bottom lip and said, "This is not for me to handle. We shall call the hairdresser."

Hitch's tailor in New York gave him fittings every time he went to and from England. He would be fitted on the way there. On the way back he had lost ten pounds so the suit had to be taken in. The following trip he had put on fourteen pounds and the suit had to be let out. After several years of inflated and deflated fittings, the poor bewildered tailor greeted him by saying, "I'm terribly sorry, sir, but I am afraid this suit is worn out." So, I am sure, was the tailor.

5

The Hatfields and McCoys, the Montagues and Capulets perpetrated insignificant little family misunderstandings compared to the feud that burned red-hot between the two queens of Hollywood gossip, Hedda Hopper and Louella Parsons. There were in the 1940s about 600 correspondents—including press services, press syndicates, fan magazines, and foreign press—covering the news of Hollywood.

The routine releases from the studios, the birthdays, the "girl next door" stories were plentiful. Plentiful and dull. Imagine 600 ravenous journalists patrolling, scratching, and bribing for copy that a handful of people were honestly qualified to generate. But on copy alone could these hovering creatures survive. Their craws and their claws demanded copy, succulent copy, at any cost to them, the truth, or anyone else. Had there been even a scent of truth in most of the stories relating to the personal lives of the handful of people who sparked their interest, the stars' bacchanalia would have rendered them much too delightfully exhausted ever to have considered going to work.

There were sharply focused eyes at every studio gate, on every stage, in every restaurant and every nightclub. The doorman, the men's room attendant, the maid in the ladies' room, the waiters were never out of reach of a telephone, with nimble fingers ever ready to dial that unlisted but lucky number.

In those days the studios worked six full days a week. That is to say, the cameras turned six full days a week.

At this time, the early 1940s, I was working again at Universal Studios on a loan-out arrangement from my boss, David O. Selznick, and at noon every Sunday I was on the air at CBS with a radio show called "Ceiling Zero," which was sponsored by Lockheed Aircraft. Then, it seemed to us that Lockheed was an intimate family company run by Bob Gross and his brother. (At the end of our initial broadcast I was summoned into the control booth for a telephone call. It was Groucho Marx. He congratulated me and said that he had not only enjoyed the show, but had also been completely sold by the commercial. "Just where can I buy a P-38?" he asked.)

Making it a noon air time meant an 8:30 A.M. rehearsal call. On this particular Sunday, after the Lockheed radio show, I went to the nearby Brown Derby on Vine Street for a leisurely lunch, thence a block or two away to NBC, where I joined the rehearsals of another radio show which was to air from 9:30 to 10 P.M.

When this was finished, so was I. I was ready to qualify for the title of Mr. Rubber Legs, and an invitation from the orchestra conductor and his wife to join them for a nightcap was the most soothing music I had heard all day. I returned to the Brown Derby, joined Alan and Roxy, settled down with them, and we all had a drink.

Before I was finished with my drink, I had told them about my Sunday's schedule, and they also knew that I had a seven thirty call at the studio in the morning.

"You're silly to drive those endless miles out to Pacific Palisades, just to sleep in your own bed for a few hours," said Alan. "Why don't you spend the night in your dressing room at the studio?"

It made good sense.

I called the house. Lenore was playing cards, so I told our Filipino gentleman not to disturb her, just to give her the message. I knew that if she needed me for anything she had my telephone number in the dressing room.

It was just before midnight when I drove up to the gate at the studio. The guard's face was a familiar one. I told him I was spending the night in my bungalow, and I held out my hand for the key.

He delivered it, I thought, with just a trace of hesitation, and I wondered why, since on two or three previous occasions I had, at our producer's suggestion, spent Saturday nights there to be near my early Sunday morning radio rehearsals.

I got into my pajamas, and as I turned off the light I saw the figure of a man moving across the lawn, gold badge flashing spotty reflections. Obviously a security guard making his rounds. I thought nothing of it and fell into bed. Two or three minutes later, the alarm clock told me it was seven o'clock Monday morning, and almost time to start acting again.

I found fresh clothes, put them on, picked up my script, and left the bungalow with it under my arm.

"Good morning," said the guard who was standing outside the front door.

Just a slight twinge of curiosity colored my response, which was, of course, "And a good morning to you." I headed toward breakfast.

The commissary was not crowded, and I went straight to the counter because it was near the griddle, and I believe that hot hot pancakes are better than almost hot pancakes. Deanna Durbin was perched on a stool, sipping coffee. I was working as leading man in her current production, which was about half finished. Deanna said, "Aren't you out of uniform, Captain?" I explained that my wardrobe had not yet made its appearance in my dressing room.

"Let me tell you about my Sunday," I said, and I did.

"You mean you spent last night in your dressing room?" she gasped.

"That's right," I answered.

She twirled on the stool and said, more to herself than to anyone else, "Then that accounts for it."

"Accounts for what?" I asked blankly.

"That policeman standing in front of my bungalow all night."

"What do you mean, *all night?*" I croaked.

Deanna covered her face with both hands, then said, "Now, let me tell you about *my* Sunday."

She had driven her husband to the Burbank Airport for a 10 P.M. departure and decided, instead of making the long trek home to Brentwood, to spend the night in her bungalow on the lot, make up there, and be fresh for work Monday. I looked around to the

East, I think, the Far East, the Near East, or any place in the east where I could be at this moment except here. Everything was at once in 3D clarity. Deanna had driven to the lot about eleven; I had come through the gate an hour later. We were both working in the same film, and our bungalows were just a few buildings apart.

The guard at the gate, in all honesty, cannot be faulted for being suspicious. But why the police at the front doors? Who were they protecting against whom? Had Pinkerton crusaded an army in shining badges to preserve the inviolability of Hollywood morals?

Deanna and I walked back toward our bungalows. We got to mine first and I went in. The policeman was still there, and he was doing a bad job of not seeing us. He was lolling about with his arms folded, his eyes rapt in admiration of a cloudless morning sky.

As I was dressing and making up, I thought that there must be some sane and simple exit to this maze. I was sure that Felix Jackson, with his never-ruffled exterior, would know how to handle it. Felix was the producer of our film and was to marry Deanna as soon as her divorce from her present husband was achieved. I dialed Deanna's bungalow.

"I think we should consult Felix about this mess," I said. "If you agree, I'll leave word in his office to call as soon as he comes in."

"He's already in," she said.

"I think we should tell him about last night's farce," I said.

"He already knows," said Deanna.

"Who told him?" I asked.

"Hedda Hopper," she said.

The item that appeared in Hedda's column was not the personal kind of reference that one would clip for a scrapbook, or care to preserve in any of those elaborate, leather-bound gift journals inscribed "Golden Memories."

If we started her story with the title of our picture, *Hers to Hold*, and finished with "Breakfast Together in the Commissary," it would not strain the most diminutive imagination to sprinkle in a spicy middle.

The area of embarrassment was wide, but as the orbit grew smaller and more personal, emotions grew larger. Embarrassment expanded to humiliation, and humiliation exploded into anger. Hot, hot anger that finally, when it reached its zenith, was transformed into icicles. The only warm thing in my igloo was my temper.

I telephoned Hedda. We were on a first name basis. I had met her during the making of *Lydia* about two years earlier. I told Hedda that as a journalist she had every right to air her opinion of my professional behavior on the screen, but that my personal life was none of her business. She replied that I was wrong, and went on with an earful of trite reasons . . . "free speech," "duty to the reading public," etc.

"Would you like me to deny it, dear?" she asked.

"Yes," I said.

"Fine. I'll simply say you called and said you did not have a midnight tryst on the lot . . ."

"Forget it, Hedda," I said. "And forget it forever. If you mention my name in your column personally again . . ." I was about to say something about a bloody nose, but I recalled the difference in our genders in time to recover and modify my threat to, "If you mention my name in your column personally again, I'll kick you in the ass!"

She did.

And I did.

It was at a dinner in the Beverly Hills Hotel honoring the vice president of the United States. The Kick was not a boot that would have carried a football over the crossbar, but neither was it a token tap. Hedda was sitting in a cane-bottomed chair, and contact was positive enough to disturb the flower garden on top of one of the outrageous hats for which she was renowned. Walter Wanger, who was presiding at this function, left his chair and joined a group of gentlemen, including Danny O'Shea, the president of my studio. They carried me from the room on their shoulders to the bar, where I was toasted in champagne by all.

At the risk of being anticlimactic, it would be unfair to Hedda not to add that her manners concerning this entire incident were better than mine. I avoided her conspicuously. My name appeared in her column in strictly industry releases. One day she telephoned and said: "I'm reading a piece here that says you once kicked me in the backside. I don't remember any such thing ever happening, do you?"

I laughed. She laughed. "Of course not," I said. We buried the hatchet and remained friends.

Perhaps reading, and rereading Hedda's aggravating and obviously titillating remarks about my infidelity had an unconscious effect on my behavior. Perhaps the columns had nothing whatsoever to do with it.

I seem to have found no difficulty in writing truthfully about my fortitude; it is not only fair, but imperative that I now admit my weaknesses.

Hedda's pen had given me "the name without the game," but I do not think she was responsible for my subsequent behavior.

I loved my wife. I had no intention of leaving her or in any way of hurting her, but I became unfaithful. It was very easy. I was a young, healthy, full-blooded American and had achieved a certain amount of fame, which of course made it easier. I was away from home a lot. Lenore did not want to fly, sail, or even travel by train, and whenever she could avoid these modes of transportation she stayed home. Although I think she would have liked us to be together, she thought separations were unharmful. And since her home was her castle, she entertained a lot, mostly musicians and card players. She was considered a snob by some people, but I think she just chose her friends carefully. Those she chose loved her sense of humor, for although she had changed, as we both had, her sense of humor remained intact.

We lived our own lives and were together whenever possible. My conscience didn't bother me too much. As far as I could see, or would let myself see, she was a completely happy wife and a very busy hostess. She was surrounded by friends whose interests were not in the movies.

I was an actor. A roamer. A lover. I made pictures, I made love, and I made martinis. I was living the life of Riley. But if the truth be faced, Riley was a temporary name I indulged in when I was lonely.

Why had we both changed? I would think often of the feelings we had for each other when we were first married. We seemed to be completely, passionately in love . . . and now, was all passion spent? Was she growing cold? Was I to blame? I was so confused and neither of us was happy. Our marriage was holding together by a very slender thread.

6

My distant relationship with westerns ended one Sunday morning in 1945 at the Fairmont Hotel in San Francisco. I was enjoying a leisurely breakfast and the view of the autumn sun sparkling on the harbor. The telephone interrupted to announce a wire coming in. "Just slip it under the door," I called in response to the knock. My eggs were getting cold.

"Please, sir, I don't think it will fit." I opened the door. The page was right, the cable wouldn't fit under the door, it would barely fit into the room. It was a memo from David. I had asked to be excused from acting in his forthcoming movie, a western called *Duel in the Sun*. He had definite and strong opinions about my regrets. By the time I had finished reading the memo, the autumn sun had set, the harbor was dark, and I had talked to David in Beverly Hills. Our conversation ended with his words: "I'll have the wardrobe man start on your riding gear tomorrow."

The love story in *Duel in the Sun* was a lusty, daring theme for its time. Today many exhibitors would consider it ideal for a children's matinee. The Hays Office, or the Breen Office, or whatever the censor's office was called then, kept sharp eyes on every frame of the film as it progressed, and David Selznick was constantly bombarded with orders and suggestions to modify or delete anything verbal or pictorial that might appeal to the libido. Rumors of censorship circulated the lot, and a word to the wise guys is sufficient. Alternative titles for the film kept popping up in the commissary.

"Lust in the Dust" and "Hump in the Sump" were the two most printable.

During that picture Old Jim came into my life. Bob Adler introduced us. He said, "They told me you wanted a tame horse. Here stands the tamest horse in the West, Old Jim. I taught Shirley Temple to ride him!" We became great pals, Old Jim and I, and I can remember only one slightly sticky moment while in his company. He pulled up rather suddenly, and I lost my balance. I grabbed his right front leg and descended gently to the desert floor. Old Jim looked down, gave me an embarrassed blush, and I swear I heard him say, "Sorry about that."

Old Jim was almost the recipient of one of David's famous memos. Though completely innocent, he accepted the blame like the thoroughbred old gentleman he was, with both ears pointed high. David was indulging in a retake of a retake of a retake. (There are fewer feet of original film in *Duel in the Sun* than there are of retakes.)

There was one particular scene that simply refused to fall into any dramatic order of interest, but David thought the scene necessary and was determined to make it fall into its place—wherever that was. Jennifer and I were the only actors involved.

We had originally shot it in the dining room. No good. Then we shot it in the parlor, then in the pool room. David gave Jennifer a scanty costume, and we tried it in the bedroom. Still no good. We were now shooting it in the stable. Six o'clock came and we called it quits for the day. The assistant announced, "We'll continue here in the morning at 9 A.M."

I turned to the boss. "We're slipping, David," I said. "We always wrap this scene in one day."

He looked puzzled for a moment, then he brightened, "Ah, but we never had a horse in it before."

There is no doubt that *Duel in the Sun* was one of the most successful westerns ever made. Europeans still talk about it. It made a star out of Greg Peck. Jennifer lost her innocent image and surprised everyone by playing a *femme fatale*.

David knew from the start that I did not want to appear in it. It was only after his long, long memo to San Francisco and our subsequent telephone conversation that he beguiled me into playing the part. But I was never happy in the role of Jesse.

To relieve my boredom, David let me choose the most elegant wardrobe. I then proceeded to call myself "Dressy Jesse." It caught on with the rest of the cast and provided diversion during many days in Tucson in a long, colorless role for me.

The evenings I took care of in the only way I knew how. Those of the company who cared to would drop into my suite for one of "Dressy Jesse's" dynamite martinis. Later, I would dine in some secluded spot (I needed no more publicity about my indiscretions) with someone kind, and pretty, and warm. It was surprising how cold I found myself in deserts when I was alone.

These little flights of mine into the realm of infidelity were not frequent. They occurred only when I had known someone first and found her attractive. I always made it clear at the start that I would never, ever leave my wife. Under these conditions I tried not to hurt anyone, including myself. As Ruby had taught me many years ago, if you walk away from an affair . . . I always walked away. I say this not with pride.

Old Jim and I also worked together on a movie called *Untamed Frontier*. One morning we were with Shelley Winters, her horse, and one of those mounted toughies usually described as "a man with a two-day growth of beard," trotting our way out of O.K. Trail, which is in Tombstone Canyon, which is an extension of Brewery Gulch, which is near Douglas, which is in Cochise County, which everyone knows is in Arizona.

Shelley Winters has never been anything less than a fine actress. Luckily her cup runneth over with solid, indestructible talent; otherwise, it could not withstand the abuse she heaps on it with her perplexing experiments, which she claims are necessary to achieve artistic honesty. Her capacity for laughing at herself is born of disarming charm, and she is a genuine, uncomplicated mixture of sensuality and naiveté, which is probably one of the reasons so many men fall in love with her.

We were out on a vast white plain now, and we must have looked like dots to the little aircraft high above us. As it began circling for a landing on the plain, Shelley cried, "That's him!" and took off at a gallop toward the landing plane. The toughie and I rode back to our base of trailers, equipment trucks, and tents. A Jeep took off carrying a wrangler in the direction of the aircraft. The wrangler returned on Shelley's horse, and Shelley returned in the Jeep with two men, the pilot of the plane and Vittorio Gassman, a very handsome and popular Italian stage and film star. Shelley introduced this visitor who had suddenly dropped out of the sky, and, with her hand in his, hastily led him to her trailer. Slam! All eyes looked in every direction other than the trailer, except two. Those two belonged to a Peeping Tom, who reported that "the trailer shook." The assistant director waved a warning finger at Tom and took his name.

When they came out, Gassman settled in a canvas chair, produced a small volume of Italian poetry, and began to read. Shelley, the toughie, and I mounted our horses and returned to the scene. Hugo Fregonese, the director, was Argentinian, but his grasp of American idiom was acute. When the camera rolled again, Hugo tactfully substituted "Commence" for "Action."

The golden thread of romance wove itself into the pattern of our production for two or three days. Finally the bird warmed up its engine and we all watched it soar away, carrying Vittorio in the direction of his native Italy.

"Didn't seem too interested in our western scenery, did he?" said Cad Number One.

"Too wrapped up in that book," said Cad Number Two. He pointed to the volume of Italian poetry lying open, face down in the canvas chair.

Shelley, I am told, says that they shook the trailer just to make us all think what we were thinking. In that case, did Mr. Gassman fly from Italy to Arizona to fake a shake and read some poetry? If Shelley said so then it must be true.

He may not have seemed too interested in our western scenery, but after all, the man was in love. Soon after the movie was finished, Shelley became Mrs. Vittorio Gassman.

In 1948 I was flying over New London, Connecticut. The pilot let me take the controls for a moment, and it was a great sensation. I was on my way to see Robert Brackman, who painted the portrait of Jenny for the movie of that title. He had invited me to his New London studio during some of the sessions when Jennifer Jones was posing for him. Mr. Brackman said he was sick of seeing actors who knew nothing about painting making asses of themselves in artist's smocks and berets, kicking over their easels and destroying their canvasses in raging tantrums.

I sat quietly in Mr. B's large studio overlooking Long Island Sound, and observed him as he brought his subject alive on canvas.

I mentally filed two or three of his gestures and stances. Some weeks later, on a Hollywood stage during the filming of Paul Osborn's adaptation of Robert Nathan's *Portrait of Jenny*, where Jennifer Jones was now posing for me in my New York attic, I executed one of Mr. Brackman's dramatic flourishes with the brush, then mimed what I considered a well-rehearsed imitation of one of his frequent acrobatic maneuvers.

I had noted, in his New London studio, that when Mr. Brackman felt the need of a more distant view of his canvas, it never occurred to him to walk away, turn around and look, or even simply to step back a pace or two. Instead, he kept both feet firmly planted to the floor and leaned his head back, back, back, curving his spine into a C not only defying but defeating the law of gravity.

Our production manager had engaged a technical adviser, a real artist, to be present on the set and assist my struggles in handling alien props such as brushes and palettes and, above all, to prevent any nonprofessional garret behavior.

On my first try at a faithful imitation of Mr. Brackman, the technical director was on his feet crying, "No, no, no, please, please—no artist was ever guilty of such overacting."

William Dieterle, the director of the film, with whom I had worked before, remained silent. I said, "The man who painted this picture did exactly that."

"I can't believe it," said the technical director.

I looked to Dieterle, who said, "Joseph, I must admit, it looks a little broad. Although I'm sure it's authentic, it is, I am afraid, another example to prove how difficult it is for art to copy nature."

I demonstrated more of Mr. Brackman's idiosyncrasies, which drew tolerant smiles from Dieterle, sneers from the technical director, and a stony silence from the crew, most of them old friends.

Dieterle was right, it is nature that copies art, not the other way around. I wish I could say that when Mr. Brackman saw our movie he modified his studio behavior to what was on the screen, but I have no way of knowing whether my performance, with its more economic albeit enforced animation, changed his habits or, indeed, his opinion of actor-painters.

He did say once, however, after reading one of David Selznick's daily memos on the progress of the portrait, "I do appreciate outside opinion. One of these days I shall accept every suggestion offered to me, then I shall paint the perfect picture."

I believe that Robert Nathan created Jenny out of a wispy fragment of time, just as he had her disappear in a violent gust of cosmic agelessness.

Barely one of us has not been touched personally by an eerie finger that clearly points, sometimes for what seems a fraction of a second, to an expansion in time, a collapse in space, an overlapping of both.

Robert Nathan relates his strange tale through the eyes of a painter, Eban Allen. And Eban tells us the story with his brushes and his easel, on which the portrait of a little girl matures into young womanhood during the passing of a few months, perhaps a few seconds.

Some believe it all true. Some believe Jenny to be a vision, an inspiration. "Perhaps," some say, "it happened before Jenny was born; before Eban was born." It has no chronological significance.

David O. and the director, William Dieterle, agreed that since the subject matter was fantasy, the style of relating *Portrait of Jenny* should be visually as realistic as possible.

We went to New York's Central Park, where much of the story took place. God was kind to Selznick and the production department. It was supposed to be winter with snow, and it was. During the days the snow got dirty and slushy, and usually by week's end it was gone. But the big production man in the sky always redecorated the set with flurries of clean, pure, white fluffy snow on Sunday night.

To achieve the effect of this dream . . . or vision . . . this mirage or brain fever that the artist suffered whenever he saw or talked to the child, Jenny, she would appear in a halo of warm light. Joe August, the cameraman, thought our modern lenses were far too sophisticated for this picture, so he sent to Hollywood for some of the primitive equipment he had used in the movies of William S. Hart. With those precious antiques he achieved his goal. He, of all of us, understood the story, and I think he truly believed that Jenny existed.

One day when Jennifer Jones and I were shooting some of his Currier and Ives shots on the frozen lake in Central Park, David came stumbling on to the ice excitedly shouting, "Stop, stop, I have reread the book, and I now understand it!" This alarming statement snapped us all out of our dream world.

"The special effects department in Hollywood can make it all look much more real," David said. "Shoot the scene with Jennifer and Jo on the bench, with a swan swimming in the background, then wrap it up, and we'll finish the job in California."

Joe August was the last to leave; he found it hard to part from the beauty of nature, but professional that he was, he slowly awakened and did as his producer bade him.

We all laughed, and called it the swan song scene. Jennifer and I were seated on the bench. In the background was the frozen lake. The crew had broken the ice, leaving enough room for the swan's activity.

At that point, Joe August announced that it was impossible to proceed. The motors of the camera had frozen and refused to turn, and the faces of the actors were blue from the cold and quite expressionless.

Runners were sent to purchase electric blankets, two of which comforted the camera. Another pair were painted to match the seat on the bench and were used to defrost the seats of the actors.

Action. "Cut," said Joe August, "the swan went out of the shot." Several rowboats were dispatched to discourage the swan from wandering by waving their oars.

Action. "Cut," said a voice. It was the voice of the animal technician, who said, "That swan is being harassed by the men in those boats. The SPCA will have us up for this. What is it you are trying to do?" Dieterle explained that what we wanted was the swan to be seen swimming in the background of the shot. "Simple," said the animal technician. "How deep is the water where we want the swan?"

"How deep is the water where we want the swan?" cried three assistants to the men in the boats.

"How do we know how deep the water is?" cried the men in the boats to the three assistants.

Several measuring devices were sent out. "Ten feet," yelled boatman number one.

"Ten feet," yelled boatman number two.

"Ten feet it is, plus enough for the circle," said the animal technician as he carefully measured out a length of rope. He tied the swan's foot to one end of the rope and a heavy rock to the other. He dropped the rock into the water. It was perfect. The swan glided in a little circle just inside the borders of the shot.

Action. The swan circled in the background, but each time the circle was smaller. The animal technician was unaware that the bottom of the lake was a quicksand of decomposed plant life and that the rock was sinking into it. The swan's circle became smaller and smaller, and his neck was struggling to stretch above the water, when from behind the camera, Joe August shouted, "Save the swan!" One of the boatmen reached it just in time.

Before our New York location, we had filmed at Graves End Light, off Boston, a real lighthouse with real waves, real fog, real wind, real water, and a great iron ladder leading to the top of the lighthouse, with real ice surrounding every single rung.

Most of the time, we were too sick and too cold to eat the real lobster dinner that the crew of one of our tug boats served to us after they had robbed the nearby traps.

It had all been *terribly* real and extremely uncomfortable. David's sudden comprehension of the story, and his decision to return to Hollywood and remake everything he didn't like, was most welcomed by Jennifer and me, by some of the crew, if not all of them, and by a dazed and delighted cameraman. Joe had worked with David before, and their taste and artistry were similar.

Home, sun, studio hours. Special effects. Fantastic special effects.

To film that New England hurricane entirely inside a Hollywood studio was a masterful accomplishment. But then, after burning Atlanta, this was but a wave of the wand to David.

Magic or not, we all worked even harder than we had on the exteriors. Our electric sun was always shining. We were early for work, late to go home. That strange feeling of the unreleased soul of Jenny pervaded the atmosphere wherever we worked.

The storm scene, shot indoors, with tons of water all over us for so many weeks, has been written about as one of the greatest location scenes ever filmed! The picture won an Oscar for special effects that year.

In our final scene, Ethel Barrymore talked about Jenny and the artist, and her character believed that the spirit of Jenny had returned. After the scene, I looked into her wise, expressive eyes. We said nothing. Without words she told me that she believed in Jenny's existence.

The picture finally had come to an end, if an end it ever had.

Joe August, our brilliant, incomparable cameraman, our master of ethereal light, as much our inspiration as anyone (even Dieterle vehemently conceded this), walked into David's office and said, "I think it's finished now, I'm satisfied." He went over to the sofa, lay down and with a hauntingly beautiful smile on his lips, closed his eyes and never opened them again.

Some time later, David's financial problems were such that he was forced to close the studio. This man had made *Gone with the Wind*. This man had had under contract Ingrid Bergman, Gregory Peck, Joan Fontaine, Shirley Temple, Louis Jourdan, Valli, Rhonda Fleming, Dorothy Maguire, and many others, including yours truly.

He freed us all. That is, all of us who wanted to be freed. Jennifer he had wisely married. For my part, I could never cut the umbilical cord from David.

I did not, however, always take his advice. He would often say, "You don't need to make that movie, Jo, the part isn't good enough." Or, "The movie isn't good enough, you've been in so many top-flight pictures. Wait for the right story." I was often aware that I should have heeded David. But I wanted to work, and I did.

It had often entered my mind that through our many separations, it was possible that Lenore might have found someone to her liking. Someone to flirt with, someone who would pay a great deal of attention to her. Someone who might even appeal to her so much that she would let him make love to her.

I always dismissed the latter thought as soon as it entered my head. Lenore was attractive, gregarious, witty, and faithful. I was sure of this, for although I knew her to be a passionate woman, she loved me. This she manifested whenever we were together.

The only reason we were apart so often was that she despised any form of travel whatsoever.

Would I have been a model husband had we been together more often? I certainly cannot say that I would have, but I liked fidelity, I admired it, and in some indescribable way I needed it.

So, when David sent me to New York to do publicity for *Duel in the Sun* and *Portrait of Jenny*, I had to fly there, and I asked Lenore if she would follow by train and join me. We could have some fun. We hadn't been to New York for some time, and the train was really quite safe. She consented happily.

We stayed at the St. Regis Hotel, suite 505. I have often wondered why I remember the number of the suite!!!

When I was not having interviews and pictures taken for publicity, I would go to the Racquet Club and have a steam bath, then a bite of lunch. I loved the Racquet Club, and the steams and rubdowns and swims eased my tiredness through years of working both in pictures and the theatre.

One morning, I left the hotel early and told Lenore that I would have lunch at the club, see some publicity people, and be back in time for us to go out for dinner together. She wished me a happy day. It certainly was a most beautiful day. After a quick swim I decided that it was far too nice a day to spend in a club with a lot of men. Also, the publicity could wait until tomorrow. I telephoned the newspaper people and made the date for the next day. I walked out of the club into the bright sunshine on Park Avenue, and sauntered back to suite 505 at the St. Regis.

I was not in the least surprised when I saw Lenore sitting in the living room, sipping a cocktail with Henry Luce. We had met Henry and Clare at the Selznicks, and I liked them both. He seemed pleased to see me, and Lenore offered me a cocktail, which, of course, I didn't refuse. I told Henry a long story about a friend of mine who was printing a new Bible. He appeared most interested, so I elaborated on my tale for quite a while. Henry said he would buy one. I sipped my cocktail happily, glad to have been able to give him such spell-binding information.

Lenore was unusually quiet, but that was understandable, for Henry Luce was not a close friend of ours, and I was sure she was happy that I had turned up and helped with the conversation.

There was a knock on the door. It was a waiter with a table and lunch for two, chilled white wine, and lobster salads!

Lenore's voice returned. "Jo, Henry and I were going to have a little lunch, so won't you join us?"

"Yes, thank you, I'll have the same thing," I told the expressionless waiter.

Henry Luce consumed his lunch with great rapidity, and then politely made his exit.

"Well, I did enjoy seeing him," I said sincerely.

"So did I," said Lenore in a voice as expressionless as the waiter's face.

Now Lenore and I never discussed this extraordinary encounter, but a friend of mine once told me he had mentioned my name to Clare. "You know Jo, don't you?" he said.

"Oh yes," said the lady who wrote *The Women*. "Yes, I know Jo, he asked me to dance once, and I said I'd rather not, as I didn't like being pushed around by men. 'That's all right,' he replied, 'I don't mind at all if you lead.' " I remembered the occasion.

Then she told my friend, "Lenore and Henry were close friends. I really don't know why Jo and I didn't become closer, if only to get even!"

Clare Booth Luce was known for her wit, for her intelligence, and for her sugar-coated wisecracks. My friend was known for his unreliability. But looking back, it is only fair to say that seeing Lenore and Henry that day in New York, in suite 505, I obviously behaved like a stupid, insensitive, unsophisticated, and conceited idiot. Why didn't I at least leave when the waiter arrived? I could have said that I had to do some publicity photographs.

Poor, poor Lenore. It may have been a harmless little flirtation, it may have been something more meaningful. Whichever, she certainly deserved a better break.

As for Henry . . . well, he had good taste, and good manners.

I do hope he bought that Bible, if only to give it to Clare.

David telephoned New York and told me to get back to California and meet him at the studio. When I met him, he told me the most extraordinary story about one of his screenplays that was soon to be done by RKO. The evolution of any screenplay is extraordinary, I suppose. More works of conjecture, for instance, have been written on the creation of the screenplay of *Citizen Kane* than Orson and Herman were ever able to cram between those blue covers.

David told me that he had bought a story for Ingrid Bergman. It had been a Finnish play called *Hulda for Parliament,* and he had assigned Dore Schary, one of his producers, to supervise the transformation of its language to English, its locale to the United States, the heroine's name to Katie, her nationality to Swedish, and, of course, Parliament to Congress. It was to be released in 1947 as *The Farmer's Daughter*, and he suggested that I consider the part of Ethel Barrymore's son, a congressman. Charles Bickford was to be the butler, H. C. Potter, the director.

"Oh, by the way," David added after telling me all this, "Ingrid is not going to do the picture."

I am not at all certain what cooled Ingrid's ardor. I thought her perfect for the part and was disappointed at her decision. Of course David knew about my insecure home life. He knew Ingrid had much the same situation. And he also knew, I now feel sure, that Ingrid and I were "compatible." To put us together in another picture at this time might cause hurt and scandal.

What he did not know, was that we had discussed just that possibility and because of Lenore and Peter, we had decided to remain just friends. Friends we remained for the rest of her life.

David said that Loretta Young liked the script but had been apprehensive about mastering a Swedish accent. He sent Ruth Roberts to work with her. Ruth was Ingrid's English coach and was helping her lose her native accent. Ruth succeeded admirably with both Ingrid and Loretta.

When Academy Award time came, a best performance Oscar went to Loretta for the Swedish housemaid-congresswoman she played in *The Farmer's Daughter*.

Loretta started film acting while in her teens. Like most thoroughly professional and talented actors, she contributes great pleasure and relaxation to the day's work. Her knowledge of her own technique, as well as the offstage mechanics of movie making, is enormous. I am not the first to observe that she could do well with no other lighting expert on the set. She can never be unglamorous, and her beautiful eyes are as innocent today as ever. At one of those big hotel ballroom do's recently, I greeted her with a peck on the cheek and was almost arrested by the security guard for child molesting. She is one of five beautiful girls. Four are sisters, the fifth was the crowning beauty of them all . . . Mama.

Darryl Zanuck, the head of 20th Century Fox, entertained in a totally different style from Selznick. The Palm Springs Yacht Club was an affectionate name imposed by their guests on the rambling,

comfortable estate of Virginia and Darryl Zanuck, a truly gregarious and hospitable couple.

During the active days of the Palm Springs Yacht Club, this ru-
ral town in the desert was a small community of private oases dotted
about in an arid, sandy basin. Today, of course, Palm Springs is a
large community of private oases, with a few grains of sand dotted
in between them.

Darryl was a croquet enthusiast. No, that won't do. Darryl was
a croquet fiend, and a passionate contestant. Perhaps because it is
played with a ball and a mallet, he was overzealous in accepting it as
a substitute for his favorite game, polo.

On the front lawn was a sprawling, beautiful court, with
heavy white wickets and other serious and advanced equipment.
Big league croquet always seemed to me to be more a game of
strategy than of skill, and the aces of the Yacht Club often made
one game last through an entire weekend. Sometimes floodlights
were brought out on Saturday nights to enable the contestants
to finish their match before the guests' departure time on
Sunday.

If you didn't play croquet, you saw Darryl and three others only
at lunch, cocktails, and dinner. Whenever the game was finished
before darkness, there was dancing to the phonograph or a wild
game of charades in the billiard room.

With the exception of an occasional banker from New York,
there were no "private people" to inhibit the natural and relaxed atmosphere of these joyous weekends.

Mary Lee and Douglas Fairbanks, Jr., were charter members of
the Yacht Club, as were David Niven and his wife Hjordis. Many
Yacht Club members shared the difficult times as well as the good
times, and rallied around when friends needed support.

Patricia Medina was at the end of a rocky trip. She and Richard
Greene, her husband, had tried their best. Their friends had rooted
for both sides, for they seemed a fairy tale couple. They were so
welcome and so adaptable to any society, but they simply couldn't
make it work. They always spoke highly of each other. Patricia confided little to anyone, but she did tell Lenore that she thought they
had married too young.

Richard would telephone her often. This extremely handsome
young man had hit a low in his career. He was a fine actor and

aspired to be a serious English stage performer. I personally think that his looks held him back.

One day Patricia called Lenore and said, "Guess what? Rick has been offered a television series. He doesn't want to do it. I think I talked him into it, though. They want him to play Robin Hood, and I think he'd be a marvelous Robin Hood."

Instead of playing Hamlet, he wound up making a huge success on television. Patricia was delighted for him. It did not, however, rekindle their love.

She divorced him, but she told everyone who asked her, "I will always be his friend, maybe his best friend, but not his wife. It didn't work, and heaven knows we both gave it a fair chance." Then she would smile sadly and say, "Marriage is not for me, and I'm sure I won't get married again."

In the midst of this personal confusion, she had transferred her professional life from the MGM studios to Columbia, which had loaned her out to Paramount studios, where she was starring in one of several films she made with Alan Ladd.

Now, living alone, her telephone was busier than she wanted it to be. She was on everyone's party list, and her answer to "We'll have so-and-so pick you up," was always, "Thanks, I'll get myself there alone, if you don't mind." Her wings remained singed, her heart shied from involvement. She felt safe with Hjordis and Lenore, and they both adored her.

Jennifer Jones and David Selznick were runners up for the charades championship at the Palm Springs Yacht Club, which was held by Mousie, William Powell's wife. Bill's charm, his old-world manners, and his wide horizon of interests made him everybody's favorite. But Bill was no social butterfly. He was always happy in a far corner, or under a tree, with his nose in a book, until exactly 6 P.M. Then he used his nose for testing the aroma of something exotic that had been poured into a long cold glass.

Charlie Chaplin, incidentally, always won the booby prize at charades. His pantomime was so perfect and elaborate that both teams forgot the game in their fascinated attention to his performance. The time-is-up bell usually rang before he had completed growing from an acorn into an ancient oak spreading its shade over the village smithy or whatever it was he was demonstrating.

Lenore, Virginia, Hjordis, and Patricia were the gamblers.

They were canasta addicts, and at the drop of a card they would gravitate to their favorite corner, from which would emanate giggles much higher, I'm sure, than the stakes.

There was other homey entertainment at the Zanucks. Noel Coward would sing, Richard Rodgers would play, and sometimes when the stars lowered themselves over the desert to within touching distance, Spyros Skouras would recite Greek poetry in his native tongue.

Darryl's favorite croquet partners were Louis Jourdan, the loquacious Russian director Gregory Ratoff (both ringers), and Moss Hart, the champion of every island in New York sound, including Long.

Douglas Fairbanks, Jr., David Niven, Tyrone Power, and I, all graduates of the "vicarage school" of Sunday croquet, were the also-rans of the green. Our chief weakness was "no strategy," we were told. Well, according to the vicarage method, there was no such thing as strategy. Style and simplicity were our strong suits. After all, the purpose of the game was simple . . . get through the wickets and hit the stake as soon as possible. The Yacht Club strategy had become so complicated that a large blackboard had found its way onto the lawn, and without an official scorer to keep accurate book, memories would either muddle or go blank.

At this point, the big cigar would be removed from Darryl's mouth, so that he could deliver some unwelcomed, if deserved, comments on cheating.

One particular Sunday, we started a game after lunch. It was Darryl and Moss Hart against Ty Power and me. Ty and I agreed that our strategy would be *no* strategy, and while Darryl and Moss were knocking our balls and their own all over the country, Ty and I kept knocking back to the playing area and making the wickets. When we hit the stakes in less than an hour, with Moss and Darryl still a telephone call away, they threw down their mallets in the kind of disgust the Olympic Committee would have shown had they caught Hitler lining Jesse Owen's running shoes with lead.

After our unforgivable behavior on the croquet lawn, the Palm Springs Yacht Club forever banished Ty and me to the white-flannel "Tennis anyone?" set.

7

No place can be more beautiful, more aesthetically stimulating, than London on a fine day. And that's exactly what it was when I woke up on my very first morning ever in this ancient and civilized city, after an endless and boring trans-Atlantic flight. Through my window I was viewing a montage of familiar postcards—Big Ben, Westminster Abbey, the Houses of Parliament, and closer, Waterloo Bridge with its supports in the Thames. Everything was in bright sunshine, except for the few moving shadows cast by the trees in the foreground. What dream could conjure up a happier omen for one's first day of work in a foreign land?

I regretted that Lenore was not with me to share this morning's rare elation. She would be arriving in a couple of weeks by ship. She tried hard but was never able to overcome her claustrophobic dread of being locked up "in that little tube." She never set foot inside an airplane.

Almost everybody arrived at Elstree studios at the same moment. There were hasty introductions, and we all went into a large empty soundstage and arranged ourselves in an enormous ring of chairs. Manuscripts of *Under Capricorn* were in our laps. This was to be Hitchcock's first personal production, released in 1949. His business partner was an old friend, Sidney Bernstein. Hitch was seated quietly with his hands folded over the front of the navy blue double-breasted jacket that was his uniform. Sidney was moving about greeting and introducing, and several assistants were taking notes on everyone's preference for tea.

James Bridie, Scotland's foremost playwright, was seated next to Hitch. Mr. Bridie had written the screen adaptation, and the atmosphere of the room was already beginning to benefit from the aroma of his flat Turkish cigarettes, which never ceased to burn. During the next three days we all would benefit from his personal explanations of his precise writing—no word, no punctuation of which was ever changed without his conference and approval.

Since I was playing Ingrid Bergman's husband, I sat myself next to her. On her other side was Michael Wilding, the "other man," then Margaret Leighton and Cecil Parker. The rest of the cast was composed of a large part of the Abbey Theatre company from Dublin, for most of the principals in this nineteenth-century drama were unsavory characters from Irish prisons who were "freed" by the authorities in exchange for settling the new colony of Australia. Ingrid and Michael were Irish gentry.

Actors in general are a clannish group and most cooperative and helpful to each other while rehearsing and acting. Formalities are quickly discarded and first names come easily. Even Mr. Bridie, whom I had come to like very much, suggested on the day he was to leave that I no longer address him as Mr. Bridie. Thank goodness some finger from above stopped me from asking whether he preferred James or Jim, and prompted me to say instead, "What shall I call you?"

He replied, "I gave up medicine for play writing and changed my name. My friends call me Dr. Mavor."

"Dr. Mavor" invited me to visit him in his native land, which he loved. "I'd like to show you Loch Lomond," he said.

"Isn't that where the monster or dragon or something is?" I asked.

"I believe you're thinking of another lake," he said. "However, under certain circumstances monsters and dragons have oft' been spotted in Loch Lomond . . . which reminds me . . . how much whiskey?"

"What do you mean how much whiskey?" I asked.

"Believe it or not," he said, "Scotch whiskey is still being rationed in Scotland, of all places, and I'll have to lay in some."

"Just a little would do fine," I said.

"That's no answer," he said. "How many bottles? How many bottles a day?"

"Oh," I said, "what about one bottle a day?" Mr. Bridie, now familiarly "Dr. Mavor," gave me a Scottish squint.

"How many days?" he asked.

Shooting proceeded smoothly. I never heard Hitchcock raise his voice on a set. He often spoke in whispers, and his quiet authority commanded concert deportment from all aboard. He knew exactly the moment when the thick atmosphere of silent concentration was ready to explode, and he always doused the fuse with low, often bawdy, comic relief.

The authentic accents of the chaps from the Abbey Theatre were beginning to worry this foreigner, who was slowly approaching the scene in which he told the story of his life in Ireland.

Ingrid and I would go for walks in the English countryside between Hitch's long takes, and I decided that on our next walk I would ask her advice about my problem with the accent. She was then in Paris for the weekend, and had promised to bring us back some meat. (Rationing in England in 1949 was more like starving!)

Lenore had not yet arrived and Peter Lindstrom, Ingrid's husband, was in California, his date of arrival unknown. So every evening I would dine with Hitch, his wife Alma, and Ingrid. Of course when Ingrid was off using her best French to bring home the bacon, there would just be the three of us.

Hitch had become an American citizen and, in doing so, decided that he disliked all things British. We had just finished "not eating" our dinner, and Hitch was being particularly sarcastic about England, when sailing into the dining room came Ingrid. I write *sailing* because it seemed her feet didn't touch the ground, and her expression was more mysterious than Hitch's movies.

"Ah, here comes the goddess bringing manna from Paris!" he said fondly.

"I didn't bring food. I didn't have time, Hitch, I'm sorry," she said. Then to me, "Jo, is it too late for you to make me one of your martinis?"

"Of course not," I replied as I guided her away from Hitch's mean and hungry look.

"Whatever did you do in Paris that you didn't have time to bring us food?" he snorted.

"I met a director from Italy, that's all," Ingrid said with complete finality. We left. There was no food and we were to hear no more about the director. Oh, but much later we were all to read such awful stories in the press: Ingrid and Roberto Rossellini had shattered the world with their romance. Ingrid's career tumbled through unjust criticism of her morality. And the people of the United States were the worst offenders.

Ingrid drank her martini in a flash, then said, "Jo, please?" She moved her glass toward me, and as I refilled it she shook her hair as if to toss away any thoughts of Paris. Back came the Bergman smile.

"Well, what's going on with the picture?" she asked. I told her of my problem explaining my heritage and my inability to assume an Irish accent. Immediately she became Ingrid Bergman, actress. "Don't come to me about accents," she said. "I am beyond confusion as far as any language is concerned. In California I worked so hard on my English to lose my native accent that I've made myself incomprehensible in Stockholm. At the moment I am going to Berlitz for Swedish, so that I can be understood at home, and I have a coach at the studio who's trying to twist my accent, whatever it is, into Irish."

For the benefit of those who preferred martinis icy cold instead of "chilled," Sidney Bernstein had installed in his private office a brand-new, clinical white electric refrigerator. After shooting every afternoon, he held open house, or, as Hitch called it more accurately, "open office." I was appointed official bartender; my responsibility to this honored title permitted no absenteeism.

As in any club, most of the conversation flowed in a very narrow channel. Ours, of course, concerned the progress of *Under Capricorn*. It was, therefore, easy for me to bring up my growing self-consciousness regarding my Irish background. "Perhaps we'd better seek the author's help," suggested Hitch.

"You know how James Bridie hates London," said Sidney. "There must be some simple alteration we can make without imposing another trip on him." Hitch reminded him of their agreement to make no changes without the author's conference and approval, and Sidney promised to call him.

The following day, Sidney told us that my friend "Dr. Mavor" was reluctantly taking the night train and would join us at lunch in the commissary the next day.

When I entered the commissary I didn't see "Dr. Mavor," but the aroma of Turkish tobacco told me he was there and in what direction to find him. He was sitting with Hitch and Sidney.

"They tell me the speech about your background is giving you trouble," said "Dr. Mavor."

"Oh no, not at all," I said. "It's a beautiful speech, a pleasure to learn, and I look forward to reciting it."

"Dr. Mavor" gave Sidney and Hitch a puzzled glance, waved his Turkish censer in my direction, and asked, "Well, exactly what are we talking about?"

"It's only the first five words," I said. "I simply find it impossible to say them with any conviction."

"What are the first five words?" he asked.

"I was born in Dublin," I said.

"Where were you born?" he asked.

"Virginia," I said.

"Well, change the line to read, 'I was born in Virginia,'" he said.

Actor's problem and dramatist's problem solved, "Dr. Mavor" caught the night train back to his beloved Scotland.

Before he left the studio that day, however, he stopped by the set for a brief visit. In between shots, I was talking to him and to Hitch about the story in general, when the devil suddenly touched my tongue (one of his frequent torments to actors) and our title, *Under Capricorn*, came out "Under Cornycrap."

I never saw Loch Lomond. I never worked in another Hitchcock film.

I finished early that afternoon and learned that I would have the next two days off. I happily rode up to London, planning to surprise Lenore with tickets for a play that night and a full day of sight-seeing the next day.

When I closed our front door, she came in from the bedroom. Her eyes were wet, her face ashen. She held a blue envelope in her hand. "I opened this by mistake," she said. "I read it."

It was from an actress I had known in California who now lived in London. I had seen her several times during my two weeks alone in the city. The letter was from New York, where she was starting rehearsals for a play. It was an indiscreet letter. It was a graphic letter. Denial was hopeless, and the onrushing sense of guilt compounded my deceit into aggression.

"If you'd behave like other wives and travel with me in the air, things like this couldn't happen," I said.

"Do you mean you can't be left alone for two weeks without a keeper?" she asked. "And what did you mean by *things like this*?"

I tried to remain on the offensive and succeeded malevolently, saying, "And since when has the opening of other people's letters been admitted into the realm of good manners?"

"Good manners," Lenore sobbed as she rushed into the bedroom and closed the door.

I now faced that dark, darkest moment of realization that I pray never haunts me again. I myself was the vile embodiment of the human elements I most despised . . . underhanded, untrustworthy, dishonorable behavior, all base spinoffs of deceit. I thought as carefully as my pounding heart would allow. I appealed to whatever sense of reason, and respectability, and truth, and consideration I could find within my hectored brain. I determined to beg forgiveness whether I deserved it or not. I opened the bedroom door. Lenore was sprawled on the chaise lounge. She was breathing heavily. On the table beside her was an empty bottle. Little yellow pills were strewn about the floor. My remorse turned to panic. I was unable to awaken her. I tried to make her drink tepid water, but it only spilled down her chin. I called Sidney. He was still at the studio. He said, "Do nothing until I call you back, which will be immediately." It *was* immediately. "Dr. So-and-so is on his way," he said, "and so am I." Thank God for those friends who not only know what buttons to push during crises, but who receive positive responses when they push them.

Shortly there was a sharp rap on the bedroom door that led into the corridor. Before I could get to it, a passkey opened it. It was our floor waiter, and behind him were the doctor, two nurses, and a porter carrying an armful of galvanized equipment with rubber tubes. The doctor ordered me out of the room and closed the door as I went into the sitting room.

I paced. I sat. I could hear muffled voices through the bedroom door. I quietly opened it. What I saw, before the doctor waved me away, was an ugly sight, a debasing procedure that, through thoughtlessness and careless inconsideration, I had brought on someone I loved.

Finally Sidney arrived. He went into the bedroom. He spoke

seriously when he came out. "The doctor thinks she'll make it, but it was touch and go for a while. He wants you to know that she'll need help in recovering, not only from the nurse, but from you."

Why is such a shocking tragedy, or near-tragedy, necessary in our lives to shame us into a clear vision of relative values? During the next few weeks I thought of nothing else, and with the help of Lenore's wisdom and love, I discovered the true meaning of fidelity.

After *Under Capricorn*, Lenore and I took a gentle vacation while she recuperated. We visited Paris, and we drove all around the beautiful spots in France.

Alexander Korda (who shared my contract with David) had a very interesting movie that was to be made in Vienna. We had many telephone conversations about it. It was called *The Third Man*.

Carol Reed, the English director, and I became good friends in 1948 during the making of *The Third Man*. We started in Vienna, and most of the locations there were night exteriors. The time required for the lighting of large squares and blocks and blocks of cobblestone streets gave the actors unusually long and tedious periods of waiting.

At various hours between midnight and sunrise, we would sit waiting in canvas chairs in the middle of some magnificent square or a mountain of bomb-shattered rubble. Some kind property man would wrap us in blankets, and we would sit drinking coffee, or, if we were waiting for a mere action scene with no dialogue to twist tongues, there was always nearby a spike for stirring the coffee.

At that time Vienna was occupied by the Allies, and its military forces were policed by the "four-power patrol": Great Britain, the United States, France, and Russia.

One evening after a particularly grueling day's work, Trevor Howard decided to case the neighborhood saloons for some company and refreshment. Trevor is a gregarious person, a superb actor, and a man who does not believe in missing the leisure hours of life. That night he intended to have an evening off from *The Third Man* crowd. Our conversations had a sameness. We all loved the picture, but we all wanted to go home.

Tired as he was, he didn't bother to change his uniform before setting out on his toot. He was playing a colonel in the British army. The four-power patrol were doing their duty policing the military at play. They followed Trevor to three or four different saloons, where his conversation grew in loudness and merriment, but they were so impressed by his high rank that they dared not caution him to be a little quieter and set a better example to the lesser ranking officers.

By the fifth wine garden he was so thoroughly relaxed, his voice became even louder and he indulged in a few songs. The patrol finally decided that it was time to arrest him. Imagine their horror when he informed them that he most certainly was not a colonel. He was just wearing the uniform in a movie! The arrest now became extremely complicated; it could not be for rowdy behavior unbecoming his rank. He was hauled into jail for impersonating an officer! The production people, and Carol, had to use all their influence and tact to get him and his seized uniform out for the next day's filming.

Trevor shrugged and said happily, "Well, I wanted a change of pace, and I certainly got it."

"Good show, old chap," said Carol and gave him the day off.

We were to shoot the ferris wheel scene that day. Orson and I had a long, excellently written and directed scene to perform while circling the sky of Vienna in this huge contraption. It was stimulating and memorable, particularly because of Orson's line, "In Italy, for thirty years under the Borgias, they had warfare, terror, murder, bloodshed—but they produced Michelangelo, Leonardo da Vinci, and the Renaissance. In Switzerland, they have brotherly love, five hundred years of democracy and peace, and what did they produce? The cuckoo clock." It is apparently memorable to the Austrians as well, for they keep a photo of Orson and me on the "great wheel." A wheel of fortune it turned out to be for us.

The Italian actress, Valli, spoke fluent German, and was an enormous help in translating for the crew and the Austrian actors. My scenes with her were sad. One felt that if she had never met The Third Man, she might have fallen in love with the character I played. But that would have been an entirely different story and not nearly such a good one. Casting Valli, with her mixture of cool beauty and vehemently determined loyalty, was indeed a fine and unusual choice. Carol and producers David Selznick and Alexander Korda had scored a bull's-eye.

Carol Reed was already one of England's top directors. His *Fallen Idol*, with Ralph Richardson, was a monumental success on both sides of the Atlantic. He was happily married to beautiful Penelope Dudley Ward, whose mother was also a great beauty and had been a favorite of the then Prince of Wales before Mrs. Simpson arrived on the scene to rock the boat and the world.

Carol's camera angles have been much imitated but, in my opinion, never matched. He was an original. He had his assistant read the script of *The Third Man* to him every night, so he knew exactly what kind of mood he would use throughout the film.

One evening, sitting in a saloon in Vienna, he heard a little-known zither player called Anton Karas. Against studio pressure, he followed his own instincts and signed him to play throughout the film as the sole instrumental background. The "Third Man Theme" enhanced the picture beyond belief and gave Anton Karas a career for all time.

After *The Third Man,* Carol's name became synonymous with big success and good taste. He never lost that reputation, although he suffered an enormous setback some time later, when he started *Mutiny on the Bounty* with Marlon Brando. He and Brando were never in accord, and because MGM depended on Brando's name more than Carol's, he was fired from the picture. His loss of face, I am pleased to say, was not as disastrous as *Mutiny on the Bounty* turned out to be without him at the helm.

After what must have been some very unhappy and unfulfilling years, he returned to the limelight in full glory by directing *Oliver* in his own beloved England and receiving the American Academy Award for the task.

During one of our verbal ramblings in Vienna, I mentioned to him that a friend in New York had written me that he was reading *The Third Man* in serial form in an American magazine. "Please beg him," said Carol, "to send you the last chapter, and do let me know how it ends." At that time no definite end had been decided on, and no final scene was ever written that appeared in the film.

We were on location in the cemetery one gloomy, biting, raw day. Carol stood staring down a long alley of trees that flanked a perfectly straight, endless road whose perspective took it to a tiny point, finishing with grey sky. He simply announced: "Now we'll shoot the ending."

When the camera was ready, it was pointing its eye directly at that distant apex. Then Carol shouted, as loudly as he could,

"Action!" From far, far away, Valli started her walk up that lane toward the camera.

The hero, smoking a cigarette, was standing in the foreground waiting for her. Like the audience, he was confident that she would join him, and they would stroll away happily together, arm in arm. Valli walked on and on, closer and closer, until at last she was a life-sized figure in the foreground with the hero. And then, without turning her head, or even glancing in his direction, she continued her steady pace, out of the shot, and into limbo.

I remained there, as directed, still smoking the cigarette. My eyes followed Valli out of the shot and, anticipating Carol's shout of "Cut," I almost strolled back to my chair to wait for the assistant to announce "Once more, please," or for Carol to say, "Print."

Nobody uttered a word. The camera kept rolling. The special effects men from their high perches continued to drop toasted autumn leaves from above. I continued to puff on my cigarette, and began to get quite panic-stricken. Was there more to the scene? Had I gone blank? What was Carol waiting for me to do? I took one more puff, then in exasperation threw the cigarette to the ground, at which point Carol shouted through his laughter the word I had been waiting desperately to hear—"*Cut.*"

And that is the way the movie ends, in spite of the studio's pleas to him to make an alternate and less stark ending, which would suggest a glimmer of hope for a happy finale. Stubborn Carol, of course, refused.

This scene and Orson Welles's sudden introduction (Do you suppose Mozart ever dreamed that another boy genius would one day darken his door?) are considered by many film buffs to be the crowning triumphs in cinema pictorial entrances and exits. King Vidor, one of our cinematic giants, always said that in the history of films, every great moment that shines in memory is a silent one.

Some thirty years later, I was making a movie in Italy. Toward the end of the picture, we had some days of filming in Vienna. On my arrival, the local press asked me if I would go and have some publicity pictures taken in the sewer where we had filmed a great deal of *The Third Man.* The newspaper had asked for them, as that classic motion picture was still being played often over there. Naturally, I agreed.

Down I went, remembering how hard we had all worked there.

It was indeed nostalgic, and I did so wish that some of the rest of the company and crew could be with me.

A sewer is not a place to be in alone. Suddenly, right in front of my eyes, appeared about ten of the sewer police—the same ones we had worked with! My friends, my colleagues. We hugged each other and slapped our "older" backs with gusto. Out came bottles of fine wine. On their nice clean floor, in which they rightly take such pride, we sat down and had a reunion party, never to be forgotten. "Come back here and make *Third Man II,*" suggested Hans.

I laughed, "We can't do that. Orson was the third man, and I shot him in the movie, down here. We can't bring him back."

Willie, who had wit and wisdom, said, "Then make *The Fourth Man,* and Welles can direct it."

"What a good idea," said his friends. After my last glass of wine and several more backslaps, I promised I would suggest this brilliant idea to Orson when I next spoke to him.

8

Lenore took the *Queen Mary* to the United States, where she visited her family in Ohio, and I made my way to Rome to begin the location filming for *September Affair* (1950) with Joan Fontaine and Jessica Tandy.

Hal Wallis, who was producing *September Affair* with Paramount, and his production staff were already there. Anticipating "slow Italian methods," they had provided our director, William Dieterle, with a liberal schedule of seventeen days to photograph exteriors in Rome, Florence (with its defensive walls engineered by Michelangelo), Capri, and Naples. The "slow Italian methods" dragged us to a finish two days ahead of schedule; therefore, Dieterle was given the added opportunity of including a pictorial tour of Pompeii and photographing inside the Blue Grotto at low tide. This was to be a cinematic first.

No cameraman had ever devised a method of pouring enough artificial light into that cave to impress its sparkling blue reflections on film. The patent office would have kicked Dieterle out, his idea was so simple. He engaged a host of night fishermen with their bright portable gas lamps, and sent them into the grotto in their little boats, with one man to row and one to control the lamp. A portable camera followed in another boat.

Joan Fontaine and I rode with an official Blue Grotto guide.

The night fishermen of Capri, in case anyone needs an introduction to this unique group of anglers, are professional fishermen who place their boats, each equipped with a bright gas lamp, in a large circle on a calm sea. The fish, or "poor fish," attracted by the light, swim innocently to the surface to investigate. Here they are greeted with a powerful THUD, which immediately transforms them from "poor fish" to "dead fish." This method of angling is not mentioned in the works of Izaak Walton, and I have no idea how it is regarded by the SPCA. The night fishermen of Capri tell us, or at least told me, that while on first impression it might seem unsporting, a sudden death is actually more humane than the torture of the hook.

When the filming was finished, we were having a farewell cup of tea in the public hall of the Excelsior Hotel in Naples. Slim Aarons, who had been photographing our location activities for *Life* magazine, was leaving for New York with his thousands of negatives.

Joan Fontaine was leaving by fastest carrier to Los Angeles to marry Collier Young, a fine producer and writer and one of my closest friends. I was going to Venice. The annual film festival was on there (this was before I learned that *festival* has little relation in definition to *festive*), and my pal Orson was on location there with his production of *Othello*. I had not been to Venice since last summer, and I believed that an annual visit to Venice was necessary therapy for restoring the magic of the spirit.

A page brought a handwritten message to our table. It was addressed to me and was an invitation to Joan, me, and "your friend" for cocktails, either in the bar or in suite number so-and-so. It was signed, "Lucky Luciano."

I had passed Mr. Luciano on the front steps of the hotel a few times during our Naples location. We always exchanged pleasant smiles in passing, and Slim told me that he had very graciously posed for his camera. I believe Mr. Luciano was residing in his native land because of some misunderstanding with our immigration authorities.

We were about to send him a note of acceptance when a gentleman, hovering over our table, presented an open wallet containing a shiny badge and muttered: "FBI. May I draw up a chair?"

"Oh, yes, please do, by all means," came the breathy response.

I am always so thrown when any of those gentlemen dressed in what we know as "plain clothes" suddenly pushes that gleaming, leather-enclosed badge under my nose; I go absolutely blank. What is it? Guilt? Fear? Anyway, one would have to be a champion speed-reader to make out what is printed on the badge, so quickly does the extended hand snap it closed and return it to an inside pocket. Who has ever been calm enough to say, "Just a minute, sir, may I take a closer look at your identification?"

Our gentleman pulled up a chair. He was very pleasant. "How did the filming go?" he asked. "How do you like Italy?"

We offered him tea.

"No thanks."

"A drink?"

"No thanks. I'll only be a minute. I take it you just received an invitation from Luciano."

"Yes, yes, so we have, yes."

"Are you going to accept?" he asked. Before we could answer, he continued, "The reason I ask is this; if you have a drink with Mr. Luciano, if you even shake Mr. Luciano's hand, we'll have to report it."

"We?" asked Slim.

Our guest laughed and looked about the packed lobby.

"About half of this crowd is 'we,' and while you might enjoy Mr. Luciano and his hospitality, and while I know your meeting will be all in fun, you should be aware that our report of your meeting will become an official record, and your entry back into the United States will probably, as a routine result, be a complicated and tedious procedure with the U.S. customs inspectors. Just thought you'd like to know."

We thanked him. As he was leaving, we all noticed Lucky Luciano watching us from the front door. Slim picked up our invitation from the table, held it high in our almost-host's direction, and slowly, gently tore it into shreds, which floated to the carpet. Joan, Slim, and I laughed. The FBI laughed. Mr. Luciano, with sorrowful dark eyes, bestowed on us that classic Italian gesture as his head tilted slightly, his elbows almost touched his ribs, and he extended his arms with the palms up.

In Venice, I went from the airport to the Excelsior Hotel on the Lido, which is the traditional headquarters for the Venice Film Festival. The concierge gave me some messages, and when I asked him if he had been able to find a room for me in Venice, he smiled,

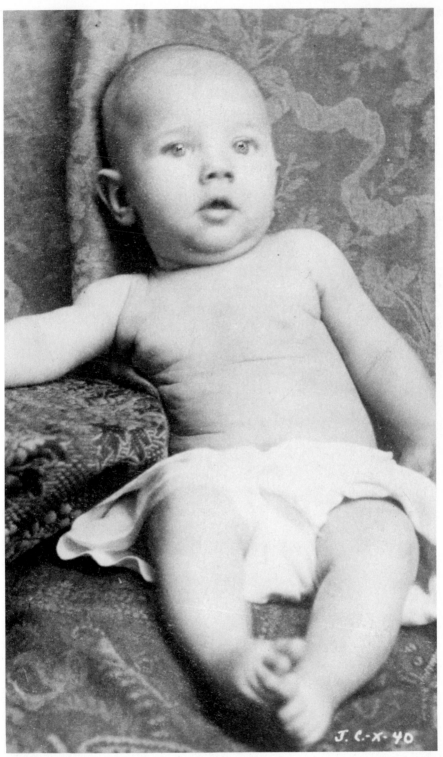

Joseph Chesire Cotten (1905). (Courtesy Joseph Cotten.)

With his parents, Sally and Joseph Cotten, Tidewater (1906). (Courtesy Joseph Cotten.)

Nanny Annie and Jo in Atlantic City (1906). (Courtesy Joseph Cotten.)

Grandmother Elizabeth Bartlett (circa 1860).
(Photographed by J. M. Ives. Courtesy Joseph
Cotten.)

Jo Jr. with his grandfather John Cotten and his
father, Joseph Cotten, Sr. (1908). (Courtesy
Joseph Cotten.)

Jo in Tidewater (1916), training for his future role in *Duel in the Sun*. (Courtesy Joseph Cotten.)

Six-year-old Jo (this photograph was used in the film *Shadow of a Doubt*). (Courtesy Joseph Cotten.)

At the age of three, already a showman (1908). (Courtesy Joseph Cotten.)

Facing page: Young, serious, suave Joseph Cotten (circa 1926). (Courtesy Joseph Cotten.)

Modeling for *The American Magazine* (circa 1930). (Courtesy Cotten Collection, University of Southern California.)

Photographed by Sarli in Miami (1928). (Courtesy Joseph Cotten.)

Lenore La Mont Cotten and her daughter, Judy, at the Cottens' cabin in James River, Virginia (circa 1938). (Courtesy Joseph Cotten.)

With Elizabeth Love in the play *Loose Moments* (Broadway, 1935). (Courtesy Joseph Cotten.)

Flanked by Arlene Francis (right) and the first Mrs. Orson Welles, Virginia Nicholson (left), in *Horse Eats Hat*, Jo's first starring role. (Courtesy WPA Federal Theatre Photos.)

Jo (center) with the cast of *The Shoemaker's Holiday* (Mercury Theatre Productions, 1937). (Photographed by Lucas & Pritchard. Courtesy Joseph Cotten.)

Katharine Hepburn and Jo contemplate time in *The Philadelphia Story* (Broadway, 1939). (Photographed by Vandamm Studio. Courtesy Joseph Cotten.)

Following page: Orson Welles and Joseph Cotten in *Citizen Kane* (RKO, 1941). Courtesy Cotten Collection, University of Southern California.)

Transformation to old age in *Citizen Kane*. (Courtesy Cotten Collection, University of Southern California.)

Sharing a joke with Orson during the making of *Journey into Fear* (RKO, 1942). (Courtesy Cotten Collection, University of Southern California.)

With Dolores del Rio in *Journey into Fear.* (Courtesy Cotten Collection, University of Southern California.)

Dolores Costello, Ray Collins, Agnes Moorehead, Joseph Cotten, Tim Holt, and Ann Baxter in *The Magnificent Ambersons* (RKO, 1942). (Courtesy Cotten Collection, University of Southern California.)

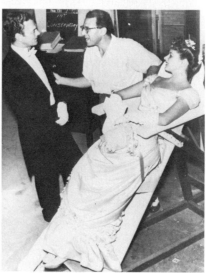

Joseph Cotten, Ingrid Bergman, and Charles Boyer in *Gaslight* (MGM, 1944). (Courtesy Cotten Collection, University of Southern California.)

Clowning for the children during the making of *Gaslight*. The boy on the left is Sir Laurence Olivier's son Tarquin (1944). (Courtesy Joseph Cotten.)

A special moment with director George Cukor and costar Ingrid Bergman during the shooting of *Gaslight*. (Courtesy Cotten Collection, University of Southern California.)

Facing page: Uncle Charlie in *Shadow of a Doubt* (Universal, 1943). (Courtesy Cotten Collection, University of Southern California.)

Instructing FDR in how to run the country (1944). (Courtesy Joseph Cotten.)

A relaxing moment (circa 1946). (Courtesy Joseph Cotten.)

Facing page, top: Admired by Jennifer Jones, Shirley Temple, and Claudette Colbert in *Since You Went Away* (Selznick, United Artists, 1944). (Courtesy University of Southern California Cinema Library.)

Facing page, bottom: Celebrating the successful opening of *Shadow of a Doubt* at the Stork Club with Lenore Cotten, Orson Welles, and a magician (1943). (Courtesy University of Southern California Library/*Los Angeles Examiner*.)

Jennifer Jones takes the *femme fatale* role with Jo in *Duel in the Sun* (Selznick, 1946). (Courtesy University of Southern California Cinema Library.)

Jo and Jennifer Jones reunited in *Love Letters* (Paramount, 1945). (Courtesy University of Southern California Cinema Library.)

A promotional photograph for the Selznick Studio (1946). (Courtesy Cotten Collection, University of Southern California.)

Painting the famous portrait of Jennifer Jones in *Portrait of Jenny* (Selznick, 1948). (Courtesy University of Southern California Cinema Library.)

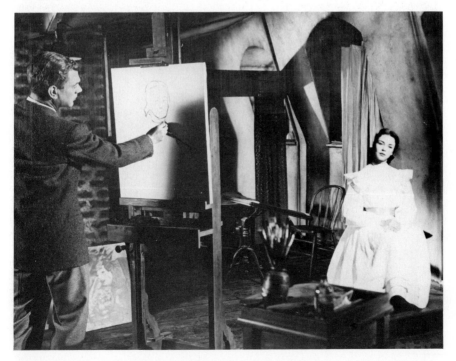

Jo admiring Loretta Young in *The Farmer's Daughter* (RKO, 1947). (Courtesy University of Southern California Cinema Library.)

With Bette Davis in *Beyond the Forest* (Warner Brothers, 1949). (Courtesy University of Southern California Cinema Library.)

Facing page, top: Alfred Hitchcock, Michael Wilding, and Jo chat during a break in the shooting of *Under Capricorn* (Warner Brothers, 1949). (Courtesy Joseph Cotten.)

Facing page, bottom: On the ramparts of the Tower of London (circa 1949). (Courtesy Joseph Cotten.)

Eye to eye with Orson in *The Third Man* (Selznick, 1950). (Courtesy University of Southern California Cinema Library.)

Jo, Cary Grant, Ann Sheridan, and Orson Welles in the London Films commissary during the shooting of *The Third Man* (circa 1950). (Courtesy Joseph Cotten.)

With Valli during *The Third Man*. (Courtesy Cotten Collection, University of Southern California.)

Joan Fontaine and Jo on the Capri beach in *September Affair* (Paramount, 1950). (Courtesy University of Southern California Cinema Library.)

Margaret Sullavan gets a leg up in the National Theater production of *Sabrina* (1953). (Photographed by Vandamm Studio. Courtesy Joseph Cotten.)

Narrating a United Nations radio program, "The Grand Alliance" (1953). (Courtesy Cotten Collection, University of Southern California.)

With Marilyn Monroe in *Niagara* (20th Century Fox, 1953). (Courtesy Marvin Paige Collection.)

Facing page: Patricia Medina (1954). (Courtesy Patricia Medina Cotten.)

Top: Patricia and Jo at their wedding (1960). (Photographed by John Swope. Courtesy Joseph and Patricia Cotten.)

Bottom: The Cottens arriving in London for their honeymoon (1960). (Courtesy University of Southern California Collection/*Los Angeles Examiner*.)

David O. Selznick at the Cottens' wedding reception (1960). (Photographed by John Swope. Courtesy Joseph and Patricia Cotten.)

The Cottens at Villa Tramonto (1962). (Courtesy Joseph and Patricia Cotten.)

Jo huddles with Olivia de Havilland in *Airport 77* (Universal, 1977). (Photographed by Peter Borsari. Courtesy Joseph Cotten.)

Charlie Chaplin and Jo in Malibu. (Photographed by David O. Selznick, who named it a picture of two hams. Courtesy Jennifer Jones.)

With Jimmy Stewart in *Airport 77*. (Photographed by Peter Borsari. Courtesy Joseph Cotten.)

Jo and Patricia at White Gables, their Palm Springs home (1986). (Photographed by J. Michael Kanouff. Courtesy Mercury House.)

"Yes." With the assistance of a cousin in the post office and the captain of the ferry, he had secured for me a room at the Grande, the very last room to be had in all of Venice. A small annuity passed between us and he summoned a waiting launch.

I never understood the great popularity of the Lido, with Venice itself so few miles away. I always assumed that Thomas Mann's memorable novelette was set on the Lido because of the beach. And a certain amount of the clannish international figures will always go there to be secure in each other's company and to enjoy good eating and effortless swimming in the buoyancy of the Adriatic. Gambling? I accept, though I do not understand, the fact that gambling is magnetizing. There comes a time during the night—and no daylight ever penetrates most casinos—when the next card, that little shiny ball, those two rolling cubes exercise their powers of hypnosis and galvanize the eyes and the mind. The stacks of smooth, multicolored chips cease to be money; they turn into exactly what they are, chips . . . only chips to be thrown about and thrown away. When a total disrespect for currency takes hold, it seems to me to hint of sickness, but I have no intention of paying a psychoanalyst one cent for a confirmation of this opinion.

What the concierge at the Excelsior had described as "the last room to be had in all of Venice," the receptionist at the Grande described as "The Barbara Hutton Suite" as he ushered me into an apartment that caused me immediately to speculate on the possible international application of our own "squatter's rights" laws. I wondered if I might take permanent possession simply by "squatting" there a while. (Barbara Hutton's launching of the first motor-driven boat in the Grand Canal is regarded by some Venetian ecologists as a dubious blessing.)

Alexander Graham Bell's first message over his invention was a command: "Watson, come here; I want you." Since that day, people have been flooding the wires with imperious demands with such frequency that at least some switchboard operators seem to have developed the occult power of anticipating them. "A call will be coming through soon from Mr. Orson Welles," the operator at the Grande informed me soon after I arrived. Certainly Mr. Orson Welles had not called to inform her that it was his intention to call "soon." Was it possible for her to hear a voice in space before that voice had actually spoken in time? This seems at least as believable as the ads put out by the telephone company when they first announced that money could now be sent by wire. Illustrations showed us endless rows of silver dollars high in the air, rolling themselves over dozens of telegraph lines toward their appointed destinations.

The slight inaccuracy of the seeress of the switchboard was forgivable. It was not Orson, but one of his assistants on the line. A boat was on its way; would I please join them for lunch on their *Othello* location? The boat docked at an island, one that I had visited exactly a year before when Orson was on location with this same picture. The company was sitting under trees about to begin lunch. Orson came out to greet me and I saw behind him the wig I remembered from last summer. It was Desdemona's headdress, blonde with interesting and complicated plaiting hanging to the waist. It was an easy wig to remember.

Orson presented me and Desdemona looked up. I was about to say, "How nice to see you again," when I suddenly realized that it wasn't the same face at all. No wonder they were back at last year's location—retakes. Same wig, different girl.

After lunch, on my way back to the boat, Orson said, "If you've nothing else to do tonight, why don't you join me at Harry's Bar. I'm dining with Maria Montez."

"I've nothing else to do tonight," I said.

The blinds that sheltered the Barbara Hutton Suite from the balcony had been lowered and the thick, beveled louvers permitted only knife blades of red, red sun to filter through. Venetian sunsets strive, not in vain, to duplicate those garish reproductions we find on giveaway calendars. My back sank into a large bed, and before I could count the many angels who supported the chandelier, I was enjoying the world's greatest nap.

There must be some hour on the clock when Harry's Bar is not crowded and chattery, but I am unable to enlighten anyone interested in this statistic.

Maria and Orson were enjoying those tiny, tiny sandwiches and those heroic cocktails that had made Harry's a haven for travelers many years ago.

Maria was a vibrant and beautiful girl. Her wit was sharp, her laughter uninhibited. Shyness was not Orson's strongest conscious trait, nor is it mine, and so our dinner was hilarious. Generosity, however, *was* one of Orson's natural traits. He not only paid the bill, but also invited me to share the privilege of escorting Maria to her hotel on the Lido.

It was late. We told the launch, when it docked at the Excelsior, to wait. We could see, silhouetted in the moonlight, skyscrapers of chairs stacked on naked tables on the terrace after bearing their burdens of the evening's film festival agenda.

The concierge greeted us, then said to me, "Where were you tonight?" Something about his expression led me to believe it was not idle curiosity that prompted his question.

"Harry's Bar," I answered.

"You should have been here," he said.

"By 'here' do you mean the festival?" I asked.

"You should have been at the festival tonight," he said.

"I was invited to Harry's Bar," I said. "Nobody invited me to the festival."

"An oversight," said the concierge, "you should have been here for the award."

"What award?" I asked.

"You won the prize for the best performance in *Portrait of Jenny*," he said. "I told them you dropped by often, and they left it in my care."

Maria and Orson congratulated me. "You can't simply pick it up from the porter's desk without a presentation ceremony," said Maria.

The concierge jumped. Two shirt-sleeved waiters appeared. One of the tables was cleared of chairs, and a white cloth quickly covered it. Glasses materialized, as did the neck of a champagne bottle from a bucket of ice. Pop. The concierge made a speech. It would be redundant to describe it as a poetic speech since, in Italy, no one has ever made an unpoetic speech. I accepted the award, a bronze and brass reproduction of the weather vane atop the customs building (today it is the Lion of Venice) mounted on a marble base.

My head descended to my knees in several more bows to out-of-uniform waiters, the concierge, and a few curious passersby. Maria kissed Orson and me good-night, and I dropped him off at his location island, whose outline was beginning to take form in the rising sun.

As the launch chugged toward the Grande Hotel, I dreamily reviewed the pattern of the award ceremony that had just touched me. I saw a surprised and overwhelmed winner, a truly humble and dignified donor, all surrounded and endorsed by happy, unenvious friends.

When I opened my door, those strong, vulgar colors that yesterday had protested their departure from Venice so loudly, were returning after an exhausting trip around the world. The knife blades of red had become fuzzy pink blushes, slowly creeping through the slats. The shy approach of dawn fled when I turned on the chandelier, and before I turned it off, I counted all of its supporting angels and offered to each a thankful and happy good morning.

The following day Orson and I had a date for lunch with two gentlemen (not from Verona, I fear). They were two tough and exceedingly wealthy businessmen. The reason for our meeting was simple; Orson needed money for his next film and he intended to acquire some of theirs.

Walking into the restaurant I saw Winston Churchill seated quite close to our table. As we passed the great man, Orson said to my horror, "Winston, how nice to see you again." Churchill made no response at all. Our lunch was a fiasco. Orson made some lame excuse about, "Winston's not feeling well." He mentioned other big names, big money, which almost caused me to say, "Big deal." Actually it was no deal, for our money men asked if we could postpone our discussion until dinnertime, as they were expecting several overseas telephone calls.

Late that afternoon, we spotted Churchill swimming in the Lido. In a flash, Orson had his swimming trunks on and was in the water beside him. He was talking, but thank heavens I couldn't hear what he was saying. Apparently neither could Churchill, for he just turned and swam in the other direction.

Later I asked Orson, "What did you dare to say this time?"

"I apologized for being fresh," he said, "but I told him I just wanted to impress two gentlemen whose money I needed for a film."

Rather unnecessarily I asked, "Did he reply?"

"No," said Orson.

That evening, we walked into the dining room, our two prospective backers following gloomily. As we reached Churchill's table, he stood up, looked directly at Orson, and bowed slowly and deeply.

We got the money.

Back in Hollywood some years later, Orson was to receive the Life Achievement Award from the American Film Institute in the grand ballroom of the Century Plaza. Of all the industry tributes paid in those vast hotel ballrooms, the Life Achievement Award from the American Film Institute is truly a high honor and one that Orson richly deserved.

It was an exciting night. My nervousness was no surprise to me. The very suggestion, the mere thought of stepping into the illumination of a spotlight turns my palms into a couple of icy, slippery clams. Who said butterflies in the stomach? On these occasions my tummy plays host to all three witches from you know where, swishing about on their scotch brooms. Orson was mopping his brow and ignoring his plate.

"Orson," I said across the table, "it may be a long evening, don't you think you should have some dinner?"

"Remember that sign we had backstage?" said Orson. He quoted it: "No drinking in the theatre except during Shakespeare." I remembered. "Well, tonight it reads 'No eating during tributes.'"

"Nervous?" I stammered.

"Not a bit," he replied in a voice so high I was surprised to see the glassware unshattered.

I reminded him of the other sign. The one that appeared on the call-board during performances of farce or bawdy comedy, such as *The Shoemaker's Holiday*. That one referred to pace, energy, tempo. It read:

Beware the Pause.
After a count of 485
It begins to Lag.

"We should have added, 'No matter how good it feels,'" said Orson.

"For a theatre with no rules, ours certainly seemed to suggest a few orders," I said.

"Not orders at all," Orson said, "just a reminder here and there of the pitfalls ahead."

I could see that our conversation was not an honest distraction for him, that he was inwardly rehearsing what he was going to say later. I kept quiet. I could feel an atmosphere in the room that was entirely different from that usual presentation aura that penetrates the music, the songs, the film clips, the jokes, and the speeches. On this night, a nervousness, an electric spark struck beyond the participants. It sizzled throughout the entire room. There was a sharp awareness that we were gathered to honor, if not a stranger, certainly a maverick, a nonmember of the club. Here was a recipient of the Life Achievement Award who didn't know how to spell *establishment,* who would remind you that a "committee" created the giraffe, who knew the first names of only a small portion of the audience.

This was a great night for Orson, a necessary night, because I think before the evening was over the "boy wonder" bugaboo that had shadowed him for nearly half a century disappeared, was consumed in the light of the truth. "He came into bloom too early." "He never could top it." Top what?! His first production on the stage in New York was a black *Macbeth* in Harlem that set the early evening traffic of Manhattan moving one way—north—for as long as the Federal Theatre Project chose to run the play. He topped this with probably the most stylish French farce ever seen west of the Champs Élysées, and the topping for this was a production of *Dr. Faustus* that led to the opening of his own theatre, the Mercury, with a production of *Julius Caesar* so vigorous, so contemporary that it set Broadway on its ear. But luckily, only one ear, for with the other it was listening and running scared with the rest of the country while O. Welles, in a Madison Avenue radio studio, was reading his adaptation of H. G. Wells's account of the Martian invasion of Earth.

This was a tale told by no idiot. Listeners who had tuned in from the start of the broadcast knew, of course, that they were hearing a story, a fantasy of outer space, of giant robots who waded knee deep across the Hudson River. But "dial fiddlers" were struck dumb, riveted, with their fingers unable to turn further, as they "saw" with their ears these metallic invaders kick over the New York skyline, crush the population beneath their advancing feet and sweep the traffic before them into the East River. Investigations into the cause and effect of this Halloween spoof will never cease to exist. Our court system, which needs streamlining more than our communications system, seemed likely never to clear the docket of suits against that program for nervous breakdowns, heart attacks, and other dire distresses it brought upon a nation of hysterical listeners . . . fingers frozen to a radio dial that tuned in a rich voice saying: "Flash . . . New York has been destroyed by Martians!" One of the remedies for this kind of airwave hocus pocus, by the way, was an official banning of the word "Flash" in all radio broadcasts except when used in genuine news programs.

On the dais after friends and officials had finished their speeches, after the last film clip had hushed the room with a reminder of the extraordinary skill and taste of tonight's guest, after Frank Sinatra had finished his last song, it was time for Orson to accept the award.

A standing ovation followed his steady walk to the microphone. No one would have been surprised had he produced another masterpiece on his way down the aisle.

His speech was honest and witty, as I knew it would be. He was modest without being surprised at the honor. His words sprung from his own personal dictionary, which never contained an obscenity. He was eloquent because he was an eloquent human being.

I played Marilyn Monroe's husband in *Niagara*, which was her first starring role. I was looking forward to meeting her, as, indeed, who would not have been?

Movie companies on location usually become a chummy lot. At Niagara Falls, Canada, where we were to make the exteriors for the film in 1952, my rooms became the gathering place for the acting company before dinner—probably because the suite was equipped with a bar tended by a host who would sooner have gone over the falls than serve a tepid martini. I wasn't needed in the opening day's shooting, and I met most of the company for the first time as they dropped in that evening before dinner.

Marilyn was the last to arrive, as was her wont. I opened the door when she knocked, and recognized her because I had seen her photographs. Millions had seen The Photograph.

"Is this where the party is?" We shook hands. She came in and bestowed a velvety sensuous "Hi!" on those assembled. Covering her feet were large white terry cloth slippers, and covering the rest of her was a large white terry cloth robe, on the back of which was written, in scarlet letters, "Sherry Netherlands Hotel, New York." Somebody behind her laughed. She said, "Oh, that. I thought I had stolen this robe, until I paid my bill."

She took orange juice and sat on the floor. One glimpse of her figure either in that bulky robe or in what she accurately described as "my little black dress," would once again prove Dieterle's theory on nature copying art to be sound. Each curve was in the right place, but like a painted illustration in *Playboy* magazine, each was conspicuously exaggerated. Socially she tried not to rock the boat. She was outgiving and charming. If you wanted to talk about yourself, she listened. She was defensively shy. If you wanted to talk about her, she blushed. If you wanted to sing, she joined the chorus.

We met again in our bedroom. It wasn't the most glamorous room, since we were in a very ordinary motel bedroom, but after all it was Niagara Falls, and after all we were married. What was even more unfortunate was that I had to murder her. Imagine being chosen to kill a lovely young girl in her first starring movie. A rather lost little girl I found her to be.

She gave the impression that she earnestly sought a specific definition, a practical and visible form of happiness, of satisfaction in achievement. At times she glowed with the joy of discovery and then, suddenly, her focus would move into outer space, thrusting her into a cloud of blankness. This dilution of thought, this quick snapping of concentration sometimes happened to her in the middle of acting a scene, and recovery was not always easy for her. At the time, it seemed to me that she was cursed with less than her share of confidence and more than her share of insecurity, both dark synonyms for fear. I am not qualified to comment beyond this obvious oversimplification. Many analytical words, however, have been written about Marilyn's distressed reveries. Words by brilliant minds who knew her well, and words by brilliant minds who knew her not at all.

I enjoyed her company. I enjoyed working with her. Her compulsive tardiness was upsetting to some. It was upsetting particularly for the production department, for all production departments are upset whenever they see a moving clock and a static camera at the same time. The director, Henry Hathaway, was upset. But there's hardly a director alive who doesn't wear four gold stripes on his sleeve and consider any lapse in discipline on his ship a direct insult to the bridge. Some of the cast were upset because they considered it ill-mannered of Marilyn to keep her fellow players waiting.

The cameraman was never upset. Like all lighting experts, he seized that extra minute, that extra hour, that creative opportunity before reluctantly saying "Ready."

Personally, I favor the latter attitude toward others' inconsiderate behavior. How do we know it's inconsiderate? Isn't it self-conscious of us to assume that we are being thought of at all?

Marilyn was blessed with a healthy appetite for laughter. She was aware of her sense of humor about herself and she called on it to rescue her from that grey outer space to which she sometimes fluttered.

She was a pretty clown, beguiling and theatrically disarming. Once, in our hotel, during cocktails in Jo's Bar, the tacitly forbidden subject of The Photograph (the nude on the calendar) came up because she herself brought it up. The innocent though spotlighted entrance of this topic brought from our gathering a reaction that probably is responsible for the popularity of the freeze action technique in films. She told us the studio had instructed her to deny that the photograph was her body, to which she had asked, "Okay to claim the face as mine?"

"Just deny everything," was their final direction.

Later, the first reporter to inquire asked, "Why did you pose in the nude?"

Her answer: "That's the kind of picture they wanted."

Next reporter: "Is it true that you had nothing on?"

"Not true," she said, "I had the radio on."

Reporter: "Oh, you know what I mean."

"If you mean was I wearing anything, well, I was," said M. M.

"What?" he asked.

"Chanel Number Five," she said.

I believe she was not seriously rebellious, although she seemed to relish the overthrow of authority—authority at this time in her life being the director, Henry Hathaway ("Go away, you annoy me."), the production department ("Am I making a picture or punching a time clock?"), and the studio, 20th Century Fox.

Besides underpaying her, she thought the studio most ungrateful for her cooperation beyond the call of duty. "Take this little black dress," she said. The little black dress was made of a dyed Kleenex, or rather a part of a dyed Kleenex. From the top, it was slit down the front, and from the bottom, it was slit up the side.

There was much speculation about how she got into that dress, or indeed, if all of her ever was in it at one time. "This little black dress is my personal wardrobe," she informed us. "The studio liked it, and hasn't bothered to thank me for lending it to them for the picture. Ordinarily, I wouldn't own such a dress . . . but I had to go to a funeral last week." Further on the studio's lack of financial generosity, she said, "By the time I pay my dramatic coach, my singing teacher, and my dancing master, there's hardly enough left for my analyst."

Many years later, I received that telephone announcement that heralds bad news. Usually terrible news. "This is the Associated Press," said a voice, and it continued, "Marilyn Monroe has just been found dead. You played her husband in *Niagara*. Will you please make a statement?" I made a statement, one of those mumbled utterances, trite and sincere. End of telephone call. But it has turned out to be the most controversial death. Suicide was announced. Suicide was accepted by most people.

At first I was sure that it had been an accident. Such buoyancy of spirit, such sparkling anticipation, such a happy and comic attitude would deny support to any other theory.

But she had such moments of fear and insecurity, and she did flutter into that grey outer space. Maybe once too often. That, of course, could make suicide a possibility.

As to all the other furtive theories—cover-up, murder, etc.—I have no knowledge or interest in such sordidness. I knew and acted with Marilyn Monroe. I am proud of having had that privilege. May she rest in peace.

9

Bob Edwards, MGM's public relations man, met me in Rome and I went with him to Catania, which was our location base for the filming of *The Angel Wore Red* (1960), a story concerning some of the religious aspects of the Spanish Civil War. Nunnally Johnson had written the screenplay and was to undertake the direction.

The original plan had been to make the film in Spain, and it's hard to believe that MGM and Nunnally were naive enough to believe that Spain would welcome a movie company with such a controversial manuscript. After many revisions of both the political and religious allusions in the story, the Italian censors gave their consent, if not their blessings, for the film to be produced in Rome and Sicily. But the basic story element (without which there was no story at all) remained. Ava Gardner, a Spanish prostitute, saves the life of Dirk Bogarde, a priest who is being hunted by one of the armies, by hiding him in her bedroom overnight.

"Evil is in the eye of the beholder," said Nunnally in many, many long vowels that enriched his Columbus, Georgia, accent, whenever he was questioned concerning the intimate details of this scene. "You will note, however," he would add, "that the good father leaves no money when he departs in the morning."

It was my bad luck not to work a great deal with Ava in the film. I played a reporter patterned, I believe, on Floyd Gibbons, the first war correspondent actually to broadcast the news from the field of battle.

Ava, besides being beautiful and glamorous, was straightforward and definite. She was born to be an actress; I never saw her make a false move or miss a word. The pattern of life seemed clear and sharp to her, which probably increased her heartache when she was unable to make it work. She valued her privacy, and if she ever carried a torch, no one saw it lighted. She was almost too glamorous, hated making dates, but knew how to get a party together at a minute's notice. She believed that mornings were made for sleeping, and the clause in her contract that allowed her not to be disturbed until noon was the envy of all actors.

"Acting is simply not a daytime job," she once said, "No wonder all actors hate matinees."

The Sicilians are an old people. On the north coast, high in the clouds above the Gulf of Castellammare, Greek architecture still houses the inhabitants of several villages. On the east coast, between Catania and Taormina (a resort where many old Americans and English go to retire with their parents), the people talk of Ulysses and Cyclops with the same casual realism that we use in referring to General Custer and Sitting Bull. You will learn that the monstrous boulders that dot the sea below the cliff of Taormina were tossed there by Cyclops himself to impede the progress of Ulysses as he loomed out of the Ionian Sea, headed for the Strait of Messina, a battle as factual and as recent as the one at the Little Big Horn. Cyclops abides never too far from the crater of Etna, for it is with this angry fire that he forges the thunderbolts of Zeus.

So much a part of Sicilian culture has this heroic giant become that a chain of Cyclops Pizza drive-ins has sprung up. A fussy minority might find the blazing eye and the gaping mouth that serves as an oven for baking thirty-one varieties of pizza an unesthetic blight, but their parking lots are jammed as full as our own that surround the ubiquitous golden arches.

It was in this romantic atmosphere that Ava's maid met Ava's driver. They fell in love, were married, and I am able to report that they live happily ever afterward for I see Mario frequently on my trips to Rome. Matter of fact, it's difficult to miss him since he now pilots one of the few Rolls Royces in the city.

The exterior footage of the Spanish Civil War was finally completed on the east coast of Sicily, and the company settled into the old Titanus studios in Rome. Titanus is certainly one of the oldest, if not *the* oldest, film companies in the world. During its many years of production, it has remained in the hands of the original founders, the Lombardos. Although grey with age, its facilities have been well maintained, its equipment modernized. The lot itself is lushly overgrown with trees and shrubbery and flower borders, with the contrived touches of neglect and unbalance so typical of Italian landscaping, so typical of Italian exterior design in general. I should think the most unflourishing business in the country would be a paint factory.

Lenore's ship would be arriving in Naples early in the morning. She was beginning to overcome her fear of trains and ships. But flying was something I could never let her do, she was so obviously terrified of it. Mr. Lombardo's production department graciously rearranged the working schedule to enable me to meet her. Nino, my driver, and I set off that afternoon for Naples, where we stayed in some dreadful hotel because Nino's cousin was married to the sister of the concierge.

At dawn, I was welcomed aboard Lenore's ship and had a nice American breakfast with her and a group of complete strangers, all of whom had become her intimate friends during the past six days. As Nino was straining to lift one of her bags into the car, Lenore explained, "Sight-seeing books."

It was nearing Christmas and a few days later our friend, David Pleydell-Bouverie, joined us at the Grande Hotel to be, as he put it, "closer to Bethlehem and farther from Bloomingdales." David's avidity for sightseeing ran Lenore a close second, and his curiosity about people required him to transport a portable library of address books. His date book, however, was made of granite; his engagements were entered with a chisel. He can tell you today where he will be having tea six months from Tuesday.

It was a crisp, sunny morning, a day off at the studio for me. Lenore, guidebook in hand, and I were exploring the Borghese gardens. We could see Nino's car parked ahead of us, where we had agreed to meet, at the foot of the steps that led up to the museum. We waved to Nino and climbed the short stairway. At the top, Lenore fainted. She was given a great deal of polite and concerned attention, and shortly was able, with supportive assistance, to return to our car. When we reached our apartment, she went to bed. She said she felt cold, dizzy. I called Jimmy Dunn.

When our government finally allowed Jimmy to retire, he and his wife, Mary, had settled down in Rome. They were one of the most outgiving, happily-in-love, generous couples I ever knew. Jimmy had been our ambassador to almost everywhere, mostly Rome, I think. From what is said of his professional ability, it's easy to believe that if we could possibly find a Jimmy Dunn to represent us in every capital city in the world, there would be no need for a United Nations or a Pentagon, because there would be no problems.

Jimmy knew, as I was certain he would, just the right doctor for Lenore. He would find him and send him. The doctor arrived in the early afternoon. He was Roman and had graduated in medicine from UCLA. His examination was short. After he lifted and looked under her eyelids, he immediately called an ambulance and arranged a hospital room for her.

On our way down to the ambulance, the floor maid who had assisted Lenore into the stretcher noticed that she was shivering and ran for an extra blanket.

Early that evening the doctor appeared at the hospital, where I was still sitting with Lenore. He wanted me to leave immediately. He already knew that I would be working the next day, and he was frankly happy to have me out of the way. There were many, many tests to be made. If the results indicated pernicious anemia, as he suspected they would, not a minute should be wasted before beginning treatments.

The next night after work, Nino drove me from the studio to the hospital. Lenore was sleeping, and the doctor had left orders for her not to be disturbed. He would meet me there the next evening at six.

The next morning, I remembered to put Lenore's reading glasses in my pocket, and at lunchtime, Nino rushed me to the English Bookshop, thence to the hospital. Lenore was sitting up in bed, and gave me a bright welcome. One end of a clear tube punctured her arm; the other end was connected to a container of red liquid that hung above her head. She was happy to have her glasses and the reading matter but really had been kept too busy to miss them, she told me. "I've never undergone so many tests in my life," she said, "and this morning, besides my own doctor, there were three others. One was a professor, long name, from the University in Milan." She laughed, put on her glasses and picked up the Paris edition of the *Herald Tribune*. As she began reading, she said without looking up, "I don't think they're worried about pernicious anemia." But before I could summon a happy reaction, she added, "I think they suspect something glamorous like leukemia."

I think I said something inane like, "Oh, don't be silly," gave her a most casual peck on the forehead, and with the cheeriest "See you at six" I could utter, I made a hasty exit.

At six, Nino's car reached the hospital. Our doctor was waiting at the front door. He took me to Lenore's floor, but not into her room; instead we entered a consultation office where three or four doctors were seated around a polished table. One of them was the professor from Milan, a world-renowned authority on leukemia. He did most of the talking; our own physician, sitting next to me, quietly translated. Lenore's guess had been correct. It was leukemia. Acute leukemia. One of the most vicious and destructive cases in his records of this consuming disease.

All the doctors except Lenore's shook my hand and departed.

"What do we tell my wife?" I asked him.

"I have already told her that the conclusion of the consultation is pernicious anemia," he answered.

"At lunchtime she mentioned the word *leukemia* to me," I said.

"She mentioned it to me also," said the doctor. "That is when I told her that the conclusion of the consultation was pernicious anemia."

We went in to see Lenore. She was receiving, as she would be constantly now, a blood transfusion. If only the red corpuscles could withstand the ravaging assault of the white, there might be some hope of a few months. Meantime there was always hope that in someone's laboratory the miracle cure might be discovered. A nurse was arranging her back pillows to improve her upright position. She greeted our entrance with, "You'll have to find me one of those pens that writes upside down, like David Selznick's," she said, "if you expect me to make out my Christmas list in bed."

"I'm sure Paper-Mate will pay you a fortune if you'll permit them to photograph that endorsement," I said. "I'll have Nino scour the town tomorrow."

"Think Nino could also pick up a few bed jackets for me?" she asked. "Particularly now that you're going to have me doing TV commercials while recuperating."

"Nino may pick out something to match his mustache," I said "I think we need daintier fingers for that job. I'm sure someone at the studio . . ."

"By the way," she interrupted, "did you speak to Bud Barton today?" Dr. Clay Barton was Lenore's doctor in California and a close friend.

"Yes," I said, turning to our Italian doctor, who was standing behind Lenore's bed, "and our doctor here agrees that his presence might help. He might even take you back to California, if you like, before I finish the film. At any rate, he hopes to arrive the day after Christmas."

Nino and I shopped with Lenore's list, which was mostly things for the sisters, doctors, and other staff in the hospital. Ava's newly married and happy little maid came up with the bed jackets.

I spent all of Christmas day with Lenore and distributed her presents at the hospital.

The next day our friend David motored off to visit the Sitwells, and Nino and I met Dr. Barton at the airport. He insisted on going directly to the hospital. The sight of him gave sparkle to Lenore's eyes, and she immediately presented him with a list. "I know this is your first visit to Rome," she said, "you're not to miss seeing a single one of these sights."

"I'll start tomorrow," he said, then went down the hall to have a conference with our doctor, who had just arrived. After that, I took him to the hotel. He told me what I had feared but refused to believe. Each day her condition was worsening. Each day she was weakening.

The word *leukemia* was never spoken in her presence. No face in her room ever reflected the truth. With the assistance of the dear sisters, the nurses, and the doctors, I somehow managed to display a mask of optimism, and she, it seemed, floated buoyantly on this atmosphere of compassion and hope, which makes itself more strongly felt in Catholic hospitals than in the cold accuracy of science. There were times, however, when after a peaceful, sedated sleep, her eyes would open slowly, then gradually seem to focus on some fearful target above her on the ceiling. I would take her hand, but in reality she took mine and held it in a viselike grip, a grip much beyond her normal strength.

Although she was never told, although she never said she knew, although we all hoped she did not know, in all honesty I believe she did know. Over the next few days I began getting suggestions from her, not too subtle suggestions.

"Remember that lapis lazuli box you found in that funny named store on Fifth Avenue?"

"Black, Starr, Frost and Gorham isn't such a funny name," I said.

"Jennifer always liked that little box, and I mean to give it to her sometime, if you don't mind."

One day she calmly started a sentence with, "If I should die, . . ." I tried to interrupt with facetious words, but when I turned and looked into her eyes, I decided the one and only thing I could do was to clasp her very white hand and listen. "If I should die," she continued, "what will happen to my pianos?"

I distinctly remember saying, "I'll simply get two instructors, one for my fingers and one for my toes."

Bless her, she ignored this and said, "Leonard Pennario likes one of them better than the other, and I hope his choice might one day find its way into his studio. . . . And I don't have to remind you of Judy's favorite clip."

Another time, another day, while her gaze was focused on the ceiling and mine, from my chair, had been rendered numb by the familiar, ever changing chips in the terrazzo floor, she spoke in a loud whispering tone, "Preserving dead bodies and shipping them all over the world in search of a compatible resting place is a barbaric custom." A sister made a blessed entrance at that moment, and mercifully ordered me to leave.

Nino drove me to the hotel. There the doorman met us at the curb, crossed himself, and told us to return to the hospital.

Lenore was buried, following a ceremony by the vicar of St. Paul's delivered in a small chapel filled with her friends, on the ancient grounds of Rome's non-Catholic cemetery. There she remains, a minute from her last breath—serene, in harmony and at peace among the musicians and poets on whose company she placed such high value.

BOOK TWO

BOOK
TWO

10

It was time to go home. The studio, with the cooperation of Nunnally and the acting company, revised its shooting schedule so that all of my work could be compressed into four intensive weeks. I was, therefore, kept busy during most of the days.

Many evenings, the Dunns and Ailene Branca would call to offer sympathetic support. Except when I was asleep, I was never alone. Mel Ferrer and his wife Audrey Hepburn stopped by every day. They "just happened to be passing." Old pal Van Heflin was in town, and the Dunns simply left their latchstring out.

Under such periods of emotional stress, nature must be credited with performing more mercy than science. Besides supplying extra, almost superhuman physical strength to the body, it also numbs the aching memory, thus allowing the brain to function clearly. Those searing wounds that are being slashed, those chasms of emptiness that are being dug inside us during these times are blocked from our consciousness until a later day when they have become chronic and bearable. I suppose we are never able to draw a real calculation of personal grief. How much of that heavy emotion is true sorrow? How much is our indulgence in remorse, self-recrimination?

Once home, I discovered that I did have friends. Jennifer and David called me every day for long chats, and I joined them at their house whenever they were dining alone, which they did often so that I could be with them.

I tried to plunge into work. I undertook to direct a production for the La Jolla Playhouse. It was Christopher Fry's *A Phoenix Too Frequent,* and it was some time before I realized the subconscious significance of choosing to direct a play, a comedy, that took place entirely in a tomb near Ephesus.

Directing the play was a real challenge. None of the actors were at all experienced. In fact, the leading lady was a young cousin of mine called Mayo Loiseau, and the leading man was her "real life" boyfriend. She subsequently married then left him, and some years later became a successful writer of fiction.

At the time I directed them, they were filled with the confidence born of inexperience. I rehearsed them for weeks, and when they resisted my direction, I became very firm. In all fairness they did remarkably well, and I was proud of them. I was also proud of myself.

A Phoenix Too Frequent had been presented in New York a short time before I undertook my La Jolla production. To my surprise and delight, *Variety* reviewed our show. Although sadly I have never kept notices, I do have a very good memory—especially for good reviews! In effect, *Variety* said that had the New York production been directed by me, it would have been far more successful. My heart, which had done nothing but ache for some time, did a little dance of joy.

Whatever the result, it helped the weeks and months to pass. The old saws about the therapeutic value of time and distraction may be oversimplifications, but their contributions to the human spirit cannot be denied. I had to face a new and different life. Part of my life was gone, and the withdrawal symptoms were strange and heavy. Sometimes they were even stranger and light—I would be a child again. I was alive. I had to go on being alive. I had been dreaming for some time in a vacuum. Waking up was strange, too, like being shocked into wakefulness.

Back home at Villa Tramonto, which was a multi-level Italian house, vintage 1935, situated on the top of a very high hill overlooking the Pacific Ocean, I had a long and much needed rest.

Ida and John Nooner were my housekeeper and butler. Ida was a superb cook, and John was the best-dressed butler in the West. I had his working clothes made in Italy, and he wore them with dignity and style. Rosendo, the gardener, whom I had known since he was a small boy (his father used to work for me), called me out to the garden, and we worked together planting all my favorite flowers. He knew flowers would cheer me up.

I needed all this attention at home, and they were sensitive to my needs, for I did not go out to dinner or lunch, or any social function (except, of course, the Selznicks, but they were family) for many months.

Sundays, I took care to be dressed properly. I did not wear my gardening clothes, or wall-building outfits. Sundays were my "special days." Good friends would drive down to the coast to visit me, and John was busy from early afternoon answering the door and then answering the house phone when it rang in the pantry. Years ago, John had named it the "martini phone." I cannot think why. It just could be that nothing else was ever asked for over that particular telephone.

My friends came in droves. They came to talk, they came to listen, they came to let me know they cared. I hope they knew how much I appreciated them. They informed me of all the goings-on in town. "You should go out soon, Jo, it would do you good," they said kindly.

Actor friends came by and told me about the films they were working on. Occasionally I felt the need to return to my career. Of course I would return to acting soon, but not quite yet.

I was content listening to King Vidor's wife, Betty, who would come with Norman Foster's wife, Sally, in the early afternoon, as would Agnes Moorehead. Dear Aggie, I had known her for so many years. Hjordis and David Niven, who lived quite close to me, would come around five o'clock, and David's stories and his unique way of telling them got me laughing. Louis Jourdan and his Quique would come, as would Norman Lloyd and his Peggy. So much needed company. I just sat back and wallowed in their kindness.

Gradually, as time went by, my Sundays became less crowded.

One Sunday, I was standing alone on the terrace watching the sun drop into the ocean, when Patricia Medina stopped by. It was an unexpected and most welcome surprise. If Helen of Troy's face launched a thousand ships, Patricia's could launch a million. She is possibly the only truly beautiful woman ever to exist who is not disliked by one single person.

Months ago she had sent all the difficult and proper words in a letter.

"I would have come to see you ages ago," she said, "but I only returned from location yesterday."

"Will you join me?" I said, lifting the glass I was holding.

"I asked John to bring me a sherry when the Fosters arrive. They told me they were coming. I do hope you are not going to take to the bottle," she said.

"And why should you expect me to?" I asked.

"Some of your friends expect you to. I would like you to disappoint them." I walked to the rail and gently poured the drink over the side. "Sorry," she laughed, and continued, "I didn't mean to touch off such a dramatic reaction."

"I thought it was rather underplayed, myself," I said. "I could have tossed the glass as well." We heard the doorbell ring offstage. "That's probably Sally and Norman," I said.

John ushered them in with Patricia's sherry on a tray, took the Fosters' orders and my empty, undramatic glass, and departed. He soon returned with three drinks. Four voices said, "Cheers!"

Looking at Patricia, I realized why so many of my friends had come to me and confided their love for her. None of them could break through her armor.

She seemed to me that day, as in all honesty every other time I had seen her, to be completely outgiving. A thought occurred to me. She had given *of* herself—but she had not given herself. At least, not as far as my friends were concerned.

Did they lack something she needed, or was she completely self-sufficient? I was lost in thought when I heard her say, "Jo, I must be going now, but I'll be here next Sunday with the Nivens." She gave me a peck on the cheek, ran to the door, jumped into that independent motor of hers and was off in a cloud of dust!

After a while, I found myself wanting to see more people. I began accepting invitations to larger groups, particularly when I knew that Patricia would be among the guests. I felt drawn to this warm-hearted witty friend. To me, we seemed to have much in common, and she was so dazzlingly beautiful.

My good friend Rex Harrison arrived in Los Angeles and telephoned me. He had rented a house not too far from mine. We had drinks together and talked of that terrible illness that had smitten his wife, Kay Kendall, as well as Lenore. Talking together was a much-needed tonic, albeit a sad and bitter one. We talked about it once, freely and fully—then, being all talked out, we both set it to rest.

Summer was coming now and the Selznicks' terrace began to get crowded on Sunday evenings. Jennifer called and asked me to join them. "Pick up Rexy," she said, "and then you can bring Patricia. That ought to please you both." She hung up before I could answer.

My car became the escort car for Rex Harrison and Patricia. I stopped by for him on the way into town, and then we picked up Patricia. Rex and I became known as her "bookends."

Every Sunday evening, we would drop Patricia at her apartment, then I would take Rex to his house, rush to my own home and telephone Patricia. The first time I rang her, she picked up the telephone and said, "Hello Jo."

"How did you know who it was?" I asked stupidly, for she must have been aware that I had watched her all evening, guarding my place at her side most possessively. After several weeks of "Hello Jo," my reply became "Hello, darling."

But Sundays were not enough. I found myself really missing Patricia when I wasn't with her, and several times she found time to have dinner with me alone. We always went to Frascati's and always were given a little corner table. It became "our" table. Try as I would to make the conversation personal, she always managed to change the subject.

I did not feel it disloyal of me to withhold this information from my fellow bookend or from anyone else. But Jennifer guessed.

It seems to me that I've always known Jennifer. She is painfully shy. Compared to her, Garbo would seem a screaming extrovert. I can't imagine how it ever occurred to her to become an actress. It must be that her tremendous talent simply refused to be denied. She is beautiful and eerily sensitive to her environment. To the pragmatic her uncompromising loyalty may seem exasperating, until it is needed personally. Then it becomes an honorable, inherent characteristic. We have worked together so often, but we have very little chitchat on the set. She reads her book; I work my puzzle. All the serious conversation we have seems to take place over the wires.

"It's Mrs. Selznick for you," said Ida, handing me the telephone.

"I hear you're off to Mexico and a new film," Jennifer said. "How long will you be away?"

"Too long," I answered.

"I thought you'd say that," she said, "and I certainly think that as one of Patricia's bookends, you're leaning in the right direction."

"She promises to write," I said.

"That the best you can do?" she asked.

"I invited her to join me, and made my invitation as hospitable as I could. I even reminded her that being half Spanish, she could practice her father's language down there."

"I'm sure she was happy to be informed that they speak Spanish in Mexico," Jennifer laughed. "Does she know that you're in love with her?"

"Jennifer," I said, "if you know it, how can she not know it?"

"Have you told her?" she asked.

"Only in English," I replied.

"Did she accept your invitation?" she said.

"'I'll look forward to your return,' was her reply," I said.

"Poor boy. I'll tell David, he'll send you some movies," she said.

I was taking off soon for a film that an old friend, Robert Aldrich, was directing in Aguascalientes called *The Last Sunset*. I found seven places called Aguascalientes on the map. This one was overnight by train from Mexico City, and when I saw it I would have traded it for any of the other six, sight unseen. But it was in the heart of the cattle country and a great deal of the footage concerned a cattle drive up from Mexico to Texas.

I must mention myself first here because it simplifies the synopsis. Either that or because every actor believes his part to be the one about which the play revolves.

Not only was I the cuckold husband of Dorothy Malone and the father of Carol Lynley (at least I *thought* I was her father), but I was a traitor, a rat who had deserted his command in the Confederate Army and carried a scar on one buttock eternally to stigmatize the shame. (Aldrich and the producer promised never to release this film in Tidewater as long as my mother drew breath.) The script called for Kirk Douglas and Rock Hudson constantly to sniff around the petticoat of Dorothy Malone and take great pleasure in humiliating her cowardly husband.

Production seemed to take forever. The cattle drive was impossible to shoot. There were literally thousands of them being prodded and driven past the cameras, but their behavior was so completely uninhibited that they could be photographed from no angle whatsoever. Always in this sea of trotting longhorns or shorthorns or no horns, there were several very prominent horny horns humped up on the back of their neighbors, or rather their neighbor's wives.

Another day we were held up because we lost most of the extras. The above kind of animal high jinks can be quite suggestive, and many of the ladies and gentlemen in the wagons accompanying the drive vamoosed over the horizon. I made a note to remind Dieterle that besides copying art, nature sometimes copies nature.

Everything happened to delay us. Heavy clouds were constantly passing between the sun and the camera and throwing the scene into darkness. And with no notice, these same clouds would suddenly let go with torrents, torrents that we later wished we had trapped and saved, for we found that in this particular Aguascalientes bottled water of any temperature was as scarce as a tree-ripened orange in Florida.

We boiled the water, we flavored it with tea, we sterilized it with alcohol, but some of us became weaker and weaker, and finally—when we were barely able to stand or pull our socks over our feet, which had turned to sandpaper—a blessed Mexican Florence Nightingale arrived with glucose and needles. Within a few hours, our hydration meters were pointing upward toward normal again. We discovered—alas, too late—that one of the largest buildings in town was the Canada Dry bottling works.

In addition to these handicaps, our production schedule seemed to be decelerating for other reasons. Artistic reasons, I was beginning to suspect.

During the multiplex discussions of the banana peel theory, there must have been a moment when Mack Sennett, a strongly opinionated producer of silent comedies, looked at his great star Ben Turpin and said, "I do not see eye-to-eye with you." On our ranch location in Mexico, as the discussions grew longer and more frequent, our footage in the camera became shorter and our setups more seldom. The discussions took place out of the range of sound. They were visually serious, and they were between Kirk and Bob

Aldrich, and Bob and Rock, and Rock and Kirk, and it was obvious that none of these various combinations was seeing eye-to-eye.

One evening Bob, with whom I've always seen eye-to-eye (through three difficult pictures), dropped by my motel for an undiluted drink. He wanted to talk about anything except the picture . . . the University of Virginia, the Los Angeles Rams, his crumbled home life . . . anything except the picture. I said, "I was talking to Patricia Medina on the telephone the other night and she sent you her love." Patricia had worked for Bob in several television shows. He smiled when I mentioned "Spanish Beauty."

"What a darling girl to work with," he said, and gave me a little squint. "Talk to her often?"

"Not often enough," I said. "It's almost impossible to get through. She's working now for Bill Frye in one of those 'Thriller' sequences."

"Oh, with Boris Karloff," he said.

"Right," I went on, "and by the time the Mexican connection gets to Hollywood, she's either asleep or on the set, and by the time the Hollywood connection gets through to me, I'm out with your happy herd of kine and their gentlemen friends, or being sneered at by Kirk and Rock, and come to think of it, most every character in the piece. I'll never play a coward again. I'm beginning to feel like a pariah even off the set."

"Just because you're lonesome you shouldn't feel like an outcast," said Bob.

"Oh, maybe I am abusing the towel. I guess these long days just sitting here on standby are making me a little itchy," I said.

As he left, Bob said, "When you talk to her again, give Spanish Beauty my love. Meantime I'll see what I can do."

I had not the slightest idea of what he meant by "I'll see what I can do," but before noon of the next day, he had done it.

He was talking to me at lunch. "You have actually very little work to finish on this location," he said, thumbing about in the script where certain pages were marked with paper clips. "If we can concentrate on these scenes for the next few days, and production thinks we can, we shan't need you again until we get to the studio in Mexico City, which should be at least two months."

"As they say on the Appomattox, I'll dance at your wedding," I said.

"Polish up your clogs, that may be soon," he said, "but don't thank me, thank production for buying my theory about what you call the happy herd."

"How's that?" I asked.

"I told them they looked starved to me. Your scenes don't involve them. I thought if we left them alone for a few days with carloads of oats, or straw, or whatever the hell they eat, they may get fed up and fucked out into some blissful serenity, which might enable us to proceed with a celibate trek north."

The windy, sand-blown hills that surround Aguascalientes greeted our machinery inhospitably, but the coward finally conquered. And eventually Bob and Regis Toomey, who shared my motel digs, gave me a hero's departure as they waved me off on the overnight train to Mexico City.

During the several hours of waiting there, I tried telephoning Patricia, with no response. I sent a telegram and kept phoning with negative results until the plane left.

As I walked onto the pavement at the Los Angeles Airport, I heard a timid honk. I peered toward the curb, and saw what I thought, what I hoped, was a familiar car. It was too dark to see inside the car and during the next three seconds, as I peered into it, all of this happened: My heart stopped, and I thought, "If I should fall here in ecstasy, if I survive this breathless moment, I shall write a book called *The Happy Heart Attack*." The face in the window was Patricia's. I opened the curb door and sat limply beside her.

On the way to town, I told her I was here by courtesy of Bob Aldrich. As instructed, I gave her Bob's love. As felt, I gave her mine. Forever.

The Last Sunset finally occurred, or rather disappeared, in Mexico City, and the one and only deserter ever to cast dishonor on the Stars and Bars compounded his crime by heading, of all directions, north!

This time, alas, there was no timid honk, no beautiful chauffeur at the Los Angeles Airport. Patricia had been claimed again by Bill Frye for one of his movies.

I suffered a frustrating few weeks. I dug a long ditch for the base of a retaining wall (certainly not the most romantic step in the pleasure of wall building) and managed to catch up with Patricia for lunch once at her studio. She was understandably preoccupied with the film, and I felt an intruder. No one is more aware than I of just how little outside distraction is needed to destroy concentration. It was a period piece, a costume picture that she was doing. Bill Frye was with her, and in between spoonfuls of soup they were discussing swatches, and color, and sketches, and texture.

Bill Frye is the kind of producer who succeeds in making his actors feel that everything about his job is easy, that studio pressure doesn't exist and that his sole function in the production of the film is to make them comfortable and happy. His attention to minute detail is in the grand style of Belasco, Welles, and Selznick. It is said that recently, during the screening of a Shirley Temple movie, Bill suddenly exclaimed, "In the last shot she had one more curl on the left side."

Over lunch, Patricia agreed that we needed a change of scenery. Not theatrical scenery . . . God's scenery.

As soon as she wrapped up this show we took off for . . . I almost said "a rest," but we were headed for a house party at Nini and Francis Martin's in Burlingame, near San Francisco. To Nini the only definition of the word *rest* is "remainder"; otherwise, to her *rest* is an obscene, four-letter word, or at least a waste of time which is, of course, a sin. Nini is a devout person who does *not* believe in sin. She also has a monopoly on energy, having discovered how to split the atom when she was a little girl.

Nini and Francis have been my very dear friends for many years. Had we lived in the same city, I think Fran and I would have seen each other almost daily. But geography cannot cool real friendship; we simply took up where we had left off the last time.

Nini, with her beautiful face and burnished golden hair (some people call it just red, but there's gold in it), is a perfect wife and a devoted mother to five beautiful children, who have all inherited her tresses.

Francis is an artist—sensitive, brilliant, self-sufficient. He is tall, dark, and handsome. He is a book collector and loves to spend hours in his library among his beloved books.

It is therefore understandable that I should decide to take Patricia out of our world and into theirs.

We drove north. Although the great serpents of highways, throughways, tollways, and freeways (how can a toll possibly be justified on a road called a freeway?) had not yet completely engirdled and crisscrossed the nation, a driver could easily span the distance from Los Angeles to San Francisco in one not-too-leisurely-but-full-time-out-for-lunch day—especially with the aid of the two big eyes beside him and an occasional focus on the rearview mirror.

I picked up a sleepy Patricia at eight thirty in the morning, and headed my covered wagon toward the Golden Gate.

Change of scenery. Change of topics. That is what holidays are meant to be. They are refreshments for the body and the spirit, not refresher courses to dig even deeper the ruts of our accustomed passage.

The Martins' house is a big house, built by gregarious people: themselves. It is a never-empty house, a teeming house of friends, relatives, hospitable dogs, and tropical jungles of flowers and always, in the midst of this gracefully contrived disorder, glide trays laden with temptation, from the pantry and the bar. The conversation is stimulatingly abstract or warmly personal, but it is never business . . . yours or theirs.

This is therapeutic hospitality. But it is fantasy; therefore, it is well that its indulgence is controlled. Left unattended, it can persuade us with the swiftness of an opium puff that it is real and unrare. Actually, it is both real and rare.

After a few days, we dragged our reflections from Alice's glass and headed them south to another land of make believe; this one composed of magical devices able to change businessmen into artists and artists into formulas, where the bank reads the script in figures instead of words, and where much, much too seldom some hidden, unsmothered fuse detonates a true imagination that too often burns itself out as a Pied Piper for the blind.

The sun had dropped into the Pacific on our right. On our left as we drove along, the towers of San Simeon rose high above us. Cardboard cutouts they seemed, far away and diminished in size, like a miniature movie set. Lights were blazing through some of the upper windows, and I couldn't help thinking of Xanadu. I could see the snow falling in the little paperweight. I could hear Orson's voice whisper, "Rosebud."

We had dinner in one of the many fast-food restaurants that dot the road along the Hearst ranch, then we set out in search of rooms in one of the motels that line the coastline below the castle.

"Have you two single rooms?" I asked the gentleman behind the desk in the office.

"Certainly," said the gentleman. "Will you please register here." He gave me two cards. On one I wrote my name, address, etc., and on the other I wrote Patricia's name, address, etc. The man read the cards, picked up two keys, and then as he was about to hand them to me, interrupted his gesture. With a straight face he said, "Would you like those rooms adjoining?"

I found myself ready to shout, "Of course not!" or "Certainly not!" or something equally clever. But instead, I muttered, "Just two single rooms, please, it doesn't matter where they are." He gave me the keys and pointed outside to the parking lot.

"Just up those stairs and around to the left."

I parked the car as close as I could to the outside stairway, and was taking the bags from the trunk when the motel gentleman appeared. He said pleasantly, "Need any help with those?"

"Thank you very much," I said, "but I'm sure I can manage."

I followed Patricia up the stairs. Our rooms were in the same wing, four or five numbers apart, opening onto the bridge overlooking the central parking lot. A few people had joined the motel gentleman, and they were losing the game of pretending not to be looking up. I unlocked Patricia's door, placed her bag inside on the luggage rack and popped outside again as if fired from the Zucchini Brothers cannon.

I bade Patricia a hasty goodnight and, bag in hand, entered my room and closed the door.

We had agreed on an early departure, and when I telephoned Patricia about seven, she said she'd be ready to leave in a few minutes. I descended with my bag, put it in the car, and settled the accounts. When I came out of the office, the parking lot was beginning to fill with people. They all stood motionless, but with their eyes they panned me up the stairs, then to the left along the bridge to Patricia's room. I knocked softly on a door that was already slowly opening. I hopped into the room and out with her bag, and then she joined me on the bridge and we started our descent to the car. The dawn patrol greeted us with enthusiastic applause. They parted ranks to allow our car through the exit, and we returned their greetings with self-conscious smiles and gestures.

On the outskirts of town we spotted a pancake house and went in for breakfast. It was shiny and sparsely occupied. Soft phonograph music bathed the room. Patricia and I followed a waitress to a corner table. The music suddenly stopped. We seated ourselves and the waitress handed us menus. The music started again. It was not so soft, and it was "The Third Man Theme." The waitress smiled. "I'll leave you to study the menu," she said, "and to enjoy the music."

We reached Santa Barbara before noon. At a phone booth I called the house and arranged for lunch there before dropping Patricia at her apartment in town.

During lunch, John announced that Hedda Hopper was on the phone. I left the dining room door open and took the call in the pantry.

"Did you get married this morning?" she asked.

"No," I answered.

"I have a report that you and Patricia Medina got married this morning in Monterey," she said.

"You're getting warm, Hedda," I said. "Patricia and I were not far from Monterey this morning."

"What were you doing there?" she asked.

"We were driving down from Burlingame," I said.

"What were you doing in Burlingame?" should have been her next question, and it was.

"We were visiting some friends . . . No, no, Hedda, don't ask who. They were a couple named the Martins, Francis and Nini Martin."

"The Martins!" she screamed. "I didn't know you knew Nini and Fran."

"I didn't know you knew them either," I said. "But, since you know everybody and they know everybody, it was pretty silly of me not to know, wasn't it?"

"You sure I'm wrong about this marriage report?" she asked.

"I'm afraid you are," I answered, "but wait a second, I'll ask Patricia, just to be sure. She's sitting right here. We stopped by my house for lunch." I held the telephone at arm's length and projected the question, "Patricia, I'm talking to Hedda Hopper on the phone here. She's heard we got married in Monterey this morning. You have any recollections on the subject."

Patricia said loudly, "I don't remember marrying you anywhere this morning."

I started to relay this to Hedda, but she stopped me. "Don't bother, I heard her," she said. "Why are you dodging the question?"

"I'm leveling with you, Hedda," I said. "Your spy was a little inaccurate. I hadn't even proposed at Monterey."

"What do you mean you hadn't even proposed at Monterey?" she asked. "Where did you propose?"

"Between Oxnard and Ventura," I said.

"What did Patricia say?"

"She said, 'I'll give the matter serious consideration.'"

Hedda said, "Sounds like a board of directors meeting."

"Nobody was there except us chickens, Hedda," I said, "unless your spy had disguised himself as the empty backseat of an automobile."

Hedda laughed again, "Joseph Cotten proposes to Patricia Medina between Oxnard and Ventura . . . that's hard to . . ."

"I know what you're thinking," I interrupted. "If she says 'no' then use it. It won't hurt me as much as her rejection. If she says 'yes,' I promise you'll be the second to know."

"What do you mean the second to know? That's no deal. Who'll be the first?"

"My mother," I said.

"Good luck, honey," said Hedda. "It's a deal!"

I hung up and returned to the dining room. Silence. I thought of that old radio direction, N.D.S.N.—"Nobody don't say nothing." I wondered what Patricia was thinking. I hoped she was "giving the matter serious consideration." In case she was, I wanted to encourage her. In case she wasn't, I thought it irresponsible of me not to steer her back to the subject. I said, "I don't mean to press on that matter you promised to consider, but," I pointed toward the pantry telephone, "Our Lady of Inaccuracy on the Times seemed to think we were being 'uncooperative.'"

Patricia's face was serious. All she said was, "I seem to have a problem."

Back to the pantry telephone went I. "David," I said, "Patricia is with me and she seems to have a problem."

"Tell her to join the club," said David. "What's the problem?"

"That's just it," I said, "I'm afraid I'm the problem."

"Like to talk it over?" he asked.

"Like to talk it over," I said.

"Make it an hour," said David, "I'm sure Jennifer would like to change into something more dignified for the occasion."

"Please tell her not to bother," I said, "what is she wearing now?" There was a pause.

"Nothing," David replied.

Our drive to the Selznicks was quiet. I don't know why, but I think both of us felt as if we were headed toward the Supreme Court, the final countdown. I had observed a little about this sensitive bloom sitting beside me. I knew her values were strong and clearly etched in black and white, with no fuzzy areas of grey to disturb the division. In her own mind, in her own way, she would make her own honest decision.

David was standing in his living room, strength and understanding emanating from his person. He got to the point, "What's the problem?"

"I have asked Patricia to marry me," I replied.

David's gaze penetrated his thick glasses as he looked first at me and then at Patricia. "That's a problem?" he asked.

"Patricia seems to think it is," I said, "and if she doesn't say 'yes' soon, I'll guarantee it is a problem."

David turned his full attention to Patricia. "Come and sit down, Pat," he said. She sat beside him. "Jennifer says she's sure you're in love with Jo," he said.

"Jennifer is right," said Patricia.

"Do you want to marry Jo?"

"Yes, I do . . . but . . ."

David came to her rescue, "But you never expected it to be Jo."

"That's right," she said, "we've known each other so long and almost in a different life, then suddenly, and frighteningly, we've fallen in love. I don't know what to think or do."

"I'll tell you what I think," said David. "I think it's beautiful. Unexpected things are usually very good things. So many people miss out, eternally, on true love, and you two have found it. It is rare and to be cherished with all your might."

David savored his well-earned pause like an actor and, then said, "Do I help dispel your doubts?" Dear Patricia's eyes flooded out her reply. She flung her arms around David's neck. "Don't kiss me," he said, "I'm married. Kiss Jo."

"Later," she said, as she gave me what I hoped was an unblushing smile.

"Let's get on with it," said David, picking up a note pad and his upside-down pen. Jennifer entered wearing a sincere blue problem-solving ensemble. "Oh," said David, "Pat and Jo are going to get married."

"What else is new?" asked Jennifer. She gave each of us a kiss then sat next to her husband. Patricia sat next to me, rather as if we had not yet been introduced.

David spoke, pen poised: "When do you want to get married?" I bit the cue before the subject could change.

"As soon as possible," I said, and then to Patricia, "No point in waiting, is there?"

"I suppose not," she said.

"As soon as possible," muttered David as he wrote "as soon as possible." His next question was, "Where are you getting married?"

"Here," spoke up my fiancée, having partially recovered from the shock of her own decision.

"Why not here, here in this house?" said David.

"That's what I meant," Patricia replied.

Jennifer asked, "Who's going to marry you? Shall we get a judge?"

"Oh, no, no, no, I may be divorced, but I did nothing wrong, and I refuse to be married by a man in a business suit," blurted Patricia vehemently. "I won't feel married unless he is a man of the church."

David was writing and talking at the same time: "Marriage HERE, no business suit, must have preacher's costume. Jo, do you have anyone in mind?"

"No," I said, "but I'll find someone tomorrow."

"Good," said my boss. "Now, where are you going on your honeymoon?" Patricia looked at me with huge pleading eyes.

"I'd like to go home," she said.

"We're going to England to see Patricia's family."

David stood up, walked over to Patricia and said, "Congratulations, Pat," then over to me, "Good luck, Jo."

"Of course we won't be leaving for England until the morning after our wedding," said a slightly hesitant Patricia, "and that

David stayed in the background, except for giving Patricia to me.

It was a Jennifer Jones production, at 6:30 P.M. with a million votive candles lighting the path from the boys' house to the terrace. The orchestra was hidden as they played sweet music. Our few real friends were on hand. Nini Martin was in the front row, Fran, the best man, was backstage, or off altar, if you will, checking every ten seconds to be sure the ring was still in his pocket. I sat beside him, as relaxed in my chair as if a dentist stood behind it.

Jennifer was nearby, listening at the door to the terrace. She sent Fran outside to his place. Then she pushed a button. The music changed. She tapped me on the shoulder and said quietly: "Jo, you're on."

God bless actors and their own particular language. It is used with an economy of words and a ring of excitement. God bless Dr. Wheatly with his beautiful short service and his beautiful long robes. And God bless Mendelssohn for finally announcing the beginning of our life together.

11

When Patricia and I passed through immigration at Heathrow in London, we separated at a sign that directed U.K. citizens to the right, aliens to the left. I handed over Patricia's blue passport to her, and she joined a short line on the right, while I stood in a long line on the left, my green passport in hand. The word *alien* had never before seemed to be such an inhospitable, downright unfriendly word. As I slowly inched toward the inspector, I could see Patricia waiting for me on the other side of the barrier. What a ridiculous situation altogether! Just a few hours ago in Beverly Hills, I married an alien. Now it is she who finds herself married to an alien. Patricia must have been thinking the same. The first thing she said when I was finally waved through, and she returned her passport to me was, "We'll have to do something about this jolly soon."

"Jolly," I agreed.

Heathrow Airport is one of the largest in the world. That day it was the most populated in the world, because most of Patricia's family was assembled there to greet us. Even the press, contrary to their nature, had shown an interest in happy news. Just a few years ago Patricia had rocked the British Isles with her beauty and wit as one of the panelists on TV's "What's My Line." She was a favorite of the photographers . . . there were simply no bad angles. Consequently, in addition to Patricia's family causing a population explosion at the airport, Fleet Street had sent a large "welcome home" detachment.

One of Patricia's sisters, Piti, almost stole the show unwittingly. The press was interviewing her while waiting for our plane. "What do the Cottens plan to do while in London?" they asked.

"Well, I should think the first thing they'll want to do is go to bed," Piti replied. Piti contends to this day that only naughty juveniles could misunderstand this forthright statement.

Father, mother, sisters, in-laws, and cousins—every single one of them greeted me as an old member of the family they had missed for a long time. Nieces and nephews, of a variety of ages, called me "Uncle" as if they were welcoming home a familiar relative. It was warm, sincere, and touching. I'm afraid the knots in my own family ties had become very loose, if indeed they ever had been drawn tight and secure. This was the dawning for me of a new and deeper understanding of the meaning and closeness of family.

In London we did not reside in a hotel. The Nivens had arranged with a friend to rent us his apartment. It had four bedrooms, three of which could be described as Siberia by a bride and groom. The living room was enormous, and this space served us well. Scout's honor, the housekeeper's name was Mrs. Faithful, and her husband owned and drove a Rolls Royce of indescribable dimensions, which he kept always warmed up at the front door.

We made a brief trip to Paris, accompanied by Piti and her husband Ken. We shopped and dined in Paris. It was in a time when one could enter the Ritz bar without showing a letter of credit, and we spent happy and leisurely hours there, crossing paths and clinking glasses with old friends.

Piti and Ken headed northwest on the Golden Arrow to London, while Patricia and I headed southeast to the Golden Strand: Venice.

It was dusk when the launch reached our hotel on the Grand Canal. It was late autumn, and the hotel, though sparsely occupied, was fully staffed. This happy equation provided the restaurant with more waiters than diners and room service that arrived before the bell had cooled.

How Patricia, in all her travels, had missed Venice was inexplicable. So was the fact that she spoke flawless Italian, since she had never studied it. Her explanation was also inexplicable. "Simply started speaking it one day when I was working in a movie in Ischia. It made the director very happy, because his English was appalling."

I looked forward to tomorrow's responsibility of introducing Patricia to St. Mark's Square. Being well aware that attention to detail and precise timing are essential in producing a casual effect, I planned the excursion with extra care.

About noon I asked a safe question. "Where would you like to have lunch?" The reply from anyone in Venice for the first time is sure to be, "Isn't Harry's Bar the place?" Patricia said, "Isn't Harry's Bar the place?"

We sauntered into Harry's Bar. The greeting was warm; the greeter removed a card that read "Riservato" from a corner table. "Seems as if we were expected," said the bride.

"No, no, not at all," said the groom, "this is strictly a first-come-first-served place." If Patricia now felt a little wary of her guide, she kept it hidden . . . or almost hidden.

From certain angles, the rows of great columns that cross the entrance to St. Mark's Square assume the appearance of a solid wall, thus blocking from view any portion of the acres beyond. Patricia was very cooperative in allowing me to steer her along one of these angles until, at a certain turn, it suddenly materialized before her. It suddenly erupted, all of it, in one vast panorama: the church, the tower, the palace of the Doges, the bronze horses, all surrounded by endless cloisters filled with music and a million pigeons fluttering in the sky.

Patricia collapsed at a nearby table, tears of emotion running down her face.

"Napoleon called this 'the most beautiful room in the world,'" I said. She silently looked at the magnificence of it all, then dried her eyes and spoke briefly in Italian to the waiter. I immediately became a postgraduate of Berlitz.

"Make it two, per favore," I said.

We took an evening flight from Rome, and it was late when we arrived at our apartment in London. Mrs. Faithful had left the mail in neat stacks on the hall table. Several cables were placed apart. They all bore happy wishes, except one. That one was anything but happy tidings. It was from Benton Real Estate.

A few days before our wedding, David Selznick had asked me, "After your honeymoon, you don't intend to take Patricia back to that house, do you?"

"Tramonto?" I said, "of course not. There are reasons too numerous and too complicated why we shouldn't return to Tramonto."

"And besides all those complicated and numerous reasons," said David, "Pat has ideas of her own on what kind of house she wants to create for you both."

"As a matter of fact," I said to David, "we've sold it. At least the deal went into escrow two days ago. It was a piddling offer, but I thought it best to get rid of it as soon as possible."

"Who bought it? Anybody we know?"

"Some young producer and his mother," I said.

"I'm sure some young producer and his mother will be very happy there," said David.

Benton's cable shattered David's crystal ball. Some young producer and his mother were never to be happy in Tramonto. For tedious reasons, the whole deal had fallen through. "We are vigorously renewing our efforts, alas, from square one," signed Benton.

This was crushing news for both of us. While I had great faith in Benton's ability to find another buyer, I was aware that their customers were not exactly clamoring for five-story residences. I assured Patricia that we would not move into that house. We'd simply take a hotel suite temporarily. Anyway, they had two or three more weeks to try to sell it while Patricia met my family in Virginia.

It turned out, actually, that she introduced my family to me. We stayed with my brother Whitworth and his wife Maybelle. Their son, Whitworth Jr., was in the Pacific. Later he became a brilliant engineer. Maybelle had the most Southern name in the family and was from Syracuse, New York. Patricia immediately became Whit's sister and my mother's daughter. She called her sincerely, Mother Cotten; and Mother Cotten, before we left for California, described her as "God's perfect child." Through Patricia's eyes I was able, at last, to see Sam as simply a brother . . . not a baby brother . . . very much not a baby brother. He was happily married to his Millie, who had given him four splendid offspring, who in turn have thickened his wallet with photographs of the world's finest grandchildren.

We then went to New York and spent several days seeing friends and catching up with the new plays. Patricia loved New York.

Before we left for California, Patricia stopped me from booking rooms in a hotel or even leasing an apartment temporarily until she could find a home for us. She thought this an impractical, even negative solution to our Tramonto problem. After all, she tried to tell herself, it would be just as easy to redecorate that house as any other one, and it would save us the trouble of looking around. Her reasoning was the embodiment of kindness. It was consideration personified. It was Patricia.

I called Ida and John at the house and explained certain changes in rooms, certain changes in furniture. Then I called Guy.

Guy Womack excelled at remodeling houses. He preferred to work alone, but he suffered me as an assistant when I wasn't plying my own trade.

Tramonto had been built by an architect and decorator named Anthony Heinsbergen. Most of his creations were on a grand scale—theatres, post offices, hospitals—therefore, it was only natural for him to build his own house in a style of magnified areas. Besides being an architect and a decorator, he was a professional painter. I can't believe that any one artist has ever painted the Paris Opera from as many angles, in as many seasons, in as many degrees of lights and shades as Anthony Heinsbergen. When he designed Tramonto, he included a studio to house his easel. The studio was slightly, but not a great deal, smaller than the opera house of his dreams.

This was Patricia's first remodeling order. Guy and I were standing in the studio. She appeared on a stairway balcony above us. I'm not sure that she waved a wand, but I distinctly remember her saying, "We can't possibly use two drawing rooms. Please make this one into a swimming pool."

"Make this into a what?" said two stunned handymen, looking up at the balcony.

"A swimming pool," said Patricia. "I realize that we can see the ocean from here, but it is too far away, too cold, and too unfriendly. Besides, neither of you has been able to cope with the leaking roof in this room, and I think a pool to catch the drip would certainly be a solution to that problem."

"Not only a solution, but a most practical solution," said Guy.

The pneumatic drill, operated by Guy and his assistant, was digging up the concrete slab floor of the studio when Patricia appeared and yelled over the din, "Paul's here!"

Paul Gregory had achieved a marked success on a national scale with his touring production of *Don Juan in Hell* with Charles Laughton, Sir Cedric Hardwicke, Charles Boyer, and Agnes Moorehead. He had also been responsible for Aggie's "one lady" show, which had justifiably earned her the title of Queen of the Road. She had truly become everyone's idol, from Eau Claire to Pensacola, from Raleigh to Scottsdale. Paul knew every theatre, every auditorium, every public hall in America. He knew them not from a list provided by some booking office; he knew them because he had seen them, because he knew their managers and the local entrepreneurs. He had excellent taste and nonstop energy and was a hypnotic salesman.

He invited us to appear in a melodrama (the script of which he left with us) on a cross-country pre-Broadway break-in tour. Agnes Moorehead and Thomas Mitchell were already set for two of the roles. William Link and Richard Levinson had written it, and it was called *Enough Rope*.

Patricia and I had never worked together and we looked forward to finding something in which we could both appear. We read *Enough Rope* and liked it. (I mention here that we read the script because after an opening night in Boston, Elliot Norton, the critic there, asked me if I had read the play before accepting the part. His tongue did not appear to be in his cheek.)

The plot of *Enough Rope* concerned a doctor (me) who murdered his wife (Aggie Moorehead) because of his bewitchment by his mistress (Patricia). The evil deed was solved by a bumbling detective (Tommy Mitchell). During rehearsal, Patricia thought of a provocative title which was endorsed and officially accepted by the writers and the producer. *Enough Rope* became R_x*: Murder.* Also during rehearsal the writers joined the Dramatists Guild and became "authors." I had never been conscious of a distinction between a "writer" and an "author." Now I pondered on the transformation that must develop when an "author" becomes a "playwright." And whence comes the mystic sword that taps a "playwright" on the shoulder and commands, "Arise, Dramatist."

It became clearly evident during rehearsals that the plot of the play did not concern a doctor who murdered his wife and was subsequently apprehended by a bumbling detective. Rather it concerned a bumbling detective who put together sufficient evidence to convict a murderer who happened to be a doctor. The detective's name was Colombo. In later years, Peter Falk would don the same wrinkled trench coat and play to more viewers in one night than our R_x: *Murder* tour could attract in fifty years, instead of a fifty-week run.

Our first curtain rose in the Curran Theatre during one of San Francisco's infrequent snow flurries. The auditorium was filled with a dressy audience who made us feel welcome to the Golden Gate. The next day's review made us feel like hurling ourselves off it. Constant lines of ticket buyers at the box office, however, quickly discouraged this emotional reaction. It is said that the phrase "Nobody seems to like the play except the audience" is anonymous. This I believe not to be true. An unqualified, completely impeachable source, "The Listener," assures us that it is a paraphrase of Harry Truman's "Nobody voted for me except the people."

Before our final curtain in San Francisco the press warmed up. Herb Caen of the *Chronicle* said, "I hear the play isn't as bad as I hear it is."

The windows of Tiffany's never sparkle in the sunshine as brightly as the white clapboard facades of the hill-climbing architecture of San Francisco. On our last Sunday there, our car glided up and down these precipitous streets in sharp reflected light, then across the Bay Bridge to Oakland. There, a polished stainless steel train was waiting. The baggage car housed our revolving scenery, where it would rest for the next thirty-seven hours, while in the window of our pullman, God would create and change the sets as we slowly climbed and climbed, until at last we crossed the Great Divide, then descended into the Mile High City of Denver, our second stop.

Tchaikovsky, needless to say, did not have Agnes Moorehead in mind when he composed his Piano Concerto in B-flat Minor. Neither did Van Cliburn, who was playing it in a concert hall under the same roof that covered our theatre in Denver.

I was slowly pulling on my gloves, about to choke my wife. She was standing, face to the window, back to the audience. The end of Tchaikovsky's third movement was approaching. The crescendo was not only building in volume, it was creeping across the hall that separated the two auditoriums and becoming a distinct and clearly audible accompaniment to the action on our stage. I hurried with the gloves, but before my hands could reach Aggie's throat, Van Cliburn ended the concerto with nothing less than an atomic eruption. This was followed immediately by thunderous applause, not only from his audience, but also from ours. Aggie, whose throat was yet untouched, immediately and correctly dropped dead.

Fourteen cities later we were in Philadelphia where, after so many one-night stands, a two-week engagement offered us the opportunity to unpack our trunks and settle down to the luxury of what now seemed a long run. It was here that Tommy Mitchell collapsed and required immediate surgery. Tommy's understudy was able and professional, but the play seemed to lose its spine without Tommy, and we abandoned all plans to take it into New York.

The remainder of the tour was an excellent lesson in American geography for Patricia, who learned that Ohio was not in Florida. Savannah seemed to fit her English imagination of what the South would look like. She loved the Spanish moss and the local breakfast sausage. "That gives dignity to the word *country,*" she said. She relaxed on the snow-white sands that edge the Gulf from Panama City to Pensacola, and she thought Montreal the most urbane of cities with its unaffected integration of two languages. The size of our country she found staggering. It was difficult to imagine 3000 miles of the same customs, the same menus, the same shops. We unpacked our trunks again in Boston, where we took our last bows for R_x: *Murder.* Then one day, in only four hours, we flew west and home, across the map that had occupied us for the past five months.

12

The wind was sweeping the sea on the night we returned to Tramonto. From the terrace we looked down on the Pacific's turbulent mountains, topped with flirting whitecaps. Its unfriendly breakers pounded the beach, quelling the sound of the dense traffic along the Coast Highway.

The next morning I put on my working outfit. Guy was there, ready to resume finishing the pool deck with me. I picked up my trowel. Ding-a-ling. I put down my trowel and picked up the phone. My friend Bob Aldrich said a movie script was on its way. I put down the phone and picked up my trowel. Ding-a-ling, doorbell. It was Bob's movie. I put down my trowel and picked up the script.

"Go and have lunch, Guy," I said as Patricia walked into the room, gold leaf in her hands. There was a ladder and white paint leaning against one of the columns.

"The man from the *Christian Science Monitor* is on the terrace, waiting to interview you," she said.

"Oh, heavens, I'd forgotten about my date with him. I'll have to read Bob's script later."

I went out on the terrace above the pool, and a most charming gentleman started to ask me a few questions. Suddenly, a bloodcurdling scream came from the pool area, followed by an unprintable oath.

"Oh, dear God, that's my wife! Please excuse me!" I said as I rushed down.

When I reached the pool, I saw to my horror that Patricia was in it, with the ladder on top of her and a full gallon of white paint completely covering her head.

I jumped into the pool and grasped her. Her hands were mercifully over her eyes. "Darling, darling!" was all I could say. She clung to me and laughed.

"Find the paint thinner. I'll soon get it out of my hair," she said. "But the pool will have to be emptied and cleaned."

I pulled her out of the water, still terrified at how much damage Patricia had done to herself.

A voice from above said, "Mr. Cotten, I'm afraid I've come at a very inconvenient time. I do so hope everything is all right. I'll see myself out."

"Oh, please don't leave," said my wife. "If you'll forgive the way I look, I'd so like to meet you."

With white paint clinging to her hair and dripping from her head, she grabbed a bathrobe, threw it over her wet clothes, and flew off to the terrace.

Guy returned from lunch, and just stared at me. We worked and worked trying to get the paint out of the pool. Tired out, I finally went upstairs to freshen up. On the way, I heard the *Christian Science Monitor* gentleman saying, "Mrs. Cotten, it has been a great pleasure. You are the most delightful woman I have ever met. I'm sorry your husband had to leave, but I think I got the best interview I've ever had from you. Goodbye, and thank you very much."

"Goodbye," said my wife, as paint was dripping all over our beautiful new carpet. "It was indeed a pleasure."

I followed the trail of paint, fascinated. It led all the way from the terrace. "Here's the paint thinner," I said politely.

"Oh, thank you. Pity, I rather enjoyed the 'new look.' Go and read Bob's script," she said as she grabbed the can I gave her and rushed into the bathroom. She was still laughing.

I settled down to read Bob's script. The press had already noted with broad attention that Bob Aldrich had persuaded, bribed, or hexed Bette Davis and Joan Crawford to appear together again in another melodrama. These two super giants of the screen not long ago had rocked Hollywood and the world with their performances in Bob's production of *Whatever Happened to Baby Jane?* I had, therefore, little intention of regretting this invitation to appear with them. I knew Joan slightly. We felt more cozy than we actually were, I suppose, because she had met her late husband Al Steele at dinner in my house some years ago.

That evening, I witnessed a literal explosion of love at first sight. When they were introduced, their eyes locked. They remained locked. I remember them not touching their knives or forks during dinner, just sitting silently, staring across the table at one another. The moment we got up, they darted out the front door, and the next we heard of them they were married.

I had always hoped that the opportunity would arise once more to work with Bette Davis. Some years before, we had worked together in a movie called *Beyond the Forest.* It was made at Warner Brothers, where Bette was the reigning queen. When David Selznick gave me the script to read, I did not like the part, nor did I very much like the story. Also there was talk that Bette did not want to do the picture. I said to David, "If Bette Davis is not starring in it, there's no point in my doing it, is there?" He was loaning me to Warners for the picture.

"Tell you what," said David, "you have a point. If Bette doesn't do the movie, I won't ask you to do it. But if she decides that since she is under contract, maybe she will be nice and do it, then I will expect you to do it, too."

"It's a deal," I said. After all, whatever was good enough for Bette Davis was certainly good enough for me.

Bette decided to do it. I decided to follow her star. The picture never got off the ground. Bette was very unhappy with it and made several most sensible script changes, at least I thought they were most sensible since they concerned me. "I don't understand why I ever leave Josefff," she said. "He is so attractive, it doesn'ttt make sense."

Well, of course I couldn't voice my heartfelt agreement. I was playing her husband, and in the story she ran away with another man. Without that, there *was* no story. This was one of the few times she didn't win her argument, but the picture was a low point in her enduring career, which she has acknowledged with her usual candor.

King Vidor, who directed it, told me that he could not remember a less rewarding moment in his long and historic life behind the camera. This film, however, has now become a cult classic for the perverse. It even earned a moment of dubious recognition in Edward Albee's *Who's Afraid of Virginia Woolf . . .* Bette's "What a dump!"

As for me, I will admit to having stumbled into several trashbins here and there, but never into quite such an important trashbin. After all, I did work with one of the all time great actresses. In spite of the script, we worked well together. I defy anyone not to enjoy acting opposite this woman. She is *all* woman; and now, here was a most welcome opportunity to clear my palate of the unsatisfactory memory of *Beyond the Forest*.

Bette claims to be a better mother than a wife. Never having been married to her, I am not qualified to judge her as a wife, but I have known her husbands and have witnessed a display of love from both parties. Perhaps they felt inferior, perhaps they couldn't keep up with her. After all, she can do everything she puts her mind to: She is a marvelous cook and a gracious, exquisitely mannered hostess, and indeed she is the most loving and giving mother of all time.

To me she is a friend. I will follow her star till kingdom come, and I savor the fact that she is one of my few friends who call me Joseph. She is also the only one who pronounces it with three syllables.

Bette's energy, her enthusiasm, her creative quest for improvement, her perfection, make the legal phrase "unique and extraordinary" seem not at all redundant. She does not play a part; she attacks it. She comes on hungry.

Bob's new film, *Hush, Hush, Sweet Charlotte*, was a blood-dipped tapestry of Southern pride and decadence. Joan was finding her refinement of style difficult to weave into the strong and colorful pattern of raw emotions. She began to worry. She, too, was coming on hungry; but when she entered the dining room, instead of devouring the dinner, she began to fear that she was the dinner. She got sick. A virus infection put her in the hospital. She returned and tried her best to carry on, but she was too weak to continue. The picture closed down. Olivia de Havilland was invited to replace her. She and Bette were old friends, but Olivia was apprehensive about playing a murderess, and was reluctant to disturb her serenity in Switzerland.

The story, the project, everything about *Hush, Hush, Sweet Charlotte* was too good to scrap. Bob Aldrich put on persuading

armor, packed handcuffs and a fountain pen, flew to Switzerland,
and brought back Olivia. With this jest he makes further reporting
on the film anticlimactic. I'm getting fed up with directors who
simply can't help stealing the show.

Olivia and I played lovers in *Hush, Hush, Sweet Charlotte*. She
was a fine replacement. She and Bette worked beautifully together;
she and I had never worked together before. Little did we know
that we were to do so again and again.

In Santa Barbara we made *The Screaming Woman*, produced by
Bill Frye and directed by Jack Smythe. Olivia had a most physically
exhausting part and she never flagged or faltered; she is such a hard
worker and such a pleasure to work with. We picked up our screen
romance in *Airport 77*, again produced by Bill Frye, and directed by
Jerry Jameson, and again she had a most physical and exhausting
role. So did I. We were in the Pacific off San Diego, battling the
waves. On the stage at Universal, they kept us drenched in a tank
after the 747 had supposedly crashed under the sea.

Jack Lemmon and my very good friend, Jimmy Stewart, were
the stars. Lemmon has received many well-deserved awards. Well
hidden in Jimmy's house is every kind of award. Many are for acting, of course, but some are for flying—he is a retired Air Force
general. But his most treasured awards are his lovely, witty wife
Gloria, and their children.

Only the other day the telephone rang. Would I do a segment of
"Love Boat" opposite Olivia de Havilland? Of course! I think, and
indeed I hope, that the saga of Olivia and Jo will continue.

Tramonto had been thoroughly Patricianized. After *Charlotte*, it
was wonderfully relaxing just to live like private people. We entertained again, mostly small dinners with close friends who lived
nearby. The Esmonds were the closest. Carl and Ruth were among
the first people Patricia had met when she arrived in this country,
and she and Ruthie have remained devoted to each other. Dr. Rod-
erick Turner and his wife Nan were neighbors and popped in and
out to play tennis or dine on the terrace.

Roz Russell and her husband, Freddie Brisson, would come in
between his Broadway productions. Hitch was usually there with
his tiny Alma. Irene Dunne always seemed happy on Bill Frye's
arm. Her beauty today is as enduring as Mrs. Moonlight's, with no

remorse to sadden her humor. James Wharton usually brought Loretta. Our dear friend and producer Collier Young, no relative of Loretta, brought his new bride Meg, whom we both came to love. (He and Joan Fontaine had divorced some time ago.) And of course, David and Jennifer, who needed no invitation.

A large English contingent would fill the house whenever they were in California. The Nivens, of course, would come, and Rex Harrison, with a variation of wives, was often there. Alec Guinness and John Gielgud always let us know when they were in town, as did marvelously funny Beryl Reid. Hazel Court, who gave up acting to become a sculptor and the wife of my good friend Don Taylor and succeeded brilliantly in both switches, was a favorite neighbor. Don was equally successful in switching from acting to directing and from Phyllis Avery to Hazel. George Sanders and his witty and pretty Benita were our house guests often when in town. Radie Harris was always accompanied by her good friend Vivian Leigh, who my mother credited with the most authentic Southern accent ever in talkies, and who added her charming drawl to frequent afternoons. And as the King said, et cetera, et cetera, et cetera.

We loved our evenings alone, too. We would swim in Patricia's exotic pool, the Venetian chandeliers dimly lit above us, and then sit alongside with a cool drink and talk—about our life, about our plans to go to Europe soon, and always, on our return, to visit Virginia and my mother and family. Patricia told me that during one of her many conversations with my mother they talked about my childhood and Patricia said to her, "Were you very surprised or shocked, Mother Cotten, when young Jo went on the stage?"

"Well, no, dear," my mother replied. "You see, Jo Jr. was always the last to come into the dining room for dinner, and when he did arrive, he would make a startling entrance, which soon became no surprise to any of us, and then he would stand and gesticulate broadly while giving quite an emotional rendition of 'Jack and Jill' or 'Little Bo Peep' or whatever nursery rhyme he fancied. When he finished, he would take his place at the table and bow his head, which was his consent for Daddy to proceed with grace."

"What a conceited little devil," Patricia had said.

"No, he wasn't conceited, just quite sure of himself. He had a natural vanity."

"So I suppose you knew you had an actor in the family."

"Let me put it this way: Daddy and I thought that he spoke so well, he might end up in the pulpit . . . or in the theatre," my mother added wistfully. "At any rate we knew that vanity would get him somewhere."

I laughed. "I don't remember any of that," I said. I reminded Patricia of a conversation I once had with *her* mother. "She told me you aspired to be a doctor," I said.

"So I did," she confessed, "but I later decided that the greatest contribution I could make to the medical profession would be to stay out of it. I made the sacrifice."

"What did you do instead?" asked the straight man, her husband, who got a dirty look.

"I took up long distance swimming," said the once and never doctor as she plunged into her pool.

I had learned during *The Last Sunset* just to play my part to the best of my ability and divorce myself entirely from anything else.

The picture was released, and it was not too well received. When people are under a strain, the result is usually less than perfect. However, the *New York Times* review said, "It is left to veteran actor Joseph Cotten to give the finest performance . . ." I'll drink to that! And I did.

My ego told me, in no uncertain terms, that what I now craved was an audience! One good notice and I could hear the applause!

Luckily, Howard Erskine, a New York producer, came round with a play by Joseph Hayes, to be directed by former movie star Robert Montgomery. It was called *Calculated Risk*. He offered both Patricia and me roles in it. We would play only one week in New Haven and one week in Philadelphia and would then open in New York.

It was a very well written play. My part was enormous and as difficult as it was long. Patricia thought I definitely should do it. She found her part considerably out of character for her (she was playing my wife and she claimed to much prefer playing my mistress), "but that's on the stage only," she hastily added. "Anyway, my part is fairly small and I know I can play it," she said. We hoped to be able to find an apartment, get familiar with our surroundings, settle down, and learn our lines during New York's most enchanting month, August.

Hume Cronyn and his wife Jessica Tandy were going away for six or eight months and we optimistically, perhaps rashly, leased their roomy and beautiful penthouse. We remembered the title of our play, *Calculated Risk*.

We worked every day. Patricia, who has a photographic memory, was letter perfect before the end of the first week. My part, though interesting, was complex and full of Wall Street technicalities—difficult to memorize. Patricia was patient but stern. She allowed me only two half-hour breaks a day, and never the *Times* crossword puzzle until cocktail time.

On the first day of rehearsal I was secure in all my words and grateful for the discipline imposed on me by my coach. I could now use the three weeks ahead for developing the character.

Try putting together a finer cast, a nicer group than Frank Conroy, John Beal, Roland Winters, and Russell Collins, with Bob Montgomery as director. You can't.

We opened in New Haven to fine reviews. Philadelphia also received us warmly. While we were there, Joe Hayes shaved his manuscript while Bob Montgomery polished and encouraged his troupe of actors.

In New York the Ambassador Theatre had been upgraded for our opening. Backstage had been painted a cheerful coffin gray (green is taboo in the theatre except at the box office), and the rat-pack that attended our rehearsals had received the attention of the fumigator.

The atmosphere in the reading room of any public library would seem bedlam compared to the silence and calm that freezes the backstage area of any theatre on an opening night in New York. This is called stage fright, which professional actors are supposed to have outgrown but which most professional actors, including this one, will tell you gets worse with age. An honest poll would surely reveal that the percentage of actors who take a secret oath at eight o'clock on opening night is 100 percent. The oath is always the same: "I hereby vow never to enter a theatre again."

The response from the audience in the Ambassador during and after our initial performance was warm and encouraging. We all took curtain calls with overt smiling relief and hidden crossed fingers.

We strolled down to Sardi's, and were applauded up the stairs to a private room where we bit our nails to await an early pulled galley copy of the *New York Times* review.

When our public relations man rushed it up to us, Bob Montgomery read it aloud. Howard Taubman had written a rave about the play, about the actors, about the direction, about everything. Joe Hayes, the author, said through his tears that had the *Times* offered him Taubman's space, his modesty would have restrained him from pulling out as many stops as Taubman had.

We went home wondering how many mounted police would be needed tomorrow to control the unruly lines at our box office, and before retiring Patricia and I were forming modest phrases to Hume and Jessica concerning an extension of our lease of their apartment.

No lines formed at the Ambassador box office. No lines formed at anyone's box office. The galley copy of our rave review was never published. The newspapers had gone on strike. Little did we know that it was to last 100 days. We went to the theatre and played to very few people.

Immediately plays began folding. The domino theory ran its course down Broadway as productions collapsed. Huge vans hauled beautiful new scenery to the boneyard. There were bad jokes about *Calculated Risk* being a prophetic title. We were hanging by a thread.

One Sunday, Patricia said to me softly that she didn't want to hurt me, but, "Jo, darling, we will have to close, you know."

"We will not close," I heard myself saying rather too vehemently.

"Of course we'll have to close. Everyone's closing."

"We will not close," I repeated.

"Jo, there are no newspapers, no way of advertising. We are not making enough money to keep the theatre open. Why in heaven's name do you think we won't close?"

I saw the Ambassador Theatre clearly pictured in my mind. I saw the sign "Calculated Risk," and above the title I saw in lights: "Joseph Cotten." It was the first time those two words had appeared alone in that position on Broadway. I answered Patricia's question. I said, as simply as I possibly could, "I am too vain to close."

I did have an awful fear that the play could not survive without any publicity. But what was it that made me refuse to accept it? Was I really that vain? Oh hell, anyone who has the temerity to expect theatres full of people not only to come and look and listen, but to applaud, had to possess more than the usual amount of . . . The telephone rang. It was the first time in my life that I remember being alarmed by the bell.

"This is James Rorimer," said the voice. "Remember me, from the Cloisters?" During the New York location days of *Portrait of Jenny*, Mr. Rorimer had gone out of his way to be hospitable to us when we were filming in his Cloisters, overlooking the Hudson. I say his Cloisters because he was very possessive about the building, its contents, and its grounds, having supervised the placing of every stone during its construction and having approved every plant in the garden after first identifying it in the Unicorn Tapestries, the backbone of the museum's collection.

He was then the curator of the Cloisters. He was now head of the Metropolitan Museum. My first edict, when I become dictator, will be an order for a movie to be made from his book *Survival*, an extraordinary adventure that he tersely describes as "the salvation and protection of art in war" and which contains the excitement of a James Bond thriller.

Mr. Rorimer explained that the Mona Lisa had just arrived at the Met from Paris. In a few days it would be his pleasure to introduce her on television. "I'm sure everybody knows who Mona Lisa is," he said, "but I'm also sure absolutely nobody knows who I am. I am hoping you might introduce *me* before I introduce *her*. And, by the way, this is not one of those favors museums are always asking. The television people tell me they will make it quite lucrative."

Television! Lucre! No bell this time! Those two words rang themselves. At their sound, a naked electric light bulb clicked on in my head. I looked into Jessica Tandy's mirror. I saw standing before me Phineas T. Barnum. I told Mr. Rorimer I would be honored to appear on TV in such prestigious company.

I told my agent nothing.

I told the TV people I wanted an unrealistic fee. With Mona and the curator in my corner, they agreed. Reluctantly. Then I doubled the sum, but before they could react, I explained that I wanted it in time, not in money. Time on the air to advertise our floundering play.

"No money?" they asked.

"No money," I said. They agreed with no reluctance.

The goose had been captured. The golden egg was within reach. Without newspapers, television had become The Medium, not just one of the media. The striking press had created a monopoly out of the competition, a monopoly whose advertising rates were beyond the reach of struggling shows.

We didn't wait for our opportunity to knock twice. Patricia and I immediately designed a television campaign. "Hard sell" understates what we did. We were shameless. We were brazen. We were determined that Forty-ninth Street would not add more darkness to Times Square. The tiny screens of New York and its surrounding area were saturated with our conceit.

What the viewer saw first was a close-up of a mini billboard. Patricia's picture and my picture stared straight out above the lettering that spelled the name of the play, the theatre, the cost, etc. As the picture on the screen grew wider, it included the backs of two people, a man and a woman, who were looking up at the billboard.

She spoke: "Look at that beautiful actress, Patricia Medina. She's always been my favorite. I can't wait to see her in her Broadway debut. What's the name of the play?" It was immediately obvious that "she" could not read, for large letters on the billboard spelled out the name in front of her.

He spoke: "The name of the play is *Calculated Risk,* and it says there that it is an exciting event at the Ambassador Theatre. But how about that handsome Joseph Cotten?" he continued, "*my* forever favorite."

"He" and "She" then turned profile. The viewers recognized them as the same couple in the ad. Same faces, same clothes. "He" looked at his watch. "He" took "She" by the arm, they exited as "He" said: "Come along, Patricia, we mustn't be late for our next performance of *Calculated Risk.*"

"At the Ambassador Theatre," "She" modestly added.

This egotistical little ploy worked. I know it worked because the size of our audience expanded instantly.

Leland Hayward, now a Broadway producer, telephoned. "How do you manage all those television commercials?" he asked. "I happen to know what your theatre can gross, which is not nearly enough to support a television campaign."

"Don't you believe all those statistics you read in *Variety,* Leland," I said.

Our "saturation" time on TV was now running down to infrequent "spot" time, and the nightly gross receipts were running down in exact proportions.

For the first time since our wedding, I thought I detected a hint of nagging from Patricia. Well, mock nagging anyway. It was during our little chat session, when each night the entire acting company gathered on stage at the call of "fifteen minutes." We would listen to the murmur of the audience through the lowered curtain. We had been cheered by the volume as, over the weeks, it had increased. We optimistically believed that "word of mouth" would stem its decline. Tonight, what we heard was the roar of a kitten. The actors were aware of the too-vain-to-close story, and they accepted with tolerant grace my reincarnation as P. T. Barnum.

Patricia said to me, "Well, Mr. Barnum, think of something. You can't let us down now."

"Hear, hear," said the assembled company, as they assembled threateningly near.

Paul Foley, the best stage manager ever to call "Act One, please," gave me temporary asylum as he called "Act One, please."

Television, it was clear, was our only salvation. Saturation television. I appealed to my agent, who was unable to collect any commission on my "time" deal. I promised never again to consider money secondary to anything, anything at all, including advertising time on the air. "I'll get *Calculated Risk* on the tube," he said, "but if you want saturation, be prepared to work all day, every day."

"We have matinees twice a week," I said.

"OK," he said. "No afternoon TV on Wednesdays and Saturdays."

I sold soap in the mornings. "You take no risk when you wash with these suds . . . and speaking of risk. . . ." Well, I told you we were shameless. I sold a local beer in the afternoons. "All New York is happy when it takes a sip of . . . just as all New York is happy when it visits the Ambassador Theatre to see, etc."

I talked on talk shows; I sang along with Mitch. Patricia played game shows all day and managed to work *calculated* and *risk* into "Password." Can you imagine getting into a New York taxi and seeing a poster in front of you that read: "This is the taxi that takes Joseph Cotten and Patricia Medina to the Ambassador Theatre." Well, that is the poster you would have read if you had entered

Milton Cohen's taxi. Milton even gave up an evening's work and brought his wife, Belle, to the play so that they could be well informed on the subject. The Cohens are dear friends to this day.

My activities grew so complex and demanding that the play itself became an anticlimactic part of the daily routine. I was exhausted. The company took pity and granted me a two-week leave of absence from my TV toils.

Before my first week's vacation was over, our precurtain assemblies on the stage were being shushed by Paul Foley. The actors' chat was louder than the audience. To John Beal's whistling accompaniment, Roland Winters softly sang, "Back to the peddling for poor old Jo, back to the salt mines he must go."

The next day it was soap and beer again for Jo. It was good attendance again in the Ambassador. We became known as The Miracle of Forty-ninth Street, and we ran the entire season. It was a balmy spring night when we closed. During our curtain calls, Patricia whispered, "Well, you stooped, but you certainly conquered."

After a nice rest at home, I was offered a picture by director Norman Foster, a good friend of mine. The picture was called *Brighty* and was to be made in Kanab, Utah. It was a very happy experience except for one awful day that will stay in my memory forever. It was one of the very few days that I was not working. Patricia and I were relaxing in our motel quarters when the telephone rang. It was Patricia's agent, Bob Sherr (who is now an interior designer). I listened to Bob, and my face must have expressed my feeling, for Patricia jumped up and said, "What is it, darling, please what is it?"

"David . . . ," I said. She burst into tears. Two minutes after friend Bob had broken the awful, awful news, the Associated Press made their usual call. Whatever I said was not what was in my heart.

Patricia said, "We must go to Jennifer. I'll go and tell Norman."

This all happened some time ago, but the shock is still vivid. David O. Selznick, my former boss, my very dear friend, my adopted brother, had died. Along with my great sorrow, I felt a deep anger and resentment toward him. How could he do this to me?

Things happened fast. His son Danny called Patricia and said that his father had left a memo directing the handling of his funeral. Part of what he wrote went something like this:

I shall need a rabbi for, though I have not been a very good Jew,
I *am* a Jew. But I would like a rabbi who doesn't know me too
well; then he can't talk too long and bore my friends. I suppose
a few words will have to be said; I would like them spoken by a
good voice, so if Joseph Cotten is in the country I want him to
say them. Also, he will be brief.

There was lots more. How typical of him to issue production
memos for his own funeral. But after all, it was *his* funeral.

We took a private plane to Las Vegas, then a regular airline to
Los Angeles. A car took us up to the Selznick house. Jennifer was
resting, or trying to rest. Patricia and Anita Colby went to sit with
her and console the inconsolable.

Danny and Jeffrey, David's two sons, were waiting for me. I
read them what I intended to say at the funeral the next day. They
thought it was too serious and should have some laughs. "He *did*
have a great sense of humor," they reminded me. I didn't mean to
seem inflexible, but I thought this was not exactly the ideal occasion
for jokes, and I said so. We could not come to any understanding. I
would not change the words that reflected my feelings about David;
they wanted a big show. It was becoming a story conference. I offered to bow out. They refused.

Irene Selznick, David's first wife and their mother, had sent a
piece by Truman Capote and suggested I read that. I refused. If
David wanted me to speak about him, it was because he trusted my
judgment; he was also aware of my stubbornness.

The size of the crowd attending the funeral was too large for the
small temple in Forest Lawn, and the ceremony was moved quickly
and gracefully into a large Christian church. I assumed that it was a
Christian church because I noticed that the stained glass windows
were adorned with saints.

At the back of the church, a large group of honorary pallbearers
waited for the signal to follow David's casket down the aisle. Sam
Goldwyn, as David's oldest friend, had strong opinions on who
should precede the casket down the aisle . . . the rabbi or himself.
George Cukor was acting as director and stage manager, and he was
losing the battle to bring quiet control to the service. Sam continued to elbow himself most audibly toward the front of the proces-
sion, which was still waiting to start.

I saw Frances, Sam's wife, motion from her pew to her son Sammy, an usher. Frances whispered something to Sammy. He hurried back to his excited father and said, "Father, please, Mother says she's ashamed of you." Sam Goldwyn didn't hear.

"What?" he asked.

"Please, Mother says she's ashamed of you," Sammy repeated.

Sam turned to George Cukor, who was trying so gently to pull him away.

"You hear, George, what Frances said. She's ashamed of you!" Sam then assumed his position at the vanguard. The rabbi followed, and then came David, propelled by the undertakers and followed by his honorary pallbearers.

When I told Jennifer this story a few days later, she said, "Sam is the Dean of Hollywood, and David adored him. I'm so glad he entered first."

I read my piece as I had written it, hoping that as a small part of this enormous occasion it would be acceptable to the family. I wrote it, however, for David. And I spoke it for David.

The night before the funeral Bill Paley wrote a delightful piece on the lighter side of David, and who ever surpassed Cary Grant in reading a light line? Truman Capote's pages were read by George Cukor, and at the Selznick boys' special request, Katharine Hepburn gave a sincere and strong reading of Rudyard Kipling's "If."

I miss David every day and have often caught myself in the act of picking up the telephone to ask for his advice. I am thankful and wiser for having known him.

After the funeral, Jennifer came and gave me a kiss and said, "Jo, thank you from me . . . and thank you for David."

At the house afterward, Sam Goldwyn said sadly to Patricia, "I don't think God loves me. He sent for David, who had so much to live for, and he doesn't send for me. I don't know why." Several years later, Sam received his call.

The day after David's funeral, his son Danny appeared at my front door. He placed a letter (below) in my hand and left.

Dear Joe,

You will never know how much you have meant to this family. There were times in the last years when Dad told me it seemed everyone else had turned away, and only you and Pat stood by. And it moved him, deeply. And it moved me to hear about it, always.

If Dad, as so many seemed to say, inspired generosity in others, he inspired something even more from you, a kind of loyalty that cannot be measured, or even spoken of. And, in a moment of profound grief, you gave yourself once again—with guts and with love—these last days the details of how you hired a plane may be forgotten in years to come, but not the words that you wrote—from your heart—and defended here Thursday night, with the kind of fierce pride that can only come from deep knowledge and the kind of thing I have inadequately called "loyalty."

It seemed at the time to be less than the full portrait of my father—but when you read it yesterday, read it with the magnificence and the conviction of a great warrior saluting his Captain, I was completely and inescapably overwhelmed with emotion. How you loved him—and what a loss this is we share. I will never forget your reading—slow, rich, with adoration— nor the original and moving way you ended your words, "Last night, I found myself writing a memo. It read: 'Thank you, David. Thank you.'"

Louis Jourdan told Jennifer that is the way he felt, too. And that is the way all of us feel. For that man gave so, so, so much. Speaking for myself, I feel my life is a rich one only because of him—but then, nothing I can write now has any feeling or meaning.

I just wanted to drop you this note—so that you knew how moved I was by your devotion—and the work (up to and including Friday morning) it inspired.

Thank *you*, Joe. Thank you.

Danny.

It was big of Danny to admit his error. He must have inherited this trait. That thought brought a smile to my sadness.

13

The roads of Hollywood were now reaching across the seas. Airplanes were making the American public world-wise. Those back lot English streets were beginning to look like just what they were: back lot streets. No longer would those cutout Italian fountains do. Almost everyone now had thrown a coin into the Trevi. People were demanding the real thing, and they were getting it. Patricia and I realized, not unhappily, that we were about to become gypsies and once more put Tramonto on the market.

Don Sharpe, a producer I had known since the old days of radio, offered us roles in a film to be coproduced by an American and a Japanese company. It was to be the first English-speaking picture ever attempted by the Japanese, and Toho, the country's largest studio, was to make it. It was a science fiction story. Its scenery was entirely imaginary. It could have been made anywhere. "Why Tokyo?" we asked ourselves.

"If not for artistic integrity, it must have something to do with money," we answered ourselves. *Money* was the magic word; our answer was correct.

Perhaps our curiosity about Japan colored our judgment of the script, but we accepted Don's invitation and departed on the long flight to the Far East.

It is an acknowledged fact that Japan boasts more cameras per square foot than any spot on the globe; and to greet us in a small reception room in the Tokyo airport they had assembled every single one of them, flashing and clicking in all directions. They handed me an enormous bouquet of orchids, which I promptly handed over to Patricia, but at the reporter's suggestion, she handed them back to me. We played basketball with the flowers until they expired in the heat of the flash bulbs. The Japanese were terribly interested in movies and filled with questions. Curiously, most of their questions were not about the one we were there to do, but about *Portrait of Jenny*.

Our hotel suite outdid an advertisement for Forest Lawn. There were flowers of all shapes, and shades, and sizes. It was somewhat overwhelming and seemed almost too good to be true. It was.

We had been working on the picture for three weeks when A. Morgan Maree, my business manager, telephoned and said that all our checks from Don Sharpe had bounced.

The head man at Toho called me into his office and said that none of the American production costs had been paid. It was a most uncomfortable and embarrassing situation. What could we do? I told him I would telephone Don and was sure there was some dreadful misunderstanding that could be cleared up.

Dreadful it was indeed. Sharpe had omitted to tell us that he was bankrupt.

Patricia and I sat in our lovely hotel suite and tried to think of some honorable solution to the situation. We were getting very alarmed after hearing some of the stories about the total difference between East and West. Were these stories true? Of one thing we were sure, the Japanese are renowned for their value of face saving. But here we were in their midst, and desperately in need of saving *our* faces.

A happy and full-of-life Cesar Romero arrived in town and came to our suite for a drink. He was to start work with us tomorrow.

"I must see the American production manager," he said.

"He's on his way down here," said Patricia. "But please don't mention money, it's a very sensitive subject."

"What do you mean don't mention money?" boomed Cesar. We told him we had received nothing, not even living expenses, that the other actors needed money badly, and that I had just cashed my last traveler's check.

While Cesar stared incredulously, Patricia picked up the phone and asked for room service. "Would you please send rice for one, creamed chicken for one, and three plates—and plenty of bread and butter," she said with an embarrassing amount of authority. "We'll keep the plates," she said, turning to us, "and buy some eggs and an electric pan tomorrow."

Cesar then went to the telephone. His business people in California were the same as mine. Having come straight from Paris, he had missed a telegram from them telling him not to report for work on our picture because there were no funds. (The picture, by the way, was called *Latitude Zero. Latitude* was redundant.)

Dinner arrived. We ate hungrily and silently.

"I should have asked for more rice," Patricia said to no one in particular. No one answered.

We had a telephone call from the chief interpreter. He asked if he could come over to speak to me with the head of production at Toho and one other gentleman. We invited them to come immediately. I asked Cesar to stay with us through the ordeal.

They must have telephoned from the lobby. In one minute, all three of them were at our door. They entered, and all sat silently for a while. I searched their inscrutable faces for some kind of hint as to what they were going to suggest.

Then finally, the head of production started to speak softly and very slowly in Japanese to the interpreter. It was the longest speech I have ever heard; I could only hope that it would shrink in translation.

As the English version started, I began to feel very weak. (Obviously I needed more nourishment than Patricia had been able to con room service into.) In effect, what the interpreter said was that Toho Films had spent large sums of money on the film so far, and that the only hope they had of recuperating their investment was to invest more. In fact, they would need to take over the full responsibility of the movie, financial and otherwise.

"The large sums you have spent so far do not include any of the American actors' salaries, or their living expenses," I said with as much dignity as I felt I could get away with. I knew the interpreter had a lot more to say. The production head had droned on for considerably more time; it could not have boiled down to just that.

"We know that none of the actors have been paid. That was the responsibility of the American producer, who was a dishonorable man. We at Toho are thoroughly honorable people. When we 'make a deal,' as you call it, we keep our word. We are willing to pay your living expense, and all of your salaries."

He paused. I no longer felt hungry. I needed a drink. I looked at Romero, whose face had a slight smile for the first time since their entrance.

"But," the interpreter continued, "because of the governmental red tape that will occur in changing this production into a Japanese one, we will not be able to pay you for six months—after the picture is finished."

I felt my blood draining, and I was angry—angry at Don Sharpe, angry at these men for daring to come to us with such a preposterous proposition, and angry at some kind of internal frustration that I could not control.

Before I could say a word, he continued, "Your living expenses we would pay retroactively immediately."

"*Big deal!*" I heard myself say. I had about six more weeks' work on the picture, and Patricia and Romero had about three.

"In any country, including our own 'dishonest United States,'" I said sarcastically, "if the production defaults, if payments are not made, however generous we as actors may feel, we are instructed by our guild, by our agents, and by our managers not to work until our salaries are paid in *full*. In this case, we shall all go home, and in six months' time, if we are available, we will return here and complete the picture for you. I apologize for what my countrymen have done to you. It is an ugly situation, but we as individuals," I waved my arms to include Patricia and Cesar and, I hoped, the other poor actors who would be waiting in their unpaid rooms, "are not to blame."

I now envisioned myself paying for the other actors' rooms and meals so that we could leave the country. That would mean a phone call to Hurley Graffins, my film manager, to come out here himself immediately with the required cash. Romero, I knew, would telephone for his dollars. Actually, Hurley could bring his money here, too.

In the middle of my financial nightmare, I heard the interpreter's voice saying, "We know you are entitled to leave, but before you do, there is something that you should be aware of. Mr. Yoshimura [the production head] has been with this company for thirty-two years. But since it was his misfortune to go to the United States to meet Mr. Sharpe, and to make all the business arrangements for this coproduction, he of course feels his honor is at stake, and he can no longer stay with us. You must understand our customs, our moral values; we judge ourselves, and if we find ourselves wanting, we know what to do about it."

Oh, dear God, what did he mean? Patricia put her hands to her face, then, catching my eye, removed them to her lap again. Cesar walked to the window and looked out on the terrace, his back to the room.

The interpreter's voice (by now any way you looked at it, it was the voice of doom) continued, "Only if you agree to stay on and complete the picture would his position be saved."

Now it was our turn to give them the silent treatment. I'm not sure whether Patricia realized what his soliloquy implied. Cesar, I knew, was thinking as I did.

I walked to the window. Patricia followed me, and the three of us stood looking out. Finally I said, "Do we need a democratic vote, or am I right in thinking both of you agree that we stay?" Patricia put her head on my shoulder. I knew her answer.

"Let's stay," Cesar said. "Their beliefs and their values are Japanese. Let us stay and show them that not all Americans are ugly."

We walked back to the expressionless little group.

"All right, we've agreed to stay and finish your picture," I said. This was translated with remarkable speed to Mr. Yoshimura, who, to our absolute astonishment, let go with a flood of tears. This so unnerved Patricia that she ran to the bar and poured the entire remains of a most guarded whiskey bottle into a glass, and then poured it into Mr. Yoshimura's mouth. In an instant he was flat on his face on the floor. Apparently he had never had a drink in his life.

"Oh my God! Have I killed him?!" said Patricia.

"No . . . thank you," said the interpreter. Then he and the third man (if you'll forgive the plug) lifted the prone but mercifully alive head of production, and carried him out of the room, bowing to us all the way to the exit.

As the door closed behind them, I collapsed into a chair, wondering what we were in for. Romero was back at the window . . . wondering.

We were jolted back to earth by Patricia's clear voice on the phone: "Room service? This is 101. Would you please send duck à l'orange for eleven persons, sautéed potatoes for ten, and baby green peas, also for ten persons. And a magnum of champagne. What's that? Oh, no. No plates, thank you." She hung up, looked at us with a smile, and said, "We have the plates, remember?"

The following morning, Mr. Yoshimura came and gave us his thanks, right in the middle of a scene.

We now settled in to working very hard. As I am six foot two inches tall and Cesar is even taller, they gave us crash helmets to enter the tiny studio doors. Before our magnanimous gesture, we had been denied such refined treatment. Actually we were so used to hitting our heads that the helmets felt peculiar. But we did everything they asked of us without argument. The thought of anyone losing face was something we wouldn't risk.

At the studio our interpreter was a woman. She was the only one who was not gracious. The director was charming and artistic, and I'm sure that had he been able to speak English, or we Japanese, he would have had some very interesting ideas for the movie.

On our days off we went to the theatre. We saw a beautiful production of *The King and I*. The little boy in this famous musical was played by a little girl, an American little girl living in Japan with her mother and father. Her Japanese was perfect and her name was Linda Purl, now no longer a little girl, but a lovely young lady and a delightful actress.

A charming Japanese actor who had appeared in the Tokyo production of Harold Rome's stage version of *Gone with the Wind* and his wife took us for a drive and showed us some beautiful gardens. He was justifiably proud of his English, which was basic and direct. I told him of my love of gardening, which he shared, but he found it most unsatisfactory with the new commercial fertilizers.

"They are not at all as good as the old natural shits," he said sadly. Patricia and her sister Gloria inherited from their mother the inability to restrain themselves when such temptations for naughty giggles arise. Now I dared sneak a look. I was proud of her. Her face was the most inscrutable in all Japan.

We had dinner in some fascinating restaurants, thoroughly enjoyed their Kobe beef, their manners, and their dignity.

We were, of course, in a rather ignominious position. We went in stocking feet whenever required, which was often. The women managed gracefully, but big men with fitted shoes are unaccustomed to jumping in and out of them. Still, we held our heads high, at least as high as the architecture would allow, and kept a shoehorn ever available.

I felt responsible for the other American actors who had elected to go along with my decision to finish the picture. The hotel gave us everything they could to make us comfortable (we were finally paying our bills).

Patricia went down to the lobby in a sweater and skirt to see the manager about getting a piece of furniture for our living room. To those unacquainted with my wife's measurements (and I must confess, she has never enlightened me with exact inches), it is sufficient to say that she would never be mistaken for a boy.

"What can I do for you, Mrs. Cotten?" asked the manager, with the customary deep bow.

"I need a chest," said Patricia sweetly. The manager's head rose very slowly from his waist. His eyes became occidental and unable to focus above her chin.

"You need a *chest?*" he managed to say hoarsely.

Romero was standing behind her, and at this point he turned away and walked to the other end of the lobby, where he joined me.

Poor Patricia struggled on without a smile. "Yes, a chest. You know, with a few drawers for my husband's socks and sweaters."

"Of course. I will see to it right away," said the epitome of Eastern culture as he bowed low. This time his head came up quite quickly, and they looked into each other's eyes with mutual respect.

Cesar completed his part first. Patricia finished hers at the same time, and she promptly got the Asian flu. She was desperately ill. I called a friend of mine who was in the army in Tokyo, and he sent over a marvelous doctor from New England. I was working every day and rushing home to see how Patricia was doing. She was getting stronger, thank heavens, but we both longed to return home. I began to feel terribly tired.

One morning, before my alarm went off, Patricia was on the phone to the doctor, saying, "Please come over now, my husband has been groaning. It's Asian flu. I know. He has a high fever. Please come, before they try to make him work."

He came. What my fever was he didn't tell me. The car came to pick me up to go to the studio. The doctor said that under no condition could I work for quite a while.

"I have to finish this picture, I haven't much more to do," I pleaded.

"If you were twenty-one and went to work in the state you are in now, you probably wouldn't make it. But at your age, you most certainly would die," said our euphemistic physician. "I will talk to the film company," he said, and he did, but apparently not very successfully.

That evening he came and gave me extra doses of antibiotics. Patricia told him that the woman interpreter had been calling all day, saying they were sure I could work the next day, as the studio was warm and they'd send a car for me.

"If he goes to work, he's no longer my patient," said the doctor.

I never saw him again. I had heard about the actor who had broken his contract, not with Toho, but with another company. After his last film with that company he refused to re-sign with them, but agreed to make an appearance at the opening of the movie. On his way to the theatre the car that had been sent for him met with an accident. He lived, but was so disfigured he could never work in any more movies again.

This story may not have been entirely accurate, but it was told to us by a Japanese actor about a friend of his, another Japanese actor.

I tried to think of a way that I could finish this picture on time. It was obvious even to me that I was not strong enough to complete all the scenes. I could not ask for the assistance of another doctor. The top American physician had already given me up as a bad risk.

I called up the unpleasant lady interpreter and asked her to suggest to the director that he find a double to use in all my active shots, and I would go and shoot all the close-ups in one day. Doing close-ups, I could be supported without it being seen.

I must have been delirious to suggest getting up at all. However, the unpleasant lady returned my call. The director said he could arrange my suggestion.

"Then we can go home," I said. We had return tickets on Japan Air Lines in two days' time.

"Finish the picture and we'll send a car the next day to take you to the airport. I have your flight number," she said.

"OK," I said, and fell back in the bed.

Patricia was frantic.

In the morning, I fell down; I got up again. I refused Patricia's pleas to return to bed. "Then I'm coming with you," she said.

"No darling," I said. "Now listen carefully. Go downstairs to the Pan American offices in the lobby and ask them to change these JAL tickets, and put us on Pan Am. I think the flight leaves two hours earlier."

I went to the studio. I don't remember finishing the picture. When I staggered back to the hotel, Patricia told me that she had called the studio to see how I was, and the female interpreter had told her, "Oh, he's fine, just pretending to be ill." Not fulfilling my obligations was what she had implied, I thought as I lay on the bed.

The room seemed to be moving. Patricia's face was a blur. "You can't go home," she said firmly. "We have to get you well."

"Didn't you change the tickets?" I asked anxiously.

"Yes, I changed them, but you'll never make it to the plane."

"Patricia, please, please, please get us to Honolulu on Pan Am. After that I'll do anything you say."

I must have sounded desperate, because she said very softly, "I promise I'll do that." Then she went into the other room, and I thought I could hear her crying.

The telephone rang, it was obviously the interpreter telling Patricia she would send our car at 10 A.M. to take us to the airport.

"What time does the flight leave?" I heard Patricia say, then, "Thank you. Goodbye." She came into the bedroom. "The flight she thinks we're going on leaves at noon. Ours leaves at 10 A.M. I won't call a car; we'll have to get a taxi." She gave me my pills and some lemonade. I knew no more until the alarm rang. The phone was also ringing, and Patricia took it in the other room.

A taxi was waiting. The driver must have thought me drunk, so unsteady was I.

At the airport I was taken immediately in a wheelchair and put on the plane. Patricia wasn't with me. What had happened? I called out, "My wife!" The stewardess came over, she put a cold towel on my head.

"She's coming, she's just saying goodbye to your friends," she said.

No, no, we had no friends. What would they do to Patricia? Pulling myself up, I looked out the porthole. In a haze, I could see Patricia shaking hands with the *male* interpreter and Mr. Yoshimura. She must have called them for help; hence the taxi and the wheelchair. Yes, of course we did have friends, and my wife had decided to trust them 100 percent.

Their honor was at stake.

We spent ten days in Honolulu, of which I have scant recollection, save for doctors and nurses. As soon as I was well again, we returned home.

Six months, to the day, after the picture was completed, they kept their word.

Our real estate agent found a young producer, Charles Tobias, and his wife Eileen, who fell in love with Tramonto and bought it. One of the conditions of the sale was a very short escrow period that would give them possession on the morning of December 24, thus enabling them to host a big Christmas Eve housewarming. The entire transfer took place in under three weeks amid comic opera confusion. Our moving men going out, and theirs coming in, all became lifetime buddies. Our cook and their caterers became lifetime enemies. Our drawing room became theirs at a decorator's flip of the wrist.

We departed Tramonto on the morning of December 24th, and decided to go to Virginia and see my mother. We would go apartment hunting when we returned. I telephoned my brother Sam and told him we were coming. He and Millie and all the children were very excited about our arrival. He said he would tell Mother we were coming, so she would not be apprehensive. After all, she was ninety years old.

We also telephoned Becky and she invited us to spend a couple of days in her beautiful Washington house. She and Patricia had become great friends, so we were looking forward to our trip.

Brother Sam met us at Dulles Airport and took us to his house in nearby Fairfax County. He had found an ideal home for our mother a few miles away in Alexandria. It was a large, most comfortable facility, efficiently operated under the supervision of the Bishop of Virginia.

Her health was demanding more attention now, and we found her resting in the clinic. To me, her eyes seemed weary, perhaps a little frightened. There had been discussions about stronger medication. A pacemaker had been mentioned. Her expression brightened decidedly as Patricia kissed her and she clasped the hands of "God's perfect child."

Before we left Alexandria, her color had returned.

It was to be a hectic month in Hollywood for us. Our hotel bungalow was snug, with accommodating closets and cupboards that invited us to unpack, hang up, sort out, and put away. This made us more anxious to settle down, to spread out. We were ready to welcome the trucks that would deliver our goods from storage. We were ready to make our own home.

Our real estate agent was ready to show us a list of apartments. When could we see them? When? Patricia would be kidnapped almost immediately by a television commitment, and I was considerably behind schedule in radio commercials for a savings bank. We were both suffering from the healthiest fatigue known to science . . . overwork.

When the networks heard the octopus knocking, they kicked radio out the back door with their pointed shoes and welcomed TV in the front with their round heels. A strongly crossed and absorbing T quickly wedged in and expanded AFRA to the television actors' union, while radio actors became ex-radio actors.

Paradoxically, radio itself grew larger than ever as its public service was reduced to the airing of commercial advertisements with sporadic interruptions by a few bars of music or a news item. It is in this graveyard of entertainment that ex-radio actors sift through the bones and often come upon a legacy not to be ignored.

I went to the studio to broadcast the bank's appeal to the community. Walter, the director, Edgar, the engineer, and I spent four or five pleasant afternoons a year with a stopwatch and miles of tape while I recorded the bank's free lessons in thrift. Walter, who had studied for opera, was very sensitive to "tone" (he never used "sound" or "audio"). He believed that voices should rest in the morning and that the vocal chords enjoyed their happiest quality in the afternoons.

One day, in the middle of a recording, Walter said from the control booth, "Cut."

"What happened?" I asked.

"I don't know exactly," said Walter, "maybe something's wrong in here. Just a minute." I could see Walter and Edgar through the glass, but I couldn't hear them. They had a short conference. Edgar turned and twisted several dials, flipped a couple of switches.

"Ready," said Walter, "let's try again." Edgar pointed his finger, and I started again. After a few words, Walter's voice once more came through the speaker, "Cut." He and Edgar had a few words. Walter came into the studio from the control booth. He handed me a glass of water.

"It simply doesn't sound like you. Did you notice anything?" Edgar came out, too.

"Some of the words sound breathy, almost strained because it *was* strained," I said. "My natural level was lost. I couldn't find it. It was more than strained; it jumped about, out of control."

"Shall we forget it for today?" said Walter.

"Forget it we certainly will not. I've never had anything like this happen in my life. This is ridiculous. Get back in there. Let's get it done."

Walter and Edgar went back. Edgar pointed his finger. I began. There was no further interruption from the booth. Walter let it roll until I was forced to discontinue with no voice at all. Walter strolled with me to the parking lot.

"Let me know how you feel tomorrow," he said to a very, very bewildered actor.

As I walked in, Patricia greeted me with a drink extended. To my knowledge, she had never before made any kind of a drink. It was easy to guess that Walter had called her.

"I've just had about the worst day of my life," I said. "Thanks." I took the drink. "Walter call you?" She sat beside me.

"It *is* the worst day of your life, darling. Walter did not call. Your brother Sam called from Virginia."

I knew what had happened and I said it. "My dear mother died." Patricia nodded. I heard myself ask, "What time did it happen?"

She replied, "Seven thirty, Sam said." I looked at my watch. "That's four thirty our time," she added.

I remember the clock in the recording studio. It had been exactly four thirty when I gasped, and my voice had deserted my body.

We had watched and listened while several hundred real estate ladies and gentlemen opened several hundred doors, pointed to

several hundred cooking ranges, several hundred plumbing fix-
tures, and said, "This is the kitchen. . . . This is the bathroom."
We noted that the qualifying *master* before *bedroom* was being slowly
"phased out," as they say in Washington. Every apartment was beginning to look like every other apartment.

Suddenly, like a mirage, it appeared before our eyes. The perfect penthouse. While I admired the long alley of sunny terrace with happy exposures to compass and sky, Patricia ran in and
out of the rooms talking to herself about colors and backgrounds
and wall spaces that might support our ever-growing collection of
commedia dell'arte figures. I had started collecting this merry
entourage years ago. Patricia was fond of them all, and after we
were married she found great pleasure in adding to the cast whenever she could find a rare authentic porcelain figurine or carving
during our globe circling. This collection is precious to us
because they are all actors. During their three centuries of popularity in Italy beginning about 1600, they were considered a ribald,
lusty element in the theatre, but most of their performances today
would be rejected as too childish for Pony Land in the Park.

We departed our bungalow and soared into our aerie in a
highrise building set on a hill, in the heart of Hollywood. Its view
would have made a postcard dealer envious. Its description as a
bourgeois Hollywood pad would have earned any blasé journalist a
top award from the *Daily Worker.*

I set to work at once, designing pots, urns, boxes, and troughs
of various sizes and shapes. I even found a nook that would hide a
potting bench. I was later to discover that I had underestimated the
labor involved in receptacle gardening. It takes only about a hundred of these containers to equal about three acres of regular gardening. True, the spade is replaced by the trowel and hedge clippers
by scissors, and astroturf bids farewell to the lawn mower. But de-
tailed attention increases enormously. For instance, one learns
quickly that steer manure and white carpets are utterly incompati-
ble. The people at my new nursery reminded me that terrace gardening is much more intimate than ordinary gardening. They were
also strongly in favor of talking to plants. I had never given this theory much thought, except once when I had impatiently cursed a
simple *Camellia japonica* for dropping its leaves, with the result that
the poor thing went into immediate shock and died. I got a rather

stern look from my nurseryman when I related this to him and he said, "Why don't you try saying nice things, even sweet things. I'm sure you'll get a better response."

I tried nice things; I tried sweet things. The petunias wilted; the geraniums faded. I stopped talking; they blossomed. After years of friendly relations with the botanical world, it was difficult to accept my position as a bore, even a tyrant in Plantland. But they will always have my silent love and attention.

Patricia was enthusiastic. She was decorating, not redecorating. Our instincts to build our own nest were being fulfilled. We were now turning a home into a castle, not trying to turn a castle into a home.

The furnishing was almost completed, my garden growing, and Patricia glowing as I had not seen her since our wedding day. We lay back on the terrace and counted our blessings. I decided to take some time off for living and loving.

"Are you going to accept that movie in Salt Lake City?" I asked Patricia, dreading the answer.

She turned my face toward hers and said quite simply, "I'm not taking that picture. In fact, I'm not taking any commitment that separates us, and as of today, I have no agent, because I won't be needing one. If someday something turns up with parts for both of us, then I'll do it. Otherwise, I've decided that being a wife is quite enough for me, thank you very much." This was what I had been wanting to hear for a long time, and knowing her so well I had guessed she would make that decision.

"We've traveled too much," I said. "England, France, Italy, Greece, Spain . . . let's just stay put."

"Don't forget the Ts," interrupted Patricia. "Turkey, Tokyo, and that dreadful opening night when the scenery fell apart in Tampa."

"No wonder I forgot the Ts," said I. "But let's stay home for a change. It's absolutely perfect here. Nothing could drag me away from this."

"Nothing?" asked Patricia.

"Nothing, nohow, and nowhere," I answered firmly. Patricia tripped inside.

I shouldn't say tripped. Her feet are so tiny that she really does trip often . . . and often with dire results. She has broken her ankles, she has sprained her wrists and twisted her knees more often than a Rams linebacker. The Dodgers' orthopedist has given her more whirlpool treatments than he has administered to his entire infield.

But this time, her steps were sure as she walked inside and picked up a script. She handed it to me. I put it down without looking at it. "Oh, no you don't," I said. "I'm having a vacation. You're a slave driver."

"And you're a gypsy," she said. "Anyway, Chuck Tobias dropped it by today. He and his wife are separating. The least you can do is read it and refuse it nicely."

I picked it up slowly, the title of the script was *Joseph Cotten and the Performing Arts of Russia.*

"Russia!" I shouted. "We've never been to Russia. Why didn't you tell me about this before?" Patricia laughed as I thumbed through the pages of the script. She walked inside. "Where are you going?" I asked.

"To pack, of course. You wouldn't want me to look like a slob while we're eating all that caviar!" Off she went.

Charles Tobias, or Chuck, as he preferred to be called, had arranged a coproduction deal with the Russians to make a film embracing the performing arts of the Soviet Union. I was to be the roaming host, the interviewer, the narrator. Patricia was to appear wherever and whenever she felt comfortable.

Off we went. My manager, Hurley, came with us. It was Thanksgiving Day.

14

It was a warm and dazzling bright autumn morning when we set down at Heathrow. The British should be eternally thankful to the state of Florida. If this strong peninsula did not divert the flow of the Gulf Stream onto a northeast course, the British Isles would be known as the British Icebergs and the inhabitants would be called Eskimos.

In London we met Chuck and worked with him on final manuscript touches for *Joseph Cotten and the Performing Arts of Russia*. His American partners arrived, and with Hurley they all took off for Moscow, where Patricia and I would join them when the actual filming was ready to commence.

We decided the time had come for us to bow to our nomad instincts. To our new apartment in Hollywood we added a pied-à-terre in London. Patricia and her sisters found us one in Mount Street, exactly in the middle of everything we wanted to be in the middle of. It was one floor in a converted old mansion with a tiny elevator and a spacious drawing room.

U.S.S.R. Day arrived and a couple of innocent and ignorant gypsy children boarded a large Russian jet.

The stewardess looked at us in disbelief when we declined Coca-Cola before takeoff. We had not learned that this is a rare nectar in Russia and that our next opportunity to sip it would be in the cafeteria of the United States Embassy in Moscow. But it was not Coca-Cola we were dreaming of. In our visions floated mounds of

Caspian caviar, quaffs of iced vodka. On the plane, these typically Russian delicacies were as conspicuously absent from our lunch menu as turkey had been from the TWA carte at Thanksgiving.

Our porters at the Moscow airport were Hurley and Chuck; not a Russian porter in sight. In our enormous hotel, however, there were men to carry bags and escort us to our rooms. These men were not reluctant to accept tips, particularly greenbacks, leading one to suspect that official exchange for rubles might be an unrealistic ratio. But little is said of this, for realistic exchange leads to black market, and black market is never acknowledged in Red Square.

Our suite, like the Coca-Cola, was their pride. To them, it was The Suite. To us, it was a disappointment. It was a duplex, two small rooms with the sitting room downstairs and bedroom upstairs. A narrow stairway raked precipitously upward with no handrails through a canyon between two walls. The treads of the steps were narrow and highly polished.

Since we decided that our sitting room was not only small, but extremely depressing, we went upstairs to read in bed. I was exhausted from the meeting with the American partners, the Russian partners, and the interpreter named Olga. It had been long and tedious, and our differences were piling up. My book was heavy; my eyelids were even heavier.

I heard my name screamed in a heartrending, frightened little voice, and I heard the terrible sound of Patricia falling down and down, a never-ending thumping, to the bottom of that dreadful staircase. She had been stretching to reach for the light switch and had lost her balance, as had so many previous guests.

Both hands and both arms were wrapped around her face and head, and she seemed undamaged above the shoulders. But she was injured just about everywhere else. Her right leg was badly sprained, and she was suffering great pain. I held her in my arms, trying to assess the damage. I put a pillow behind her head, then ran down the corridor to Chuck's room for help. He was having a meeting. They all came to the rescue: Chuck, Hurley, Bob Estes (one of the American partners), his wife, and the ubiquitous Olga. Patricia bravely assured the frightened assembly that nothing was broken, that everything was bruised, and that her sprains were certain to render her nonambulatory for a while. Olga attempted to take over. She wanted to call for a doctor. This suggestion was greeted with an immediate and firm "Nyet" from the Esteses, who were no strangers to Russia. They sent Olga home, then explained to us that any Russian doctor (which is all we would be allowed) immediately sends all foreign patients to a hospital, and Russian hospitals are beyond the limits of international jurisdiction.

Two very large men appeared, wearing badges and broad smiles. They were the same two who had accepted the greenbacks from us when they ushered us into this architectural booby trap. Now, they had been sent by Olga to move us to a suite across the hall which was on one floor with a flimsy partition between the bedroom and the sitting room. We would have settled for a dungeon if it had been on one floor.

Chuck darted down the hall to fetch a pain pill and a sleeping pill from his traveling pharmacy. Hurley and I made an attempt to assist Patricia across the hall. We were brushed aside by one of the Happiness Boys, who lifted her gently and easily, and softly deposited her on a bed in our new quarters while his colleague transferred our baggage with equal facility. They lumbered off through a shower of greenbacks, happily displaying several acres of bad dentistry.

Our new suite had many windows, all overlooking Red Square and the Kremlin. This historic landmark had never shone so brightly, had never asserted itself so strongly, so mysteriously, so beautifully as it would during this celebration of the fiftieth anniversary of the revolution. The leaders and minions of the satellite countries would be meeting and reuniting here. The pomp, the decor, the lighting of the city for this festival made our Hollywood premieres pale into somber events. Hundreds of hidden spotlights and arcs turned night into high noon. The gilded onion domes shone opulently through the falling snow.

Portraits of Lenin hung everywhere, bathed in strong rays from unseen sources, and covering the facades of six- and seven-storied buildings. St. Nicholas (Santa Claus to us) was much in evidence in his white beard and red suit, as were Japanese tinsel and tree decorations. The origin of St. Nicholas (the Bishop of Myra) has been forgotten, Christmas having lost its place and significance in the Russian calendar. This jolly old character continues to remain a beloved symbol of friendship, and he has never stopped his annual trek from the North Pole bearing presents and greetings of

happiness. Now, however, he represents the coming of the New
Year instead of the coming of Jesus Christ.

The next morning, poor Patricia's brain received nothing but
pain messages from every muscle in her body, which was a spotted
pattern of bruises. Somehow, she managed to smile. "I look like a
dalmatian," she said.

"A hungry dalmatian?" I asked, remembering that the last meal
had been that disappointing lunch en route.

Room service does not exist unless you qualify as a tourist,
which is not too difficult since the hotel accepts only tourists as
guests.

Soft-boiled eggs, bread, butter, and coffee arrived, all borne by
a smartly uniformed Intourist guide named Luba. Luba smiled
when my hand went to my pocket. Luba grinned when it came out
with U.S. dollars.

I was excused from work for the day while the company hunted
exterior locations. The snow was falling heavily now, and filming
was impossible anyway. Mrs. Estes dropped by with medications
for Patricia, who had fallen asleep after breakfast. I donned my
nursing cap and found a quiet corner with my script.

I looked over at my Sleeping Beauty in her bed of pain. Her
huge eyes were closed. She was much too pale, too helpless. I wondered what I would do if she were not here with me? Silly question,
I told myself. . . . I wouldn't be here. We had not idly repeated the
vows Dr. Wheatly had spoken when we stood in front of him that
evening at the Selznicks. They were solemn and sacred. We loved
each other that night physically and spiritually. Here, some years
later, in this vast, most uncustomary and cold country, we loved
each other the same ways . . . and a little bit more.

The next day I started work. First stop was the office of control for
the performing arts. The performing arts in the Soviet Union, I was
reminded, included everybody and everything that performed.
"What do you mean *everything?*" I asked stupidly.

"How about puppets and bears?" they answered brightly. I
mentioned the beauty of Red Square. "Oh, then you expected to
find it bristling with armor and soldiers?"

"Well, that does seem to be the way the newsreels find it interesting," I said.

"But we mustn't slide into political ideology," said the man in charge. He was charming, and he was, indeed, in charge. "Let us keep our discussions on a purely artistic level, and I'm sure the cameras will roll faster. If you need anything, anything at all, come directly to me. Our red tape is probably even redder than yours." Ha, ha, ha, all around.

Patricia was soon well enough to hobble about with the assistance of a stick. We attended the circus, to which we were transported by what must be the most beautiful and efficiently maintained subway in the world. We were told that it was one of Stalin's gifts to the people. (This was the only time we ever heard his name mentioned.) Each carpeted station was a museum displaying the spirit and the strength of the phoenix that arose from the revolution.

The ministry had not exaggerated when they included bears among the performing arts. The bears were gigantic, and seemed even more towering for they never walked on four legs. They acted as the property men for the show, and as such, they dressed the stage (or rings) and cleared them, using their front legs as arms and hands for carrying scenery and properties. A first for the eyes of this old circus fan.

The cloakroom used to represent privilege. In the old days, only the wraps of the upper classes were closeted. Others either kept them on or sat on them. In the Soviet Union today, the checking of hats and coats is beyond privilege. It is compulsory. The cloakrooms of public buildings, such as theatres and arenas, cover an unbelievably large area and are staffed by dozens of elderly people. It is somewhat less aromatic than the wild animal quarters.

Everywhere, we were met with complete and friendly cooperation. No camera had ever been admitted to the Bolshoi Theatre; tonight we would have five to photograph a new ballet, *Anna Karenina*, and tomorrow afternoon, with the auditorium empty, they would dance the adagio especially for close-ups, with lighting designed by our cameraman. We had never seen a more elaborately produced ballet. The list of dancers was endless. In one scene the hundred pieces in the orchestra pit were augmented by a sixty-piece band on stage, splendid in their white and gold uniforms, playing highly polished silver instruments and being led by the pit conductor from a hidden television screen.

After the final curtain, Chuck and I had planned to take some portable equipment and Olga, our interpreter, backstage for an interview with Plisetskaya, who had played Anna to thunderous applause and a storm of flowers. That is, of course, if she would consent to receive us. No, no. Olga had made other arrangements. We were to wait in our box. When the chilly theatre had emptied, Plisetskaya would come to us. We waited in our box, and possibly because it had once been a royal box, the cloakroom relaxed its rules and allowed us to retain our coats.

The cameras now had placed themselves in front of us. We were making close-ups—reading the program, applauding, throwing flowers, etc. These shots would be cut into the film later in their proper sequence. Plisetskaya's face peeked through a curtain of the next box. I immediately rose to greet her, but a shout from Olga caused the first lady of the Bolshoi Ballet to vanish.

"We will complete our work here," said Olga. "I will then tell her when to appear." Eventually Olga gave the signal, and before I could offer our excuses to Plisetskaya for keeping her waiting, she was apologizing to us and to Olga for intruding. She was still in costume, wrapped in a flowing velvet cape. Accompanying her was her costar, who happened also to be her ex-husband. The other man with her was her present husband, who had composed the ballet and conducted the orchestra.

It was an awkward interview, with Olga correcting their English, and even their Russian, whenever they made any small, polite observation about the United States, where they had toured and where the composer had become addicted to the banjo.

"The what?" said Olga in surprised English. She was now prepared for a curve, any kind of a typically Russian, indirect, gobbledygook curve. She received, instead, a straight from the shoulder fastball that split the plate.

"The banjo," softly repeated the composer. He continued, to us, "What a sophisticated development your Kentucky has applied to the old African Kimbundu *mbanza*." Olga, the bat on her shoulder, just stared. Strike three.

The uncompromising gourmet will spend his happiest hour thumbing through the pages of a Russian menu. Inside the covers of this epicure's dream is listed everything, literally everything you have ever been offered by all the menus you have read in your lifetime. And in every single restaurant, that is every single restaurant that foreigners are allowed to enter, you will find this Escoffian marvel of composition.

The bubble bursts, the dream ends, the palate withers as you begin to order. It is then you learn that only the dishes marked with a discreet red number (the price) are available. Now your discouraged eyes hunt for the "available dishes." They boil down to three, and *boil* is the operative word. If it were true that time heals all wounds, I certainly would have forgotten by now what those "available dishes" were. But indigestion has scarred my memory too deeply. I am still hoping one day to forget the green soup, the Cossack Hat stew, and the cold soft-boiled eggs. We thought we would do better in the nightclubs. The ministry had asked us to include some of their acts in our film. We hoped they might add to the list of "available," if only for the evening of filming.

Wrong. In the nightclub we found the same enticing menu (more luxuriously bound) and the same "availables" (prices higher). We looked around us. The diners seemed thoroughly relaxed and happy. They danced through their dinners to the most ordinary renditions of American jazz, and then enthusiastically applauded cabaret acts that couldn't have made it in a five-a-day house in Colonial Heights, Virginia, in 1915. (Letters concerning the theatrical history of Colonial Heights are not invited.) How interesting, I thought, to see the artistic and intellectual culture of this bleak land slipping comfortably into the eighteenth century. "It's either Kremlin or crumbs," was Patricia's phrase. Either one dances perfectly in satin slippers, as in the ballet, or one clobbers about in unpolished shoes, as in the cabaret tonight. One either applauds opera, or bounces to the pathetically executed strains of Cole Porter.

Our crew had become fascinated with English names. The cameraman, who had been in charge of photography during President Nixon's visit to Russia, leaned toward Richard as his favorite because of its interchangeability with Deek and Deeky. We called him Deeky for a while, but the crew exaggerated the babytalk possibilities of Deeky, and he suddenly announced his name was Jack. His assistant's real name was long and almost unpronounceable in Russian. He was attracted by the brevity of Ed and it pleased him to chant it over and over, up and down the scale while working. Besides being bewitched by English names, Ed was smitten by my English wife. Whenever she called him Eddie, the snow melted from around his feet.

Now, as we set out for Leningrad, Eddie was rushing to her rescue in the railroad station. Again, Hurley and I were trying to assist her—this time, to scale what she called "the enemy of the people," a flight of stairs. Eddie swept her up in his gallant and powerful arms and we all followed them to the top where a long, long train awaited us. Olga also awaited us there, with clipboard, tickets, and all sorts of official papers. Eddie gently placed Patricia on her feet. I handed over her stick.

"Your sleeping car is the ninth in that direction," said Olga, pointing toward the front of the train. We all looked down the platform that reduced itself to zero in the fading perspective. She handed me some tickets. Patricia handed me her stick. Her slave gathered her up. We started toward the engine in the distance, a toy engine, it looked, puffing in unison with the chivalrous Eddie.

Chuck and I were not at all sure just what Leningrad had to offer a film on the performing arts. The opera house was closed, but the ministry was most anxious for us to include the People's Theatre and a war memorial cemetery. Trying to fit a cemetery into the performing arts can tempt one into making statements in appalling taste; therefore, we sensibly and respectfully added to the abundant record already filmed on the Siege of Leningrad and the unbroken spirit of its inhabitants, who withstood the German armies for two years.

The People's Theatre was immense. It was on the scale of the Radio City Music Hall in New York, perhaps larger. It was imaginatively and efficiently equipped technically, with perfect lighting, motorized curtains, revolving stages, elevator stages, and just about every mechanical gadget an idealistic stage manager could dream of. But the entertainment! The acts! Rejects from Uncle Billy's Hay Seed Varieties. Costumes by Mother Hubbard, shoes by Farmer John, music by Ivan the Terrible. How I envied them all . . . playing to such easily pleased, such enthusiastic, such well-behaved audiences.

There came a sudden lull in the entertainment. Actually, it was more than a lull. It was a cold halting of time, a victory of emptiness. Nothing is so barren, so lonely as a brightly lighted stage awaiting its forsaken lover, the tardy actor.

The audience sat quietly. No exasperated walkouts, no loud catcalls from the balcony. Just an exhibition of good manners, or patience born of fear.

Finally, a gentleman cut his way through the iceberg on stage and came down to the footlights. If he hadn't been wearing a necktie, he could have been mistaken for any of our young men at home who affect those atrocious poor folks' clothes. He told the audience (Olga's translation) that the balalaika ensemble, which was to close the show, had not yet arrived. He explained that the bus driver was not from Leningrad and had lost his way in the city.

"You can go home now," he added. The audience gave no response. They dutifully rose and followed their noses in the direction of the cloakroom.

As they went up the aisle, we moved our equipment down the aisle and nearer the stage for closer shots of the local Melba from Minsk and of the flashing feet of Ginger and Fred from Vladivostok. The young gentleman in the poor folks' clothes suddenly reappeared on stage.

"Come back, everybody, come back," he shouted to the departing audience. "The balalaikas have arrived. Please take your seats. The show is not yet over."

The balalaikas strummed away. Our equipment went back up the aisle while the audience started back down, but by the time most of them had rechecked their garments and found their seats, the show was over once again. In this empty mammoth cage of a theatre we finally completed our filming. When we headed back to the hotel, it was dawn. The city was motionless and deserted. Its perfectly restored Italian and French stone edifices—the Hermitage, the Winter Palace, St. Isaac's Cathedral—stood in quiet and elegant dignity in the early cloud-filtered light.

A few highly colored tugs brightened the grey river Neva on its way to the Gulf of Finland. And towering against the mackerel sky, still dominating his city—St. Petersburg, then Petrograd, now Leningrad—sat the heroic figure of Pushkin's Bronze Horseman, Peter the Great, the Czar and father of this architectural masterpiece.

We got back to Moscow late one morning, and Olga insisted on escorting us up to The Suite. The corridor on our floor was very busy with traffic, and when we opened our door we were greeted by a lady, a rather strong looking lady who rose from a chair where she had been reading. Olga explained that she was a policewoman. We bowed to her, she bowed to us, then she sat, opened her book and resumed reading. We looked to Olga, who told us that the Kremlin would be holding meetings for the next few days. Not only would Soviet high officials be attending, but presidents and VIPs from "sympathetic" neighbors and allies would also be present.

"Like Fidel Castro?" I asked.

"I do not have a list of those present," said Olga. The police person's eyes left the pages of her book for just a moment. "Every room in every building overlooking the square will be guarded," Olga went on. "Your old apartment across the hall is headquarters for this floor."

I peeped out. As I did, the door of our old apartment opened. It was stuffed with guards, overflowing into the corridor, some armed with rifles and bayonets. One of them was leading a new reel of recording tape into the locked cabinet in the wall by our front door. We had guessed before what it was, and we had been reasonably discreet in our conversations for the benefit of "big ears," as the bugs were commonly called. Sometimes we pantomimed by cupping the palms behind the ears.

"Your policewoman will be relieved by another if she has any reason to leave your apartment," said Olga. "And when the meetings adjourn in the afternoons, naturally, she will leave."

"Isn't it rather overdoing security? Certainly you could have done with less elaborate arrangements," I said.

"You could have done with more elaborate arrangements in Dallas," said Olga as she closed the door on her last word.

Our Shostakovich episode was to be a very exclusive event. The ministry had arranged for Maxim, son of the renowned Dmitry, to conduct a short informal rehearsal of one of his father's orchestral pieces. Since Papa's compositions before a certain date were out of favor with the Soviets, and lest his music after a certain date be considered excessively pro-Soviet, a harmless pictorial suite that had been written for a film was chosen. The music had never been published, but it was loud and brilliant and emotional; more Showoff-sky than Shostakovich.

Maxim would conduct a full orchestra in a concert hall that had been designed by someone who obviously loved concerts and believed they deserved sympathetic surroundings and large attendances. The hall was exquisite and immense. In the midst of this vast arena would sit one listener . . . me . . . and after the music I would be joined by Maxim, who would make a few statements on Soviet music in general and his father in particular. Maxim had a keen sense of humor and I looked forward to our interview. I sent him a telegram saying "Break a leg," the common international theatrical substitute for "good luck."

We were ready to go. Our cameras were set up all over the place, most skillfully camouflaged by Jack so as not to photograph each other. I sat in my exclusive seat in the middle of the hall, in splendor to be envied by dear, mad Ludwig of Bavaria. I waited for my own concert, with full orchestra, Shostakovich by Shostakovich, in the heart of Moscow.

The orchestra was never to play the music of Dmitry Shostakovich that day. Maxim was never to conduct a concert that day. We waited—me in solitary elegance, seated in the center of the great hall, and the orchestra positioned at stiff concert deportment—ready to arise at the entrance of the maestro.

The maestro never entered. Who did enter was a stage manager bearing a little slip of paper. He read from it, "Mr. Shostakovich, on leaving his house for today's concert, unfortunately slipped and broke his leg."

The promise of an exciting venture was trying to reach me from London, but Greenwich time and Moscow time seemed unable to get themselves together on the very long distance wires that stretched between them. Hurley seized this opportunity to fly the coop.

"I can't grapple with this Mickey Mouse telephone service," he said. "I'd better get to London right away and firm up this deal."

"But, Hurley, you'll miss the puppets. I thought that was high on your list," said Patricia.

"Puppets!" said Hurley. "Puppets! I taught Bill Baird to tie a granny, don't talk to me about puppets! Besides, I know that Jo would be upset to miss being with Katharine Hepburn again."

"Jo sure would," said Jo, "what a pity to break that constant record of working together every thirty-two years."

"Here's the key to the apartment," said Patricia, "help yourself to the guest room."

"Just leave the contract on the hall table before you return to California," I added.

"And stock up the fridge with everything except soft-boiled eggs and boiled potatoes," continued Patricia. The Grumbling Gourmet took the key. "No tears, please," she said.

Some of the puppets were tiny, some life-sized, others in between. They were operated from above and from below, always expertly and wittily. The music was recorded, and it was good. The entire show was first rate.

After the theatre had cleared, our crew moved in for closer shots, as had become our pattern. While waiting for them, I joined the puppeteer in his museum below the theatre. We strolled along through alleys and mazes of glass cases where lived figures in costumes that ranged from realistic to exotic. It was a perfectly beautiful, somewhat eerie dream world. The puppeteer, in excellent English, told me of his life with these sleeping figures. "But they do not sleep always," he said, "they have led me on many happy tours around the world."

I asked him what he wanted to talk about tomorrow when we returned to his museum for an interview.

"I don't care," he said. "Ask me anything. Would you like me to tell you about America?"

"I think not," I answered, "perhaps just a description of the puppets . . . the merging of reality and fantasy . . . something like that."

"Well," he laughed, "anything at all. Anything. I'm eighty-odd years old. What can they do to me? Ask me anything." I didn't know what he was getting at. I still don't know. I do know that I determined to be very careful with my words in tomorrow's interview.

When I arrived the next day, the lighting was far from ready. Jack was going crazy trying to find light positions that would not reflect in the hundreds of polished glass cases. My puppeteer friend offered me coffee and introduced me to our "interpreter for the day," another Olga. Our Olga was home with a cold. The new Olga was very blonde. She had big square shoulders and big square feet and her accent was low, rough, and just-off-the-boat.

Jack finally marked off a course between the cases, a line the old puppeteer and I could follow without having the camera lenses blinded by flashing reflections. The old gentleman and I started walking. I said, with the charm of Dick Cavett, "Yesterday I asked you if these figures, these characters sometimes didn't come awake particularly during the darkness of night, didn't have lives and experiences of their own." He looked at me with eyes that were glassier than those of his marionettes, with a face that was blanker. His tongue was equally mute. I continued with the security of Dick Cavett . . . the security of Dick Cavett during his interview with Sophia Loren and Marcello Mastroianni. "Yesterday you told me," I said, "that often you find some members of your troupe in the wrong case. I mean, not in the cases where you last put them . . . and, er, that is, what led me to speculate on the fact that they may, at times, wander off on their own secret adventures."

The old man now pulled himself together. He spoke. "I couldn't possibly have said anything like that. The movements of these figures, these characters, are entirely mechanical, entirely controlled by my trained puppeteers. You are suggesting that a realm of fantasy exists here. Ridiculous. If I believed in fantasy, I'd be in a lunatic asylum."

Two voices said "Cut" simultaneously. A light reflection on the lens had spoiled the shot for Jack, and the puppeteer's reflection on the subject had ruined it for me.

The old gentleman murmured, "Sorry." To whom, I have no idea. He then joined the two new advisers from the ministry. I joined Chuck, who was talking to our new blonde Olga.

"I don't know what we're talking about," I said to Chuck.

"You sure don't," said Olga.

"He and I were on the same wavelength last night," I said."

"Maybe you thought so," said Olga. "Right now he's talking about reality. Reality exists. It's here. You're talking about fantasy. Fantasy exists in the dreams of madmen."

"I seem to remember a very pretty book in my shelves at home," I said. "It's called *Russian Fairy Tales*." Olga gave me a look of real contempt.

"You believe that crap?" she said as she walked away. We walked away, too.

We finished the picture on New Year's Eve. That night Chuck gave a party on the roof of what must be the highest point in Moscow. All of the crew attended. Olga Number 1 was there, the ministers were there, *the* minister was there. There was more toasting than eating. *The* minister made a speech. We drank and applauded. I made a speech. Ditto. Chuck made a speech. Ditto. Patricia rose to speak, but the crew picked her up and passed her around for a goodbye kiss. When she got to Eddie they all cried in English, "Two. Two for Eddie." A glorious display of fireworks circled the entire city while we toasted the fiftieth anniversary of the revolution, the beginning of the new year, and the ending of our trip to Russia.

On our way back to the hotel we saw the wrecking crew as they began their task, putting out lights and dismantling the city. A few hours later, when we arose and were having our last soft-boiled eggs, while the Happiness Boys were carrying down our luggage, we took a long look out of our window. The huge portraits were gone, the lights were gone, the red-clad St. Nicholases were gone, the decorations were gone, the tinsel had been swept away. We thought we saw one tiny crystal slipper on the steps to the Kremlin and a few mice who last night were horses attached to a golden coach. We looked down and said goodbye to Pumpkin Square.

15

"As ordered. Signed, Hurley" was written on the card. The card was clipped to a contract that greeted us as we entered our apartment in London. On the refrigerator was another, "as ordered" card signed "Grumbling Gourmet." Inside, we found everything imaginable—except soft-boiled eggs and boiled potatoes.

I made us a drink. We sat with a great relaxed sigh and, for the first time in our lives, clinked a thankful and serious toast to what we had always taken for granted . . . *freedom*.

Our apartment was almost ready for entertaining, and when I say "almost," I mean that it will be eternally almost ready. Patricia and her two sisters haunted the auctions nearly every day, ferreting out that exact chair for here, that perfect mirror for there. My acting engagements in England and on the continent were becoming more numerous now, and the apartment on Mount Street meant that we could stop over in London on our way to and from almost anyplace abroad. There were ample closets for changes of clothes, particularly winter coats and those evening things that are always needed if you don't pack them, and a damned nuisance to tote about when you don't need them. And it meant that the three sisters— Patricia, Piti, and Gloria—could be together more often. They had become even closer, if that is possible, since losing their father and their mother. The three of them and their husbands firmly believed in Family, a belief their parents would have approved.

This film version of *A Delicate Balance* would keep us in London for two or three months. We had seen the play when our friends and ex-landlords, the Cronyns, had acted in it in New York. I thought it the best Edward Albee play I'd ever seen; at least, I thought I understood it better than any Edward Albee play I'd ever seen. I don't mean to imply that I did not like his other works or that we must understand everything in order to enjoy it, appreciate it, and identify with it. How many people who have been spellbound by the *Eroica* Symphony can tell you what it's about?

I do not, however, believe it unfashionable to produce or write a play with a plot that can be followed by the gallery. Is it fear of being thought shallow that causes playwrights to change the subject the minute the audience becomes involved . . . particularly emotionally involved? What a pity our writers banished sentimentality to the hospital, almost to the cemetery, for so many years. And give a rally, blow a horn, award a prize to Neil Simon, who has single-handedly restored L-O-V-E to the stage and screen as a respectable four-letter word that can be spoken by actors and heard by audiences without bringing blushes to the faces of either.

Katharine Hepburn and Paul Scofield were to lead the cast in this version of *A Delicate Balance*. I had admired Katharine strongly since her first film, *Bill of Divorcement* with John Barrymore, and even more strongly since my long run with her in *The Philadelphia Story*. Her presence weighed heavily in my eagerness to be involved in *A Delicate Balance*.

Our three weeks of holiday literally evaporated. With calm patience Patricia assisted me every evening with Albee's lines, which sometimes punish the tongue while they are being learned, but which once mastered, always ring out in exact and often poetic cadence. (I hope never to forget Arthur Rubinstein's advice to young musicians: "Learn the notes. Learn the notes. *Then* we'll discuss interpretation.")

The daylight hours would see the Medina sisters, demon shoppers, charging on their constant rounds. For many years, Harrods, Peter Jones, and indeed most of Knightsbridge, had bestowed on Piti the coveted title, The Electric Mouse.

London had made me feel so welcome, so at home over the years, that I now felt quite at ease strolling about with furled umbrella and homburg, quite comfortable as I called my club for a lunch reservation with Ken; Gloria's husband, Gerry; or some other English or American friend who, like me, had been saving up for the pursuit of leisure.

Suddenly my opium pipe went cool. The telephone rang. To-morrow I would commence the pursuit of another happiness. Act-ing. Tomorrow morning a car would pick me up at the dark hour of six thirty and would return me twelve hours later at the same dark hour. In between, I would spend the day in an old mansion in the Crystal Palace section of London. In this house and its garden, we would film *A Delicate Balance*. In this house, until we finished, we would make up, we would change, we would work, we would rest, we would be refreshed by a midday meal. A guard at the front door excluded the curious and rerouted heavy traffic. The neighborhood dogs had been cajoled into silence, as had the hi-fi enthusiast next door. In his case, however, *cajolery* should be changed to read *bribery*.

I have never been in the middle of a more dedicated, harder working, more professional group of people. Tony Richardson was our director, and bless him, he believed, along with Orson and Bob Aldrich, that it was fruitless to attempt acting without thorough re-hearsals. Tony not only knew when a scene was ripe for plucking, he also knew what might be stunting its growth and how to nurture it to maturity.

Katharine's manners and social graces would make Lord Ches-terfield seem untutored. She is, however, not renowned for being professionally indirect. Lest I be guilty of perjury, of breaking a commandment, I dare not say that she and Tony "hit it off." There existed certain conceptual differences between them, and as we lis-tened to some of their verbal exchanges, we all marveled that every word was uttered in laughter, that first aid was never administered. Whatever the friction, it was a God-ordered tonic for them both. The picture was one of Tony's best jobs, and I don't know how I can say that Katharine, in that mammoth, complex role, was any-thing less than perfect.

I must here be allowed another superlative. *Great* is the accurate word for Paul Scofield. But not the only word. He is that unique creature who could be an international superstar, perhaps *the* inter-national superstar and billionaire, if he chose to follow the tempting fingers that constantly beckoned to him from every direction. It is almost disturbing to encounter this degree of creative loyalty, this joyful and satisfying integrity. Money? He seems to ignore completely the fact that today's most influencing four-letter word ending in K is *bank*, preferring rather to indulge in another one, more dear to him . . . *work*. Happily married, he lives in the country, artistically fulfilled. He truly must be what is meant by the phrase "actor's actor." We became good friends during our engagement in the mansion in Crystal Palace, and whenever we go to London, the first play we see is always Paul's chosen work.

The daughter's part was played by Lee Remick. I remembered that she had enjoyed a moment of fame in her own country in Otto Preminger's *Anatomy of a Murder.* She was young, beautiful, and talented. Then she seemed to disappear, but not for very long. She married an Englishman, moved to his country and became a television star. During the making of *A Delicate Balance,* I watched her acting more than I acted with her, and I agreed with Katharine that her talent could not be ignored. It has not been. Only a few episodes of "Jenny" had appeared on British and American television screens before she had become firmly established as an international star.

Before the movie finished, Katharine, with her usual good manners, said one day, "I haven't met Patricia. Why don't you both come and have dinner with me tomorrow? I live just around the corner from you."

"Katharine," I said, "I'm not as young as I was when we first worked together. Today, when I'm working, I'm finished and out of the dining room before eight."

"Oh, I hope so. I do hope so," she quoted in that much imitated line she spoke from a play we were in years and years ago.

The next evening, after work, I changed quickly and, with Patricia on my arm, left Mount Street and strolled around the corner. Promptly at eight o'clock we strolled back to Mount Street, having had a lovely dinner with a lovely lady.

We were happy to be back in our Hollywood apartment. I hoped it was a welcome-home look my plants were giving me, for in spite of their yawns at my affectionate conversation, I preferred to believe that they did rely on my prescribed and carefully administered diet, and that they were confident about my knowledge of the difference between amputation and pruning whenever I approached them, clippers in hand.

Even gypsies (and we had ceased to pretend we were not) have a place they call home. It is that one special place in the world, or out of this world, with its own perpetual welcome, its own sequestered aura of comfort.

Patricia lay on the sofa giving me definite instructions about the color my flowers were to assume when they bloomed. "Remember, every window opens onto the terrace, and your plants must complement the interior." She pointed around. "A little rust there, orange over there and a vivid purple in between would be perfect, and please, please, no pink anywhere."

"Who ever heard of a garden without pink?" I argued reasonably. "Flowers must be given their own autonomy, they must be allowed to bloom according to their natural instincts." Patricia picked up a book.

"What's that I so often hear you say about nature copying art?" she asked, and went back to her reading. I went to the nursery.

With the heroic assistance of large areas of white, the sum of all colors, I was able to persuade nature to copy art. I produced a little rust here, a little orange over there . . . well, sort of over there, with a not-so-vivid purple in between, all peeping through cascades of white everything. Green leaves were tolerated.

"It not only complements my interior," said Patricia, "but God's firmament as well. Look how happily they dance in front of that flat blue backdrop up there."

I long ago reached the age when my conscience smiled on easy accomplishment, and California living is easy. Brother Whit tells me that I never gave Tidewater a fair shake if easy living was what I was shooting for; but in the days when my spirit was humming and driving me onward with youthful fires of determination, the words *easy* and *difficult* were interchangeable in definition. Or perhaps in my ignorant blindness of the obstacles ahead, they did not exist at all.

California is our place. Our home. We love it, but we leave it often, and I hope we shall be considered well adjusted, rather than indifferent, when we say that we really don't miss any place we ain't at. We are no-nonsense nomads, pitching our tents in the long shadows of the setting sun wherever we may be. The face of the earth is ours to wander. Together. Always . . . together.

Don Wolff smiled at last. During the past two hours he had worn out his slide rule, exhausted his patience, and spent a substantial part of his agency commission on international telephone calls; but he had succeeded in tidying up every possible aspect of *The Perfect Crime* contract.

The Perfect Crime was an ingeniously conceived film; the title was not at all immodest. It was to start within a few days in Rome, and Patricia and I were to leave tomorrow for the Eternal City. Don ushered me to the door of his office. He was counting on his fingers.

"Your reservations are confirmed. TWA is holding your tickets at the airport. Humberto [my Italian agent] is holding your salary in escrow. Your concierge at the Bristol in Rome is holding an envelope containing your living expenses." He stopped counting and wiped his brow. "I can't possibly think of another thing, can you?" he asked.

"Not a thing," I said. "Thanks. Sorry this one was so much trouble, but I thought the script was worth it."

"I'll say bon voyage now, and love to Pat," he waved.

In the cozy check-in corner at TWA, we were received by an old friend who was expecting us. "Make yourselves comfortable in the club upstairs. I'll join you later with your tickets and see you to your flight," he said.

He joined us later with our boarding passes. As I was pocketing the envelope, he said, "You know, of course, those tickets are one way only."

I can't imagine why I called Don Wolff at that moment, because I knew what he would say and I knew what we would do . . . had to do, really, because our cargo of baggage was already on board, tagged for Rome. Don said, "Don't get on the plane." We got on the plane.

We stopped at Kennedy Airport to refuel. A few hours later, we revisited Kennedy Airport to calm down a rebellious door. Finally, in something under twenty-four hours after departing the shores of the Pacific, we were looking down on the late morning sunlit sands of the Tiber's mouth, where it surrenders to the Mediterranean Sea. That meant the airport was nearby and the pilot's voice came on . . . not, however, with the usual reminders about seat belts, smoking, etc. His speech to a very sleepy and sloppy load of passengers started with, "After that mess-up in New York last night, I simply don't know how to tell you this."

Everybody sat up, just as sloppy but less sleepy. The pilot continued: "We're landing now. There is a ground strike at the airport. That means no luggage from plane to terminal, no bus from plane to terminal, no porters, and I'm sorry, no information on the duration of the strike." He left a moment of silence while we sat in stunned despair. Then our captain, who had never missed a single edition of "The Rover Boys," continued: "I suppose we should all be thankful that this is a day arrival. At least I can see the airstrip. Tonight, arrivals with no field lights must seek landing spots in Naples, Milan, military bases, or wherever they can find a ray." I didn't know what kind of "ray" he meant, but assumed it was "of hope."

Our pilot sat us down in the middle of the vast acreage, and after about an hour, we saw a group of soldiers approaching, heavily armed and riding in a jeep. The jeep was towing a portable stairway that from a mile away, looked like a better fit for a Piper Cub than a 747. They rolled it up to our front door. Oooops . . . not q-u-i-t-e high enough, by about ten feet. Away they went—Jeep, rifles, and stairs—leaving us all feeling lucky that we had arrived on a day flight. Finally we reached the asphalt and were surrounded by police and army, who all pointed in the same direction. There in the far distant background sat the terminal building of Leonardo da Vinci Airport. Leonardo da Vinci would never have sketched that flying machine had he known that anything as ugly as a modern airport would one day be given his name.

It would be quibbling to deny that the center of this airport is just on the outskirts of Ostia (about eighteen miles away!), and off we started, sharing between us hand luggage, over-the-shoulder bag, and two fur coats, in the direction of the horizon. I say *horizon* instead of *terminal* because the latter word had now begun to assume a depressing connotation.

Sometime the same day we reached the customs control, and I can tell you that going through customs with no baggage can be quite exasperating, especially if you're already exasperated. Lots of questions about money, what's in the over-the-shoulder and long stares at the toothpaste. In Italian the man asked Patricia, "Why have you brought two new mink coats?"

"I may stay two days," she replied in Italian. This explosion of Latin logic happily satisfied the inspector, and he graciously waved us through.

Outside. Nobody. No Humberto. No driver. It turned out Humberto had the flu. It turned out the driver went to the wrong gate.

"But there is only one gate," I said.

"Then perhaps there was no driver," they said, "and if this is true we will fire him immediately."

Karl Malden had not yet warned me about what not to leave home without, but Patricia uncovered in her handbag a fistful of Italian bank notes, all with attractively long numbers, left over from some nonshopping she had done on a previous trip to Italy. Therefore we were able to arrive at our hotel with a purse almost as heavy as our hearts.

Although we had touched down before noon, it was now after sunset. In the lobby of the Bernini Bristol, the Venetian crystals were glowing and reflecting the rosy marble of its walls and mirrors. Checking into a Roman hotel with foreign passports and no baggage could be considered a wee bit irregular, but the staff greeted us warmly, and we were ushered to our apartment by a familiar face.

It was cheering to be in our usual apartment, a cozy and well-maintained couple of rooms with ample cupboards, which we hoped soon to fill. Meantime we shed our clothes, now about two days old, had nice soaks, and redressed in the same rags that didn't seem *too* unsavory because at least we ourselves felt clean. We also felt hungry, so we made drinks from the well-stocked fridge, sat down with our feet up and relaxed. Patricia telephoned for the waiter. "Waiter's strike" said the voice at the other end. Patricia's flawless Italian saved total despair. She talked to the manager, and soon a man dressed as Paul Muni in *I Am a Fugitive from a Chain Gang* rolled in a plate of cold meats, hard bread, and, forgive me, hard cheese.

We woke up in some of our California departure clothes. A proper waiter brought in a proper breakfast, and a messenger came from the studio with an envelope marked "Living Expenses." He was followed by a train of porters bearing our luggage from the airport. Patricia opened the bags. I opened the envelope. Inside was a check signed by a Mr. Maimoni. I was surprised I had not heard the name Maimoni in any of my talks with Don about this film. Although the salaries of actors from foreign countries are put by check into escrow until completion of a film and then transferred to the United States, it is customary to pay living expenses in cash. Patricia steamed up the bathroom and hung up some clothes as I called my agent. "Maimoni is pronounced 'my money,'" she said.

Humberto's wife-secretary, who answered, said that although he had the flu she expected to "listen to him" sometime later that day. "May I tell him what you are calling about?" she said.

"I have a check from Signor Maimoni for living expenses. Please tell Humberto I'd like to cash it."

"You have a check from Maimoni?" she screamed and hung up. She must have "listened" to Humberto immediately, for he called at once.

"How's your flu?" I asked.

"Much better," he said. "Did I hear correctly that Maimoni has given you a check?"

"You heard correctly," I said.

"A check," he said, "a check, oh my God. Oh my God."

Humberto's Cuban blood slowly cooled, and he suggested a rather violent disposition that was physically impossible without Mr. Maimoni being present and reasonably cooperative. I stuck the check instead into the pocket of the smart if slightly wrinkled blazer that I donned for escorting my wealthy wife to our first choice in Roman restaurants, Passetto's.

They remembered the corner table we liked, and we were joyfully sipping the cool Garva and watching the waiter shave slivers of white truffles over the tiny buttery noodles when, out of nowhere, like a Houdini illusion, there materialized before our very eyes . . . in Rome, in the shadow of the Vatican . . . the two most unholy, least trustworthy, most deceitful-looking beings created by any imagination. They introduced themselves as Puglieri the producer and Antony Maimoni, his chief executive.

In Rome everybody knows where everybody else is at all times. Usually they are wrong. Today we were the exception that proves the rule.

Maimoni's eyes darted around the room behind thick, thick lenses, stopping here and there for a quick snap of the "numbered bank account" types lounging around the restaurant. When his focus picked up John Ringling North, sitting four or five tables away, his spectacles suddenly turned into zoom-in lenses. Puglieri's eyes, though uncovered, were not as warm as Maimoni's glasses. They were two slanted slits—not at all oriental, more reptilian, sort of asplike. I presented them to Patricia. Maimoni gave her hand an oily kiss and the asp bowed deeply, his eyes warming to the torrid degree they must have reached just before giving Cleopatra the hit-on-the-tit.

They had heard from Humberto about his apprehensions concerning the check and had come to exchange it for cash. They handed me an envelope, and I handed them one from my pocket containing their check. Maimoni took a quick peek into the one he received. I put the one I was receiving into my pocket. It was sealed, and I knew that whatever its contents, its value could be no less than what I was surrendering.

"Won't you sit down and have a drink?" I said. They sat down and ordered lunch.

Humberto, whom we had known for several years, arrived at our hotel early the next afternoon to take us to a preproduction reception being given at the Hilton Hotel.

"How's your flu?"

"Oh yes, my grippe. Much better, thank you." Remarkable recovery. "Well, we'd better be off; I'm parked almost under the porter's desk."

At the party we met the director, Nino Ricci, the producer and the cast, which included Valli. This was a happy surprise and reunion. She was with her son, Roberto. I remembered him as Robert in Los Angeles, a golden-haired, pink-faced toddler of five. Now a heavy dark beard bristled from his pink cheeks, and when he rose he towered over me.

"Excuse me," he said, "I'm afraid I've changed more than you have. Please sit down."

"Have you met the star?" asked Valli.

"We thought you were the star," said Patricia. Valli laughed.

"No, dear," she said. "She is that tall blonde . . . you can see her just through there." We saw her. "She is twenty-one years old," said Valli, "and this is her twenty-first picture."

"My, my," I said.

"My, my," said Patricia, "and what a striking dress."

"Odd thing for you to say," said Roberto. He and his mother smiled.

"You see," explained Valli, "this will be the first picture in which she has worn any clothes at all."

It was indeed every kind of crime except a perfect one to see this excellent story fall victim to chaotic and irresponsible production and slip down the drain. Nino Ricci directed with charm, humor, and sound technical judgment. Valli's brief appearance lent beauty and authority, and the tall blonde virginally enrobed ("How about 'Venus Unobserved,'" Patricia suggested) was never less than gracefully ornamental.

But *The Perfect Crime* was fated never to be completed. On the set bill collectors outnumbered actors. Maimoni's checkbook smelled like a rubber factory and the Asp kited himself into the ozone, his sting now rendered impotent by deceit. Poor Humberto revived his grippe and retreated behind his doctor's orders. Poor Don flew in from California with an important-looking briefcase. When he opened it, a lot of lawyers jumped out. Voices became loud. Tempers showed color.

In the streets, Christmas lights were twinkling. Children and toys had displaced traffic in the Piazza Navona. The bells of St. Peter's hung silent, waiting impatiently to ring out the joyful tidings as soon as that brilliant star had guided the Magi into Bethlehem.

"I feel sad, really sad about this whole unfortunate situation," I said to Patricia. "Now is no time to exchange misunderstandings, no time to move among men of ill will."

"Very poetic, darling," she said, "and very true. It is, however, a time to be practical."

"What do you suggest?" I said. "I'll do anything except fight."

"Remember what Jean Cocteau once said about French plumbing?" she asked.

"That question certainly steers us into the realm of practicality," I said. "No, Mrs. Bones, I do not happen to remember what Jean Cocteau said on the subject of French plumbing."

"His exact words were, 'Whenever anything goes wrong with the plumbing, simply throw a lace curtain over it and go to the theatre.' "

"Try the housekeeper," I said. The housekeeper came in. She

was an old friend. Patricia gave her a kiss and a present. She gave Patricia a lace curtain which she threw over the script of *The Perfect Crime*. We ate Christmas pudding all the way to London.

The first thing on our agenda was to go to the theatre and see Paul Scofield in *Volpone*.

Tom Swift predicted it would happen, and it did. We had lunch on the Concorde and arrived in New York in time for a late breakfast— about two weeks of late breakfasts, we hoped—before boarding a pokey old 707 for California and a resumption of the easy way.

We settled ourselves comfortably into our familiar apartment at the Gotham Hotel in New York, a few hours after landing. We had several times experimented elsewhere in New York, but found ourselves always drawn back to where we felt completely at home, in these generous, well-proportioned rooms, furnished in a style of contrived neglect and of seedy gentility that only the very, very secure could afford. Like the upholstery, the faces of the floor waiters and maids seldom changed. The bellmen's hair matched their grey uniforms, and the valet refused to believe that I knew anything at all about unpacking. "Remarkable how this old blazer stands up, isn't it, sir?" one of them said to me as he hung it in the closet.

Patricia's favorite hairdresser was downstairs, and while she was submitting to whatever happens to women's heads during these long beautifying hours, I settled down with a script Hurley had sent to the hotel. I had finished the script and also a telephone call to Hurley in California when Patricia, who had forgotten her key, was let in by our floor waiter. She started opening cases and throwing clothes about until she found a robe. "This is all I'll need for tonight," she said, and flung herself on the sofa, shaking her meticulous new hairdo carelessly.

I went over and stroked her head. "Very pretty," I said.

"Well it ought to be, I was under the dryer forever. I'm absolutely exhausted."

I had to get right to the point. "Darling," I said, "remember on the plane, you said how sorry you were we hadn't visited Venice on this last Italian saga?"

"Yes, somehow that's always been so soothing to us both . . . St. Mark's Square, how I love it. We must go there again," she said.

"Would you like to go soon?" I ventured nervously.

Patricia lay down on the sofa and closed her eyes. "Umm . . . Yes, when shall we go there? Maybe in the spring or the summer for a change?"

"Tonight," I said, and turned my back quickly so I wouldn't see her reaction. Long pause.

Patricia changed her position ever so slightly and said very softly, "What time tonight?"

"The plane leaves at nine. I must call Hurley right away. It's really a beautiful script and of course, it's set in Venice. It's called *Shadows on the Sun.*"

"Call Hurley," she said as she started throwing her clothes into a suitcase, and some of mine too. "We'll leave most of our bags here. They can keep them till we get back. I'll call the porters," she said, then, "Oh my gosh, room service!"

"What about room service?" said I.

"Never mind," she said as she went to the phone. "This is Mrs. Cotten, I just saw our waiter in the hall and ordered a large bowl of minestrone for two. Would you cancel that order please? Thank you." Click.

I called Hurley, who said the producers had meant to start shooting a month later, but the Palazzo in Venice wouldn't be available then.

Patricia called sister Gloria in England. She knew husband Gerry was on a business trip. How would Gloria like some Brenta Canal sightseeing?

I called a limousine. With one suitcase each, instead of our usual carload of baggage, we sailed into Kennedy Airport. A nice gentleman was awaiting us with tickets and the little motorcar with the fringe on top.

"Hop on, you'll just make it," he said. We ran up the gangplank and collapsed into our seats. "Long way to go to get a bowl of minestrone," said Patricia.

Gloria was waiting for us at the airport in Rome, where we changed planes for Venice.

My last day's work in the picture would be a large ballroom scene. This was scheduled to be made on February 25, the next day, and I was slated to finish my work by three P.M. so that I could catch the six P.M. plane from Venice to Munich, where I was to start in Bob

Aldrich's *Twilight's Last Gleaming* at Bavaria Films Studio on the next morning, February 26. Reservations, tickets, production departments of both films coordinated . . . nothing could go wrong. In today's parlance, "No problem."

Patricia was busily attending to our last minute packing. She was also arranging Gloria's bags for a last-minute getaway. Gloria herself was otherwise engaged. She was making her film debut! She was sitting, rather elegantly costumed, in the middle of an immense sofa, watching the prancing of the children through her domino mask.

The director sympathized with my growing concern about missing the six o'clock plane to Munich, and as he looked around at the general chaos and absence of progress, he gave me such a sad look and executed a shrug of such helpless beauty that it seemed insensitive of me not to applaud.

The producer appeared. He told us that he had just talked to Bavaria Films in Munich and had asked for an extension of my time.

"What did they say?" asked the director.

"They reminded me," said the producer, "that we are already working on an extension." He continued, "Let us make a compromise. First we must cancel your plane tickets to Munich."

He snapped his fingers. In the code books of movie producers, snapped fingers is an international gesture which automatically causes two people to materialize on the spot, both saying "Yes sir." In Italy they are always Mario and Angelo. He ordered Mario to cancel the Munich flight.

Again, the director's reaction, a sigh of relief, deserved a round of applause. He ordered Angelo to go to bed until midnight, then appear with a huge car in which he would drive Patricia, Gloria, and me to Munich.

"Munich?!" shouted Angelo. "Munich? We'll never make it across the Alps tonight. Innsbruck is six feet under snow."

"How fortunate for Innsbruck," said the producer. "They have been praying for snow there. The Brenner Pass is the one road that will be kept clear tonight. No problem."

Angelo went off looking for a bed. The producer went off screaming, and I went off biting my nails.

Soon after midnight the director cried "Cut." He came over, shook my hand, said "Thank you, and happy motoring. And now," he continued, "we'll have a close-up of the lady on the sofa. Sans mask." Gloria powdered her nose and did her close-up, then she was snatched from her seat by Patricia.

"Sorry, darling, but your career is over. Get changed at once. We've got to get Jo to Munich as soon as possible."

It was a long, dark, cold, and beautiful drive. Angelo was right; heavy snow was falling over Innsbruck. The producer was right; the Brenner Pass was kept clear by the plows. Somewhere near the summit, in this ridiculously overscaled and much-too-white scenery, we opened Angelo's hamper and refreshed ourselves with champagne and sandwiches for the approaching greyness of the descent.

The Hilton Hotel in Munich is outside of town and surrounded by forest, a topographical detail I was to notice two or three days hence. At seven, when we arrived, the receptionist handed me a notice that my car would pick me up at eight and take me to the studio.

And that, Mr. Ripley, is how I finished a movie in Italy on February 26, and after a leisurely drive through the Italian Alps, the Swiss Alps, the Austrian Alps, and the Bavarian Alps, started another picture the same day, February 26 in Germany.

Gloria left Munich after a week to join her husband in England. Patricia bought a million books and cuddled up reading in our suite until I got home from work. Sometimes it was late. We were trying to catch up our delayed film, but it became increasingly clear that I was either getting the flu or heading for an acute case of laryngitis. My voice, my most needed instrument, was beginning to get more than husky. It was faint, it was thin, it was reedy. To me, it was frightening, and many times Bob Aldrich, after several takes, would say, "Don't strain, Jo, we'll reshoot the sound in California when you're better."

But I continued, and said, "No, I'll shoot it here." I just couldn't lose my voice. I kept completely quiet when I wasn't actually speaking in the picture.

We finally finished filming in Munich, and stopped off in London. There I went to a throat specialist in Harley Street. He gave me some antibiotics. Back home, in California, my physician sent me to the man who was considered by many to be the best in the field, Dr. Richard Barton. Barton ordered me not to say a word for two weeks. I had some nodules on my vocal chords. The silent rest was amazing. Within three weeks my voice was normal, and I was given a clean bill of health.

Patricia and I were offered roles in *The Reluctant Debutante* some weeks later. It was for a tour of the United States. I needed the stage badly, and the stage is not only Broadway. Oh no. We found out that Broadway is not the mecca anymore. After all, the audiences and the critics are just as kind, and just as cruel, in Chicago, Cincinnati, or even Los Angeles. For better or worse, and I believe better, the theatre has taken over the entire country. And the entire country has taken over the theatre.

We had a marvelously successful tour with *The Reluctant Debutante*. We also thoroughly enjoyed it. By the time we got to Phoenix . . . I was husky. Reaching the audience with my once resonant voice was a painful, faint effort.

I had been swimming on Sunday and had an earache. The ear, nose and throat man in Scottsdale said my ears would be better in a couple of days, but he ended by saying, "When you get back to Beverly Hills, have your throat examined immediately."

I rushed back to Dr. Barton. By now I was experiencing something close to panic inside. What was happening to my throat? Barton said, "I think we'll have to operate and remove the nodules." He saw my face whiten. "Don't be alarmed, you've nothing like Jack Hawkins had." That did it. Jack, a good friend of mine and a wonderful actor with a very distinctive voice, had suffered terribly. Cancer. His voice box had been removed . . . before he died some years later undergoing another operation.

"You've nothing like Jack Hawkins had!!" That line haunted me, terrified me. Patricia was strong, gentle, supportive and tried so hard to hide her fear. She was at my side always, and at six A.M. on the morning of the operation, she and Dr. Forde, our own dear physician, stood on either side of my bed. She held one of my hands; he took my pulse with the other. Dear God, I had never known such fear, such a living nightmare. I had always been so fit, and my voice was my identification, my ego, my living. I would have to find some strength if the worst happened.

In a haze, I saw Patricia's face. I opened my mouth to ask her if the operation had been successful, but she put her hand over my lips. "Don't speak darling, you are not to speak at all."

I gestured in my groggy state for a paper and pencil and wrote, "What have they done to me? Why can't I speak?"

"The biopsy was negative. They have done nothing to you except remove the nodules. You may not speak at all for six weeks; then you'll be healed." I closed my eyes and thanked God.

For six weeks, I never said a word. I wrote questions and answers to Patricia, and she replied by speech. One day she said, "If anyone listened outside the door, they'd think that a crazy woman lived here alone, talking to herself all the time."

It worked. We waited eight weeks, just to be sure. Then I spoke one hour a day for a week, then two, and so on until I was gabbing away in my normal full voice.

On my first day's work after this ordeal, I was very nervous for about an hour, then I realized that people would wonder why I was perspiring. It was me, and the sound, that precious instrument so valuable not only to actors, was completely unimpaired.

I hope anyone reading this will find courage. The treatments available for more serious throat problems can and have been highly successful. Also, like most surgery, the operations are improving every day. I was lucky. I am grateful. Had it been otherwise, I should have had to find a way to live with it, and I would have. But thank you, dear God. I say this with all my heart and soul, and with a very full voice.

We are told that the memory has no filing space for physical pain. This is not true. And the fact that fear shows no incision, no blood, does not disqualify it as pain. Most of the scars of fear remain in memory for life.

Looking back, I sometimes suspect myself of being masochistic, so often did I push myself across those unstable bridges that actually never needed to be crossed. And when I at last realized this, when my whispers slowly expanded into my normal voice once again, my reaction was violent. I wanted to scream with joy, I wanted to act, I wanted to shout. No matter what, just let me shout!

I did exactly that. I shouted in a lot of international junk. But it was therapy, good therapy, I believe. It was sound therapy mentally, from the trauma of having been voiceless for what to me seemed like aeons. "Keep working," I told myself, "work begets work! Take anything. Everyone flirts now and then with a little trash." My sense of humor, or my sense of the ridiculous, pulled me up short. I was offered a part in which I was to appear nude.

I called Don Wolff, my agent, who had sent me the script. "I don't think my strip act will sell many tickets, Don," I said.

"I was wondering when you'd wake up," he said. "Now, let's move to the sublime," he continued, "read the script that's on its way to you now."

The script from Don Wolff was actually from John Woolf, Sir John Woolf, the English producer of such great films as *Room at the Top* and *Moulin Rouge*. My script was a sequence of one of Roald Dahl's "Tales of the Unexpected" that John was producing in East Anglia. This one was to be with Wendy Hiller and a perfectly horrible cat.

Wendy is one of Great Britain's top actresses. When you see her or work with her, you can easily understand why she will always remain on the summit. It was a perfectly delightful engagement, and I long to appear in her company again.

Before Patricia and I left England, John Woolf tapped me for another of Roald Dahl's eerie tales, this one directed by Alan Gibson.

Packing clothes is an art that deteriorates with experience. That may be because it is a boring procedure. In our favor, there was no way for Patricia and me to know when we left California for England that we would be returning by way of Mexico. I had been offered a picture about the Guyana Massacre. I hoped it might be interesting, but the director, Rene Cardenas, had made two financially successful films and the effect on him was unfortunate. He was the most arrogant man, with the least reason for it, that I have ever worked with. I was, for once, delighted when the movie ended, and not too upset when it was a flop. Rene's father should have directed; he had talent and was charming.

It was lovely and tropical in Acapulco. Of course, that meant a different wardrobe and that meant more bags—more bags to pack untidily in Mexico, to unpack untidily in California, to repack almost immediately in California and set off again for England, which, thank God, there will always be an!

Alan Gibson had asked me to join the acting company he was assembling for the BBC's three-hour television play entitled "Churchill and the Generals." It was not only to be the longest single drama ever attempted by that network, but was to follow strictly the relationship of the prime minister with all the allied generals.

Since George Marshall has always been one of my favorite American historical figures, I was flattered and honored when Alan said, "You'll be playing General George Marshall, of course."

"Of course," I said.

I spent many hours in the public library reading whatever I could find on the life of General Marshall. I talked to Frank McCarthy, an old friend, who was himself a general and, like Marshall, a graduate of the Virginia Military Institute. Frank had been Marshall's aide for a couple of years, and was generous with his help. I suppose this kind of laborious research is helpful to an actor in forming some sort of general overall concept of a character. But in the end the actor must rely most heavily on what the author has given him to say, and on how the director has planned him to say it.

My research taught me that General Marshall was a disciplinarian, a brilliant soldier and statesman, and had great difficulty remembering anyone's name. Well, so much for research! When it came time to play the role, I let the makeup man part my hair where it didn't want to be parted. I waited for Alan Gibson to say "Action!" and I started reciting. I was, after all, Joseph Cotten playing General Marshall, not General Marshall playing Joseph Cotten.

"Churchill and the Generals" took a long time to make. It was given loving care by all concerned. I shall be forever thankful for all the directors and producers who keep cropping up in my life who believe steadfastly in rehearsals. I can't imagine why a box-office study of the relative merits of this system hasn't been made.

On the flight back to California, I looked at Patricia's lovely face sleeping peacefully beside me. Her breathing was steady and heavy. Her peaches and cream complexion was more cream than peaches. I realized that I was pushing our travels to the brink; I realized what strain she must have suffered while nursing me so tenderly and firmly while I was ill.

My nephews Sam Cotten and young Joe Cotten III, and Joe's little wife Penny, would meet us at Los Angeles Airport. Sam was making a name for himself as an actor. Joe was a most skillful artist and musician, as was Penny. Since they had moved to California to find fame and fortune, we had found untold pleasure in having them over on Sundays, laughing with them, hearing their news and telling them ours.

"It's just family," Patricia would tell them, "come as you are and say what you like."

Two big dark eyes slowly revealed themselves and looked up at me. "How about a couple of months at home of absolute nothing?" I whispered. I felt a warm snuggle of approval.

16

It has been four and a half years since I wrote that last line. "I'll finish the book tomorrow," I thought. Tomorrow was June 8, 1981. I have total recall of that dreadful day.

I was having a shower. I felt something snap in my chest, then I fell to my knees on the floor. How I finally got up and dried myself I do not know. I called Patricia, and she rushed in. When she saw me she shouted for our beloved housekeeper, Shirley, who helped me put my pajamas back on and took me to our bedroom while Patricia called the paramedics.

I had had a heart attack, followed by a stroke that struck at my speech center. Having come through my throat operation successfully and regained my normal voice, I now couldn't speak at all. It seemed so unfair.

As soon as I was well enough, I started speech therapy. Patricia would drive me to the hospital daily. After four and a half years, I still go twice a week. She still drives me there and back.

We have moved to Palm Springs, as the doctors said the weather here would help me, and it has. We have a lovely house that my wife found, and I have flowers in my lovely garden.

I can now speak to them.

I am a very lucky man.

One day when we were returning from buying some lamps for our new house, the telephone started ringing. It was Orson asking me to have lunch with him when we went to Los Angeles the next day. When I was first stricken, he had spoken to Patricia every day. Then later, he and I talked each week for a couple of hours. He was strong and supportive, and whenever I used the wrong word (which was frequently) he would say, "That's a much better word, Jo, I'm going to use it."

Our lunches the last few years were mostly reminiscences about our early success, but he was still determined to make one more film, one more great film.

I told him I had written a book. "Bring it with you when we have lunch, I'll take it home and read it as soon as I can." I did just that.

He called us the same night, and said he had read it, couldn't put it down, and would I let him find the right publisher. "Do you mind if I interfere with your writing career?" he said. Good heavens, how would I have started a movie career without him? Patricia and I were delighted.

We still had workmen working on the house. One day on returning from lunch, we found them lined up outside, looking rather somber.

"Anything wrong?" asked Patricia.

"The telephone has been ringing constantly," said the foreman, "Orson Welles . . . ."

"Is Orson Welles on the telephone?" asked Patricia excitedly as she started in the house.

"No, Mrs. Cotten. Uh, eh . . . I'm afraid he's dead."

I walked up to Patricia, who stood frozen in shock.

I still miss David Selznick very much. I had known Orson considerably longer. He had cheated death for so many years (being overweight and having a heart condition) that he had seemed somehow indestructible. I know what his feelings were regarding his death. He did not want a funeral; he wanted to be buried quietly in a little place in Spain. He wanted no memorial services, saying that a lot of hypocrites would get up and say how much they loved him.

I respected his wishes. I refused to appear at any memorial service. The telephone kept ringing, and people said that I ought to make an appearance. I was stubborn about doing what I felt David wished as he left this world, and I was equally stubborn about not appearing at Orson's memorial. I sent a short message, and I ended it with the last two lines of a Shakespeare poem that Orson had sent me on my most recent birthday . . .

But if the while I think on thee, dear friend,
All losses are restored and sorrows end.

We talk about him often. Somewhere among his possessions is a manuscript of this book. He would have had it published. He would have made another great film. But it was not to be.

Patricia and I have become co-chairs of David Gest's American Cinema Awards Foundation, and last night I made my first public speech in four and a half years. I presented an award to my friend Olivia de Havilland. When I returned to the table, the applause was second in joy to the embrace I received from my wife, who cried unashamedly and stood by my side as she has done every single day of our ordeal. She is as beautiful today as she was the day I realized I could never be happy without her.

With these big ears and these dim eyes I hear and read that love, *per se*, is making a comeback—although, for actors, it seems that it is most unfashionable to be happily married. Divorce, public brawls, and kinky sex are supposed to be the rage, and please be informed whenever you consider this observation that the operative word is *rage*.

Perhaps you remember Mr. Belasco telling Lynne Overman that absolutely nothing is corny if you really believe it. Well, I believe in LOVE. I believe it to be a blood relative of LIFE, and that each depends on the other for its fundamental existence.

I continue to love my wife passionately, spiritually, and completely. That she calmly and unregretfully closed the door on a thriving and glamorous movie career to be at my side, tells of her love for me.

We are ordinary, extraordinarily lucky people. For that, all I can say is "Amen."

Filmography

Citizen Kane   (RKO, 1941)
Lydia   (United Artists, 1941)
The Magnificent Ambersons   (RKO, 1942)
Journey into Fear   (RKO, 1942)
Shadow of a Doubt   (Universal, 1943)
Hers to Hold   (United Artists, 1943)
Gaslight   (MGM, 1944)
Since You Went Away   (United Artists, 1944)
I'll Be Seeing You   (United Artists, 1944)
Love Letters   (Paramount, 1945)
Duel in the Sun   (Selznick, 1946)
The Farmer's Daughter   (RKO, 1947)
Portrait of Jenny   (Selznick, 1948)
Under Capricorn   (Warner Brothers, 1949)
Beyond the Forest   (Warner Brothers, 1949)
The Third Man   (Selznick, 1950)
Walk Softly, Stranger   (RKO, 1950)
Two Flags West   (20th Century Fox, 1950)
September Affair   (Paramount, 1950)
Half Angel   (20th Century Fox, 1951)
Peking Express   (Paramount, 1951)
The Man with a Cloak   (MGM, 1951)
Untamed Frontier   (Universal, 1952)
The Steel Trap   (20th Century Fox, 1952)
Niagara   (20th Century Fox, 1953)

Blueprint for Murder   (20th Century Fox, 1953)
Special Delivery   (Columbia, 1955)
The Bottom of the Bottle   (20th Century Fox, 1956)
The Killer Is Loose   (United Artists, 1956)
The Halliday Brand   (United Artists, 1957)
Touch of Evil   (Universal, 1958)*
From the Earth to the Moon   (Warner Brothers, 1958)
The Angel Wore Red   (MGM, 1960)
The Last Sunset   (Universal, 1961)
Hush, Hush, Sweet Charlotte   (20th Century Fox, 1965)
The Great Sioux Massacre   (Columbia, 1965)
The Oscar   (Paramount, 1966)
The Tramplers   (Embassy, 1966)
The Money Trap   (MGM, 1966)
Brighty of the Grand Canyon   (Feature Film Corpo-
                                 ration of America, 1967)
The Diamond Spy   (Embassy, 1967)
Jack of Diamonds   (MGM, 1967)
Some May Live   (RKO, 1967)
The Hellbenders   (Embassy, 1967)
Days of Fire   (Italian, 1968)
Petulia   (Warner Brothers, 1968)
Latitude Zero   (Japanese: Toho, 1969)
The Abominable Dr. Phibes   (American International
                                 Pictures, 1971)
Tora! Tora! Tora!   (20th Century Fox, 1971)
White Comanche   (RKO, 1971)
Scientific Cardplayer   (Italian: Cinecita, 1972)
Soylent Green   (MGM, 1973)
A Delicate Balance   (American Film Theatre, 1973)
F for Fake   (Janus Film and Les Films de
                                 L'Astrophores, 1974)
Twilight's Last Gleaming   (Lorimar and Bavaria Films
                                 Studio, 1976)
Airport 77   (Universal, 1977)
Caravans   (20th Century Fox, 1978)
Guyana, Crime of the Century   (Mexico Films, 1979)
Heaven's Gate   (United Artists, 1982)

*Unbilled guest appearance.

Index